Disaster Recovery

EC-Council | Press

Volume 1 of 2 mapping to

E|CDR™   E|CVT™

EC-Council | **Certified DR Professional**   **EC-Council** | **Certified VT Professional**

Certification   Certification

COURSE TECHNOLOGY
CENGAGE Learning™

Australia • Brazil • Japan • Korea • Mexico • Singapore • Spain • United Kingdom • United States

20110805

COURSE TECHNOLOGY
CENGAGE Learning

Disaster Recovery
EC-Council | Press

Course Technology/Cengage Learning
Staff:

Vice President, Career and Professional
Editorial: Dave Garza

Director of Learning Solutions:
Matthew Kane

Executive Editor: Stephen Helba

Managing Editor: Marah Bellegarde

Editorial Assistant: Meghan Orvis

Vice President, Career and Professional
Marketing: Jennifer Ann Baker

Marketing Director: Deborah Yarnell

Marketing Manager: Erin Coffin

Marketing Coordinator: Shanna Gibbs

Production Director: Carolyn Miller

Production Manager: Andrew Crouth

Content Project Manager:
Brooke Greenhouse

Senior Art Director: Jack Pendleton

EC-Council:

President | EC-Council: Sanjay Bavisi

Sr. Director US | EC-Council:
Steven Graham

For product information and technology assistance, contact us at
Cengage Learning Customer & Sales Support, 1-800-354-9706

For permission to use material from this text or product,
submit all requests online at **www.cengage.com/permissions**.
Further permissions questions can be e-mailed to
permissionrequest@cengage.com

Library of Congress Control Number: 2010928097

ISBN-13: 978-1-4354-8870-0

ISBN-10: 1-4354-8870-9

Cengage Learning
5 Maxwell Drive
Clifton Park, NY 12065-2919
USA

Cengage Learning is a leading provider of customized learning solutions with office locations around the globe, including Singapore, the United Kingdom, Australia, Mexico, Brazil, and Japan. Locate your local office at: **international.cengage.com/region**

Cengage Learning products are represented in Canada by
Nelson Education, Ltd.

For more learning solutions, please visit our corporate website at **www.cengage.com**

Printed in the United States of America
1 2 3 4 5 6 7 12 11 10

Brief Table of Contents

Table of Contents

CHAPTER 4
Business Continuity Management

CHAPTER 5
Managing, Assessing, and Evaluating Risks

CHAPTER 7
Data Storage Technologies 7-1

CHAPTER 8
Disaster Recovery Services and Tools 8-1

Hacking and electronic crimes sophistication has grown at an exponential rate in recent years. In fact, recent reports have indicated that cyber crime already surpasses the illegal drug trade! Unethical hackers better known as *black hats* are preying on information systems of government, corporate, public, and private networks and are constantly testing the security mechanisms of these organizations to the limit with the sole aim of exploiting it and profiting from the exercise. High profile crimes have proven that the traditional approach to computer security is simply not sufficient, even with the strongest perimeter, properly configured defense mechanisms like firewalls, intrusion detection, and prevention systems, strong end-to-end encryption standards, and anti-virus software. Hackers have proven their dedication and ability to systematically penetrate networks all over the world. In some cases *black hats* may be able to execute attacks so flawlessly that they can compromise a system, steal everything of value, and completely erase their tracks in less than 20 minutes!

The EC-Council Press is dedicated to stopping hackers in their tracks.

About EC-Council

The International Council of Electronic Commerce Consultants, better known as EC-Council was founded in late 2001 to address the need for well-educated and certified information security and e-business practitioners. EC-Council is a global, member-based organization comprised of industry and subject matter experts all working together to set the standards and raise the bar in information security certification and education.

EC-Council first developed the *Certified Ethical Hacker*, C|EH program. The goal of this program is to teach the methodologies, tools, and techniques used by hackers. Leveraging the collective knowledge from hundreds of subject matter experts, the C|EH program has rapidly gained popularity around the globe and is now delivered in over 70 countries by over 450 authorized training centers. Over 80,000 information security practitioners have been trained.

C|EH is the benchmark for many government entities and major corporations around the world. Shortly after C|EH was launched, EC-Council developed the *Certified Security Analyst*, E|CSA. The goal of the E|CSA program is to teach groundbreaking analysis methods that must be applied while conducting advanced penetration testing. E|CSA leads to the *Licensed Penetration Tester*, L|PT status. The *Computer Hacking Forensic Investigator*, C|HFI was formed with the same design methodologies above and has become a global standard in certification for computer forensics. EC-Council through its impervious network of professionals, and huge industry following has developed various other programs in information security and e-business. EC-Council Certifications are viewed as the essential certifications needed where standard configuration and security policy courses fall short. Providing a true, hands-on, tactical approach to security, individuals armed with the knowledge disseminated by EC-Council programs are securing networks around the world and beating the hackers at their own game.

About the EC-Council | Press

The EC-Council | Press was formed in late 2008 as a result of a cutting edge partnership between global information security certification leader, EC-Council and leading global academic publisher, Cengage Learning. This partnership marks a revolution in academic textbooks and courses of study in Information Security, Computer Forensics, Disaster Recovery, and End-User Security. By identifying the essential topics and content of EC-Council professional certification programs, and repurposing this world class content to fit academic programs, the EC-Council | Press was formed. The academic community is now able to incorporate this powerful cutting edge content into new and existing Information Security programs. By closing the gap between academic study and professional certification, students and instructors are able to leverage the power of rigorous academic focus and high demand industry certification. The EC-Council | Press is set to revolutionize global information security programs and ultimately create a new breed of practitioners capable of combating the growing epidemic of cybercrime and the rising threat of cyber-war.

Disaster Recovery/Virtualization Security Series

Disaster recovery and business continuity are daunting challenges for any organization. With the rise in the number of threats, attacks, and competitive business landscape, it is important that an organization be prepared and have the ability to withstand a disaster. Using the disaster recovery process, an organization recovers the lost data and gains back the access to the software/hardware so that the performance of the business can return to normal. Virtualization technologies gives the advantage of additional flexibility as well as cost savings while deploying a disaster recovery solution. Virtualization lessens the usage of hardware at a disaster recovery site and makes recovery operations easier.

The *Disaster Recovery/Virtualization Series* introduces methods to identify vulnerabilities and takes appropriate countermeasures to prevent and mitigate failure risks for an organization. This series takes an enterprise-wide approach to developing a disaster recovery plan. Students will learn how to create a secure network by putting policies and procedures in place, and how to restore a network in the event of a disaster. It also provides the networking professional with a foundation in disaster recovery principles. This series explores virtualization products such as VMware, Microsoft Hyper- V, Citrix Xen Server and Client, Sun xVM, HP virtualization, NComputing, NoMachine etc. The series when used in its entirety helps prepare readers to take and succeed on the E|CDR-E|CVT certification exam, Disaster Recovery and Virtualization Technology certification exam from EC-Council. The EC-Council Certified Disaster Recovery and Virtualization Technology professional will have a better understanding of how to setup disaster recovery plans using traditional and virtual technologies to ensure business continuity in the event of a disaster.

Books in Series
- *Disaster Recovery*/1435488709
- *Virtualization Security*/1435488695

Disaster Recovery

This product provides an introduction to disaster recovery and business continuity, a discussion of the relevant laws and regulations, how to plan and implement a disaster recovery plan, how to manage, assess and evaluate risk, certification and accreditation of information systems and much more!

Chapter Contents

Chapter 1 *Introduction to Disaster Recovery and Business Continuity*, discusses the different types of disasters and how to recover from them and explains the difference between disaster recovery and business continuity. Chapter 2, *Laws and Acts*, familiarizes the reader with the laws and regulations relevant to disaster recovery, and serves as a reference for the full text of some of these laws and regulations. Chapter 3, *Disaster Recovery Planning and Implementation*, discusses system security, in order to prevent disasters in the first place, and planning for disaster recovery. Chapter 4, *Business Continuity Management*, introduces the fundamentals of business continuity management (BCM) including sample forms for business continuity plans, contingency plans, and virtualization data recovery. Chapter 5, *Managing, Assessing, and Evaluating Risks*, discusses the importance of risk management, various risk management methodologies including a list of responsibilities of an information systems security office (ISSO). Chapter 6, *Risk Control Policies and Countermeasures*, explains system security and change control policies and how to conduct configuration management. Chapter 7, *Data Storage Technologies*, introduces three different data storage technologies, network attached storage, direct attached storage, and storage area networks. Chapter 8, *Disaster Recovery Services and Tools*, explains the importance of backing up data and how to implement effective and efficient data backup procedures. Chapter 9, *Certification and Accreditation of Information Systems*, introduces the concepts of certification and accreditation including what is involved in the process and how threats and vulnerabilities are related to the certification and accreditation process.

Chapter Features

Many features are included in each chapter and all are designed to enhance the learner's learning experience. Features include:

- *Objectives* begin each chapter and focus the learner on the most important concepts in the chapter.

- *Key Terms* are designed to familiarize the learner with terms that will be used within the chapter.

- *Chapter Summary*, at the end of each chapter, serves as a review of the key concepts covered in the chapter.
- *Review Questions* allow the learner to test their comprehension of the chapter content.
- *Hands-On Projects* encourage the learner to apply the knowledge they have gained after finishing the chapter Center. Note: you will need your access code provided in your book to enter the site. Visit *www.cengage.com/community/eccouncil* for a link to the Student Resource Center or follow the directions on your access card.

Student Resource Center

The Student Resource Center contains all the files you need to complete the Hands-On Projects found at the end of the chapters. Access the Student Resource Center with the access code provided in your book. Visit *www.cengage.com/community/eccouncil* for a link to the Student Resource Center.

Additional Instructor Resources

Free to all instructors who adopt the *Disaster Recovery* book for their courses is a complete package of instructor resources. These resources are available from the Course Technology web site, *www.cengage.com/coursetechnology*, by going to the product page for this book in the online catalog, click on the Companion Site on the Faculty side; click on any of the Instructor Resources in the left navigation and login to access the files. Once you accept the license agreement, the selected files will be displayed.

Resources include:

- *Instructor Manual*: This manual includes course objectives and additional information to help your instruction.
- *ExamView Testbank*: This Windows-based testing software helps instructors design and administer tests and pre-tests. In addition to generating tests that can be printed and administered, this full-featured program has an online testing component that allows students to take tests at the computer and have their exams automatically graded.
- *PowerPoint Presentations*: This book comes with a set of Microsoft PowerPoint slides for each chapter. These slides are meant to be used as a teaching aid for classroom presentations, to be made available to students for chapter review, or to be printed for classroom distribution. Instructors are also at liberty to add their own slides.
- *Labs*: Additional Hands-on Activities to provide additional practice for your students.
- *Assessment Activities*: Additional assessment opportunities including discussion questions, writing assignments, internet research activities, and homework assignments along with a final cumulative project.
- *Final Exam*: Provides a comprehensive assessment of *Disaster Recovery* content.

Cengage Learning Information Security Community Site

This site was created for learners and instructors to find out about the latest in information security news and technology.

Visit *community.cengage.com/infosec* to:

- Learn what's new in information security through live news feeds, videos and podcasts.
- Connect with your peers and security experts through blogs and forums.
- Browse our online catalog.

How to Become ECDR-ECVT Certified

The EC-Council Disaster Recovery and Virtualization Technology certification will fortify the disaster recovery and virtualization technology knowledge of system administrators, systems engineers, enterprise system architects, hardware engineers, software engineers, technical support individuals, networking professionals, and any IT professional who is concerned about the integrity of the network infrastructure. This is an advanced course for experienced system administrators and system integrators scaling their organization's deployment of the virtualization technologies. The ECDR-ECVT Program certifies individuals and explores installation, configuration, and management of different virtualization products. A certified EC-Council Disaster Recovery and Virtualization Technology professional will better understand how to recover after a disaster so that there is proper business continuity.

To achieve the certification, you must pass the ECDR-ECVT Professional exam 312-55.

E|CDR-E|CVT Certification exam is available through Prometric Prime. To obtain your certification after your training, you must:

1. Purchase an exam voucher from the EC-Council Community Site at Cengage: *www.cengage.com/community/eccouncil*.

2. Speak with your Instructor or Professor about scheduling an exam session, or visit the EC-Council Community Site referenced above for more information.

3. Attempt and pass the E|CDR—E|CVT certification examination with a score of 70% or better.

About Our Other EC-Council Press Products

Ethical Hacking and Countermeasures Series

The EC-Council | Press *Ethical Hacking and Countermeasures* series is intended for those studying to become security officers, auditors, security professionals, site administrators, and anyone who is concerned about or responsible for the integrity of the network infrastructure. The series includes a broad base of topics in offensive network security, ethical hacking, as well as network defense and countermeasures. The content of this series is designed to immerse the learner into an interactive environment where they will be shown how to scan, test, hack and secure information systems. A wide variety of tools, viruses, and malware is presented in these books, providing a complete understanding of the tactics and tools used by hackers. By gaining a thorough understanding of how hackers operate, ethical hackers are able to set up strong countermeasures and defensive systems to protect their organization's critical infrastructure and information. The series when used in its entirety helps prepare readers to take and succeed on the C|EH certification exam from EC-Council.

Books in Series
- *Ethical Hacking and Countermeasures: Attack Phases*/143548360X
- *Ethical Hacking and Countermeasures: Threats and Defense Mechanisms*/1435483618
- *Ethical Hacking and Countermeasures: Web Applications and Data Servers*/1435483626
- *Ethical Hacking and Countermeasures: Linux, Macintosh and Mobile Systems*/1435483642
- *Ethical Hacking and Countermeasures: Secure Network Infrastructures*/1435483650

Computer Forensics Series

The EC-Council | Press *Computer Forensics* series, preparing learners for C|HFI certification, is intended for those studying to become police investigators and other law enforcement personnel, defense and military personnel, e-business security professionals, systems administrators, legal professionals, banking, insurance and other professionals, government agencies, and IT managers. The content of this program is designed to expose the learner to the process of detecting attacks and collecting evidence in a forensically sound manner with the intent to report crime and prevent future attacks. Advanced techniques in computer investigation and analysis with interest in generating potential legal evidence are included. In full, this series prepares the learner to identify evidence in computer related crime and abuse cases as well as track the intrusive hacker's path through client system.

Books in Series
- *Computer Forensics: Investigation Procedures and Response*/1435483499
- *Computer Forensics: Investigating Hard Disks, File and Operating Systems*/1435483502
- *Computer Forensics: Investigating Data and Image Files*/1435483510
- *Computer Forensics: Investigating Network Intrusions and Cybercrime*/1435483529
- *Computer Forensics: Investigating Wireless Networks and Devices*/1435483537

Network Defense Series

The EC-Council | Press *Network Defense* series, preparing learners for E|NSA certification, is intended for those studying to become system administrators, network administrators and anyone who is interested in network security technologies. This series is designed to educate learners, from a vendor neutral standpoint, how to defend the networks they manage. This series covers the fundamental skills in evaluating internal and external threats to network security, design, and how to enforce network level security policies, and ultimately protect an organization's information. Covering a broad range of topics from secure network fundamentals, protocols & analysis, standards and policy, hardening infrastructure, to configuring IPS, IDS and firewalls, bastion host and honeypots, among many other topics, learners completing this series will have a full understanding of defensive measures taken to secure their organizations information. The series when used in its entirety helps prepare readers to take and succeed on the E|NSA, Network Security Administrator certification exam from EC-Council.

Books in Series
- *Network Defense: Fundamentals and Protocols*/1435483553
- *Network Defense: Security Policy and Threats*/1435483561
- *Network Defense: Perimeter Defense Mechanisms*/143548357X
- *Network Defense: Securing and Troubleshooting Network Operating Systems*/1435483588
- *Network Defense: Security and Vulnerability Assessment*/1435483596

Penetration Testing Series

The EC-Council | Press Security Analyst/Licensed *Penetration Tester* series, preparing learners for E|CSA/LPT certification, is intended for those studying to become Network Server Administrators, Firewall Administrators, Security Testers, System Administrators and Risk Assessment professionals. This series covers a broad base of topics in advanced penetration testing and security analysis. The content of this program is designed to expose the learner to groundbreaking methodologies in conducting thorough security analysis, as well as advanced penetration testing techniques. Armed with the knowledge from the Security Analyst series, learners will be able to perform the intensive assessments required to effectively identify and mitigate risks to the security of the organization's infrastructure. The series when used in its entirety helps prepare readers to take and succeed on the E|CSA, Certified Security Analyst certification exam.

Books in Series
- *Penetration Testing: Security Analysis*/1435483669
- *Penetration Testing: Procedures and Methodologies*/1435483677
- *Penetration Testing: Network and Perimeter Testing*/1435483685
- *Penetration Testing: Communication Media Testing*/1435483693
- *Penetration Testing: Network Threat Testing*/1435483707

Cyber Safety/1435483715

Cyber Safety is designed for anyone who is interested in learning computer networking and security basics. This product provides information cyber crime; security procedures; how to recognize security threats and attacks, incident response, and how to secure internet access. This book gives individuals the basic security literacy skills to begin high-end IT programs. The book also prepares readers to take and succeed on the Security|5 certification exam from EC-Council.

Wireless Safety/1435483766

Wireless Safety introduces the learner to the basics of wireless technologies and its practical adaptation. *Wireless|5* is tailored to cater to any individual's desire to learn more about wireless technology. It requires no pre-requisite knowledge and aims to educate the learner in simple applications of these technologies. Topics include wireless signal propagation, IEEE and ETSI Wireless Standards, WLANs and Operation, Wireless Protocols and Communication Languages, Wireless Devices, and Wireless Security Network. The book also prepares readers to take and succeed on the Wireless|5 certification exam from EC-Council.

Network Safety/1435483774

Network Safety provides the basic core knowledge on how infrastructure enables a working environment. Intended for those in an office environment and for the home user who wants to optimize resource utilization, share infrastructure and make the best of technology and the convenience it offers. Topics include foundations of networks, networking components, wireless networks, basic hardware components, the networking environment and connectivity as well as troubleshooting. The book also prepares readers to take and succeed on the Network|5 certification exam from EC-Council.

Acknowledgements

Michael H. Goldner is the Chair of the School of Information Technology for ITT Technical Institute in Norfolk Virginia, and also teaches bachelor level courses in computer network and information security systems. Michael has served on and chaired ITT Educational Services Inc. National Curriculum Committee on Information Security. He received his Juris Doctorate from Stetson University College of Law, his undergraduate degree from Miami University and has been working over fifteen years in the area of Information Technology. He is an active member of the American Bar Association, and has served on that organization's Cyber Law committee. He is a member of IEEE, ACM and ISSA, and is the holder of a number of industrially recognized certifications including, CISSP, CEH, CHFI, CEI, MCT, MCSE/Security, Security +, Network + and A+. Michael recently completed the design and creation of a computer forensic program for ITT Technical Institute, and has worked closely with both EC-Council and Delmar/Cengage Learning in the creation of this EC-Council Press series.

Chapter 1

Introduction to Disaster Recovery and Business Continuity

Objectives

After completing this chapter, you should be able to:

- Understand disaster recovery and types of disasters
- Perform disaster recovery
- Describe a disaster recovery team
- Enumerate the disaster recovery phases
- List the best practices of disaster recovery
- Understand business continuity
- Understand the difference between disaster recovery and business continuity
- Perform business continuity and disaster recovery planning
- Develop a security management plan

Key Terms

Business continuity   the ability of an organization to keep the business running even after a disaster strikes

Disaster   a natural or human-caused incident that negatively affects organizations or the environment

Disaster recovery   the processes, policies, and procedures necessary for the recovery of operations and the continuation of the critical functions of an organization after a disaster

Security management plan   a documented set of policies and procedures to ensure the security of an organization's operations and assets

Introduction to Disaster Recovery and Business Continuity

Developing plans for disaster recovery and business continuity is important for any organization. Disasters may happen at any time, often with little or no warning, so it is important for an organization to have these plans in place to ensure its ability to quickly recover from disasters. This chapter teaches you about the different types of disasters and how to recover from them. It goes through the different phases of the disaster recovery process and the best practices to use during this process. It also goes into business continuity and the difference between disaster recovery and business continuity. The chapter finishes with a discussion of security management planning.

Disaster

A *disaster* is a natural or human-caused incident that negatively affects organizations or the environment. It disrupts business continuity and may affect long-term business objectives. Disasters are often seen as the failure to effectively manage risks to different business entities.

In the present global economic scenario, organizations are more susceptible to natural, human, or technical problems. Any disaster, from floods and fires to viruses and cyber terrorism, can affect the accessibility, reliability, and privacy of major business resources.

Disasters can lead to the following:

- *Loss of life*: This is the most damaging and traumatic impact of any disaster. Individuals may lose their family members and colleagues, whereas organizations may lose their key personnel. Disasters often leave many with temporary and permanent disabilities. Epidemics after disasters leave many more people with diseases that affect their employability and economic conditions.

- *Loss of property*: Property loss is a consequence of many disasters. Disasters leave man-made structures collapsed and ruin necessary services such as communication and transportation systems.

- *Relocation or displacement*: Individuals or organizations may, at times, need to shift or completely relocate to a new site.

- *Disruptions in business continuity*: Disasters may cause disruptions in business activities due to failure in processes, machinery, and communication, and these disruptions ultimately result in loss of revenue or cessation of all business activity and closure.

Statistics: Different Sources of Disaster

The graph in Figure 1-1 indicates the major causes of disasters. It shows that human interference is the major cause of concern for protecting organizational resources from disastrous events. Human inference is also considered the most challenging aspect of information security controls.

Types of Disasters

Natural catastrophes, technical failures, manual errors, and malicious activities have led to an increased disruption in business operations. Enterprises should be aware of such happenings and accordingly plan and prepare themselves to avoid or face them. Disasters are broadly categorized into the following two categories (Figure 1-2):

1. *Natural disasters*: Natural disasters are sudden events caused by environmental factors, resulting in damage to life and property.

2. *Man-made disasters*: Man-made disasters are caused by human error, ignorance, negligence, or individuals with malicious intentions. These disasters are unpredictable and can spread across a wide area. They are sometimes unpreventable as well. System failures, power and telecommunication outages, terrorism, and cyber terrorism fall under this category.

Data Breach Investigations Report 2008/2009

Data breach incidents in which unauthorized people acquired access to or tampered with confidential data have been the main security concern for most of the top Fortune 500 companies over the last five years. Statistical analysis of various data breach reports highlights a worrying scenario for organizational

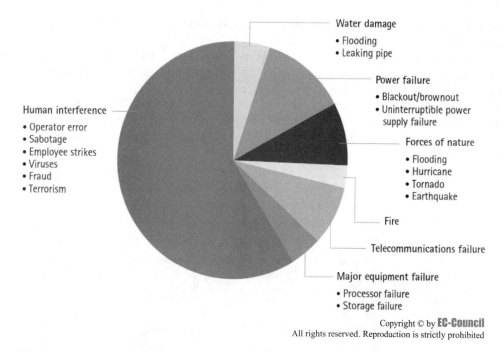

Figure 1-1   Human interference is a major cause of disastrous events.

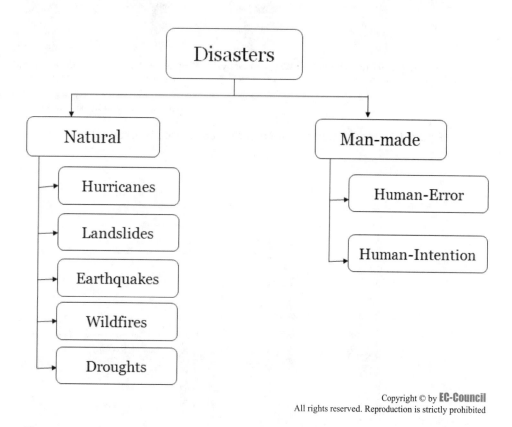

Figure 1-2   Disasters can be categorized as either natural or man-made disasters.

security and business competitiveness. According to Verizon's 2008 Data Breach Investigations Report, which analyzes the data breach incidents from more than 500 forensic engagements handled by its Business Investigative Response team over a four-year period, to the question "Who is behind data breaches?" almost 73% of responders answered that they resulted from external sources, whereas 18% of responders answered that they came from the inside. The graph in Figure 1-3 highlights the major perpetrators of data breach incidents.

Similar to the Verizon's 2008 report numbers, most data breaches continued to originate from external sources in 2009. The majority of total records lost still resulted from external sources. Additionally, 91% of all compromised records were linked to organized criminal groups.

The graph in Figure 1-4 illustrates the major causes of data breaches. To the question "How do breaches occur?" almost 62% of responders answered that their organizations experienced data breach incidents due to significant technical errors. This highlights the need for a well-trained and aware workforce that can effectively handle and respond to incidents.

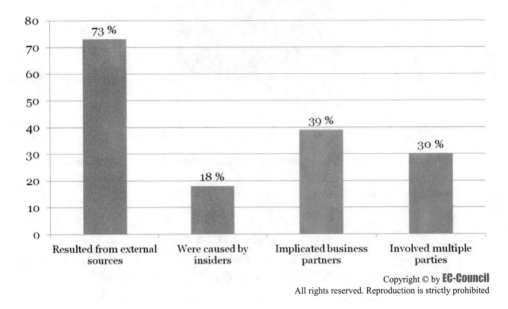

Figure 1-3   Most reported data breaches are caused by external sources.

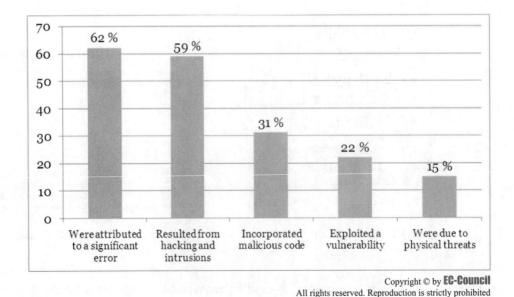

Figure 1-4   A great many data breach incidents were due to significant technical errors.

Disaster Recovery

Disaster recovery involves the processes, policies, and procedures necessary for the recovery of operations and the continuation of the critical functions of an organization after a disaster. Issues such as physical violence, hacking attempts, computer malware, and the rising incidences of information security emergencies have forced governments and corporations to focus on disaster recovery.

Disaster recovery strategies should consider the type of organization and the elements required to keep the organization running.

Disaster recovery is important to organizations for the following reasons:

- It returns the organizations to normal operating conditions.
- It limits the effects of the disaster on business functions.
- It minimizes the occurrence of certain types of disasters in the future.

Operational Cycle of Disaster Recovery

Disasters have various causes and origins, ranging from natural disasters to intentional man-made disasters, and lead to a certain period of business discontinuity. Disaster recovery efforts start as soon as there is an indication or report of an incident. Disaster recovery teams first verify the occurrence of the disaster and then execute disaster recovery plans to overcome disasters and restore operations to their normal state. Figure 1-5 presents an overview of a complete disaster recovery operations cycle.

Disaster Recovery Cost

As businesses are becoming increasingly dependent on technology, a serious failure or loss in technology will have a great impact on an organization. The disaster recovery statistics in Figure 1-6 show the relationship between cost of disruption and recovery time. As time goes on, the cost of disruption increases and the cost of recovery decreases.

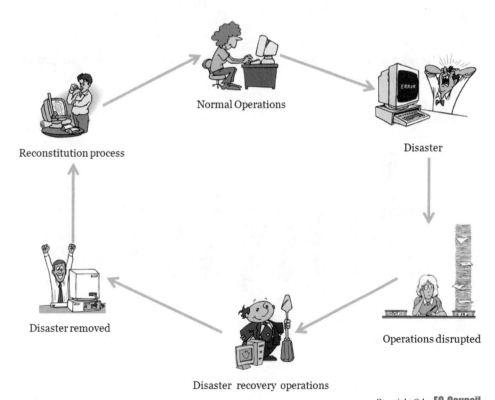

Normal Operations

Reconstitution process

Disaster

Disaster removed

Operations disrupted

Disaster recovery operations

Figure 1-5 This represents the cycle of disaster recovery.

Incidents That Required the Execution of Disaster Recovery Plans

Symantec's Global Disaster Recovery Survey highlights the importance of disaster recovery plans. Disaster recovery planning is a major driving force in business continuity planning and strategic business decisions. According to the survey (Figure 1-7), out of the organizations that executed disaster recovery (DR) plans, 59% of organizations were forced to execute DR plans to overcome incidents involving computer system failures. External computer threats and natural disasters were other major issues of concern.

Evaluating Disaster Recovery Methods

Evaluation of disaster recovery mechanisms is important for implementing any DR strategy effectively. Disaster recovery teams should analyze the available recovery mechanisms for all entities directly related to the organization's normal functioning and determine the appropriate recovery procedures according to need and feasibility.

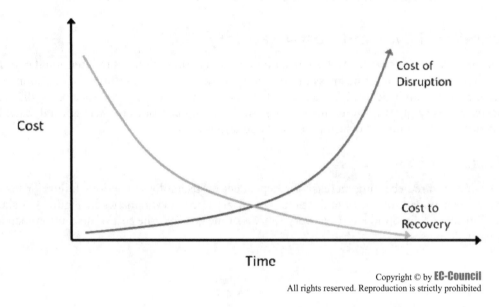

Figure 1-6   As time goes on, the cost of disruption increases and the cost of recovery decreases.

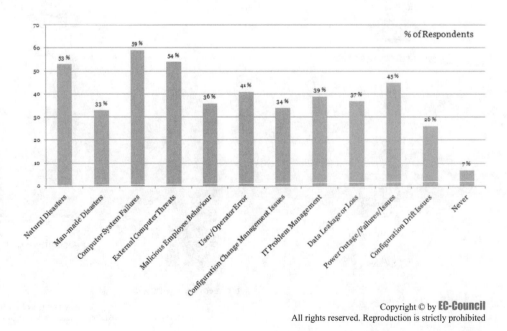

Figure 1-7   Computer system failures are a major cause of disaster for organizations.

Evaluation of DR mechanisms involves a careful consideration of the resources already employed in the recovery process. Recovery mechanisms vary according to different entities. Data storage and processing systems, power supplies, networking infrastructure, and telecommunication systems are some of the basic and most important organizational entities. There are one or more recovery mechanisms available for these entities.

Recovery mechanisms for critical information processing and storage systems may include data backup solutions. Organizations may opt for an off-site hot backup service, in which all the operational data are synchronized in real time, or a cold backup service, in which data are synchronized at regular intervals according to data criticality and synchronization medium. For less critical information systems, organizations may opt for local hardware and software redundancy. The redundancy in the organization may result in extra costs, but it can save organizational data in case of a limited disaster. Organizations decide on which disaster recovery mechanisms to implement by considering their budget, cost-benefit analysis, and availability of human resources to manage these solutions.

Similarly, to prepare for disasters related to power outage, organizations may arrange for multiple alternative sources of power, such as generator systems and UPSs. Selection of these solutions is also dependent on an organization's budget and feasibility.

Overall, selection of different disaster recovery mechanisms for an organization depends on the following:

- Acquisition, maintenance, and operation costs of the solutions
- Disaster recovery budget of the organization
- Desired recovery time
- Availability of human resources to operate and manage the solutions
- Availability of third-party solutions

Disaster Recovery Team

A disaster recovery team is responsible for developing and managing disaster recovery operations and procedures. The team includes representatives from different departments and third-party associates of the organization. The members of the team have predefined roles and responsibilities in different stages of the disaster recovery process. All departments in an organization—such as management, human resources, IT, customer service centers, security, and finance—should be adequately represented in the disaster recovery team.

The disaster recovery team builds, implements, and maintains the disaster recovery plan. It is also responsible for coordinating various disaster recovery processes between different organizational units, third parties, and public services such as police and legal systems.

The major roles and responsibilities of disaster recovery teams include the following:

- Developing, deploying, and monitoring the implementation of appropriate disaster recovery plans after analysis of business objectives and threats to organizations
- Notifying management, affected personnel, and third parties about the disaster
- Initiating the execution of the disaster recovery procedures
- Monitoring the execution of the disaster recovery plan and assessing the results
- Returning operations to normal conditions
- Modifying and updating the disaster recovery plan according to lessons learned from previous disaster recovery efforts
- Increasing the level of the organization's disaster recovery preparedness by conducting mock drills, regular DR systems testing, and threat analysis
- Creating awareness among various stakeholders of the organization by conducting training and awareness sessions

Organizations should consider the following points to develop an efficient disaster recovery team:

- Roles and responsibilities of each team member should be clearly defined and communicated.
- Reporting structure should be transparent and easy.
- Team members should be equipped with the required skills and tools.

Additional human resources should be designated to fill any vacancies in case the primary member is unavailable. Backup team members should be aware of their responsibilities and should be able to join disaster recovery efforts on short notice. Team development and skill enhancement trainings should also involve backup team members so that they are equally able to effectively handle incidents.

Management's decision concerning having backup disaster recovery team members is generally based on perceived level of risk, availability of human resources, and the organization's risk tolerance. Financial factors are also a major determinant in having backup teams. According to recent surveys by Verizon and Symantec, prevailing economic conditions are forcing organizations to cut their disaster recovery budget, which can reduce the organization's capability of having backup disaster recovery plans and teams.

Disaster Recovery Phases

Activation Phase

Immediate and proactive handling and response to disasters can reduce the impact on an organization to a large extent. The ability of disaster recovery teams to detect precursors of disasters on time may help the organization avoid the disasters altogether. In situations in which detection of disasters beforehand is not possible, a swift implementation of disaster recovery procedures and plans plays an important role in minimizing the impact of disasters. The activation phase is the first step after the symptoms of a disaster are detected. Disaster recovery teams need to verify the occurrence of a disaster before activating the disaster recovery process. The activation phase involves the following:

- Notifying the affected entities and other stakeholders that will be actively involved in the disaster recovery process
- Assessing the damage to ascertain the urgency level of response
- Making a decision concerning disaster recovery process activation

Notification

The notification makes all affected entities aware of a disaster in the organization. It puts the organization into a disaster mode of operations, and activates the disaster recovery mechanisms implemented in the organization. It gives a formal instruction to disaster recovery teams to shift to disaster recovery mode.

Disaster notifications can be communicated by different telecommunication systems such as e-mails, faxes, and telephone calls. Organizations should have a notification policy that clearly outlines the type of communication mediums to be used in different scenarios and details of personnel to be contacted and notified in different situations.

A call tree is a general notification technique that can be used in the activation phase. It documents the primary and alternate contact methods and includes procedures to be followed if the personnel could not be contacted.

Notification information consists of the following:

- Nature of the disaster and the damage it may cause
- Loss of life, injuries, and damage to critical infrastructures
- First-response details
- Estimation of recovery time
- Alternate arrangements to minimize the impact on life and property
- Information on the briefings, meetings, and discussions for further response instructions
- Information and instructions for relocation if there is a need for short-term or permanent relocation
- Instructions for whom to contact for further information and assistance if required

Damage Assessment

Damage assessment is important for initiating an appropriate disaster recovery response. It is necessary for determining the urgency level and implementing the appropriate disaster recovery solution. For example, if damage assessment results for a power-failure case show that the power supplies will be restored before the systems run out of battery power, disaster recovery team will not have to go into panic mode.

A proper damage assessment also helps in avoiding unnecessary alarms. Damage assessment procedures and outcomes after disaster differ depending on the following factors:

- Nature and cause of disaster
- Criticality of operations and systems affected by the disaster
- Possibility of further damage due to the disastrous event
- Nature of loss to critical infrastructures
- Expected recovery time for affected systems and operations

Decision on Disaster Recovery Process Activation

The decision to activate the disaster recovery process requires a careful consideration of various factors, such as whether the alarm is true, how people will react to the situation, and if there is a need to really activate a comprehensive disaster recovery procedure. The decision to activate the disaster recovery process should be based on the damage assessment findings. Before deciding to activate the process, disaster recovery teams should also decide which plan is appropriate for the situation.

Execution Phase

The execution phase involves the implementation of disaster recovery plans, procedures, and solutions. It starts after the disaster recovery activation phase, when disaster recovery teams are ready to implement specific solutions to contain and overcome disasters. The execution phase includes activities such as opening emergency doors, starting power generators, making arrangements for relocation, and contacting law enforcement agencies to help in the DR effort. The following are important aspects of this phase:

- *Prioritization of disaster recovery activities*: Prioritization of critical operations and systems to recover after a disaster is important to ensure that the most critical assets and operations are restored first. This helps in minimizing the impact of the disaster.

- *Recovery procedures*: A well-defined methodological approach to disaster recovery is important for the execution of disaster recovery procedures. Disaster recovery teams should be aware of the sequence of processes they need to perform under various circumstances.

Reconstitution Phase

In this phase, the affected operations and systems are restored to normal operating conditions. The affected systems that cannot be restored to original conditions are replaced with completely new systems. Disaster recovery teams should ensure that the systems are free from disaster aftereffects before restoring them to the original facilities.

The reconstitution phase also involves the periodic inspection of restored systems to check their performance. The execution team should be involved until the restoration and testing is complete. This terminates with the shutdown of the disaster recovery systems and processes.

Disaster Recovery Objectives

The following are the three different types of objectives for the disaster recovery process:

1. *Short-term recovery objectives*: After the occurrence of an emergency, the first few hours and days are spent restoring the required structural (facilities) and nonstructural (power, water, sanitation, telecommunications, etc.) functions. The DR team should provide the direction and the required operational support to achieve and manage these objectives.

2. *Medium-term recovery objectives*: During the first weeks after an emergency event, the primary goal is to restore all the preidentified business functions that are found to be critical to normal business operations.

3. *Long-term recovery objectives*: The main objective of a DR effort is to resume normal operations. The long-term objectives focus on the resumption of operations to predisaster conditions. A long-term recovery team may be employed to consider and coordinate strategic planning for long-term recovery efforts. The timeline to restore to normal operations is dependent on the level of the disrupted critical services. In case of a major disaster, the recovery efforts can last for months or even years.

Disaster Recovery Checklist

Table 1-1 shows a sample checklist for disaster recovery procedures.

Plan: Technology	Yes	No
Is a written disaster recovery plan available?		
Is the plan current?		
Has the plan been tested?		
Are the legal or regulatory compliance requirements addressed in the plan?		
Are all the critical data and applications (including e-mail) part of the plan?		
Is there a clear recovery time objective for each business requirement?		
Is that recovery time objective tiered based on criticality to the business?		
Is a designated recovery site present for data?		
Are hardware, software, facilities, and service vendors part of the plan?		
Are critical data backed up on a frequent and regular basis?		
Are backups located off-site?		
Are backups tested?		
Are you located in a mandatory evacuation zone?		
Plan: People	**Yes**	**No**
Does the plan include employees (with current contact info) critical to recovery?		
Do those employees know their roles in the plan?		
Do you have a designated recovery site for people?		
Will your staff relocate?		
Has your staff participated in an actual test of your disaster recovery plan?		
Does your staff have access to documentation online and offline?		
Do you have an alternative if your staff is not available during an actual disaster?		
Do you require contractors or business partners to be available?		
Do those contractors/partners know about your plan and expectations?		
Do you have an alternative if your contractors/partners are not available?		
Plan: Data Center	**Yes**	**No**
Is your platform for critical data and applications located in a secure data center (DC)?		
Is access to the DC secured with badge, PIN, or biometric?		
Do you have access to a second DC networked to/with the primary DC (hot or cold)?		
Does your DC monitor and ensure proper temperature and humidity?		
Does your DC have adequate fire suppression?		
Is your hardware adequately secured and monitored inside the DC (or cage)?		
Does your DC provide fully conditioned power to all hardware?		
Does your DC provide redundant power with a UPS and generator?		
Does your DC have a power plan and scheduled maintenance?		
Does your DC test on a regular basis?		
Plan: Network	**Yes**	**No**
Does your network have multiple fiber connections to a SONET-based network service provider?		
Do you have multiple carrier-class ISPs to the Internet?		
Is your network failover integrated into the network topography?		
Do you perform BGP routing to facilitate failover?		

Table 1-1   Sample disaster recovery checklist

(*continues*)

Plan: Data Protection and Support	Yes	No
Are your data automatically backed up daily?		
Do you secure backup data off-site?		
Do you have a comprehensive security strategy with policies and procedures in place?		
Do your data have virus protection?		
Do you perform intrusion detection?		
Is your firewall managed and monitored?		
Do you employ or have access to live engineers, 24 hours a day, 7 days a week, 365 days a year?		

Table 1-1   Sample checklist for disaster recovery (continued)

Best Practices for Disaster Recovery

The following are some best practices for disaster recovery:

- *Dedicate and empower staff*: There should be a separate team in the organization to manage the business continuity planning. The team members should have access to a set of resources required to perform their roles during disaster recovery. The staff should be given proper training and should be well prepared to counter any disaster.

- *Divide and conquer*: To ensure business involvement, the organization should divide the business continuity and disaster recovery plan into two initiatives. Both have their own governance and goals. In case of disaster recovery, the goal is technical recovery, and the plan is created and managed by developers and engineers. The goal of business continuity is business process stability.

- *Design an independent plan*: DR teams and strategic planners should ensure that the disaster recovery plan is effective, even without the help of other plans and the involvement of people from other organizational teams. The plan should be implemented even when the key personnel in the recovery plan are unavailable. Proper backups should be maintained to take on the responsibility of key personnel.

- *Provide facilities*: Organizations should determine the right staffing to be involved during a disaster. They should also provide the appropriate services that are required to recover from disasters.

- *Align disaster recovery with application development*: Organizations should develop an isolated test environment that allows for full-time access and testing of all systems and applications. This allows the functions to be updated and tested regularly in order to minimize the occurrence of a disaster. It is advantageous to test the DR functions before a disaster strikes.

- *Try (and test) before you buy*: Organizations should make sure to try the trial version of any disaster recovery solution product before purchasing it. As there are different types of disasters and disaster recovery solutions, it is advisable to test the most appropriate recovery solution for that particular disaster.

Business Continuity

Business continuity is the ability of an organization to keep the business running even after a disaster strikes. It ensures that critical activities are available for users who have access to those activities. Business continuity also helps to prevent or reduce the interruption of operations and services.

Business continuity is not implemented at the time of a disaster, as it refers to activities performed daily to maintain service, consistency, and recoverability. Business continuity plans and processes help an organization in the following ways:

- Ensure uninterrupted critical business services
- Minimize business losses
- Ensure that the business is able meet its short-term and long-term objectives

Disaster Recovery Versus Business Continuity

The following are characteristics of disaster recovery:

- Disaster recovery deals with recovering systems to their normal state in the event of a disaster.
- It tends to deal with systems and data affected by a disaster.
- It is reactive, as its focus is to restore the business after a disaster.
- It includes plans and procedures that enable businesses to deal with a crisis.
- It ensures that the business is out of the crisis.

The following are characteristics of business continuity:

- Business continuity involves prioritizing various business processes and recovering the most important ones first.
- It is concerned with the overall business operation.
- It is proactive, as it focuses on avoiding or mitigating risks.
- It guarantees the survival and functioning of the business during and after a crisis.
- It does not ensure that the business has completely recovered from the crisis.

Business Continuity and Disaster Recovery Planning

Disaster recovery plans enable organizations to analyze and identify the different ways to handle a disaster. Business continuity planning helps organizations to develop and document procedures that enable them to achieve predefined business objectives before, during, and after a disaster. Business continuity plans should be tailored according to the particular needs of the organization. The objectives of business continuity plans are to:

- Protect corporate assets
- Provide management control for risks associated with the organization
- Ensure the survival and continuity of the business after a disaster
- Ensure practical management control over any business interruption

The following are the basic steps in any BC/DR plan:

1. Project initiation
2. Risk assessment
3. Business impact analysis
4. Mitigation strategy development
5. Plan development
6. Training, testing, and auditing
7. Plan maintenance

Security Management Plan

A *security management plan* is a documented set of policies and procedures to ensure the security of an organization's operations and assets. It includes guidelines on the procedures to minimize the perceived risks to an acceptable level and provides appropriate response measures for disasters. The main objective of the security management plan is to establish a secured organizational environment by reducing the risks.

A security management plan enables organizations to effectively manage security issues. It educates the faculty, staff, and visitors about the basic security measures to be taken during an emergency. The plan also helps an organization coordinate its response to different security incidents.

A security management plan generally includes the following:

- List of identified threats or risks to the organization
- Description of different countermeasures for identified threats
- Guidelines for reporting incidents
- First-response strategies for different disasters
- Description of risk mitigation strategies
- Assignment of roles and responsibilities in case of emergencies
- Guidelines for auditing and updating established plans

Disaster recovery teams and senior management are responsible for developing, testing, implementing, and monitoring security management plans according to the organization's requirements and business objectives.

Natural Threats to Consider While Preparing a Security Management Plan

Natural disasters are often sudden, giving organizations only a small amount of time to deploy any security measures. They have a negative effect on the environment and people. These types of disasters include natural hazards such as volcanic eruptions, earthquakes, and landslides that result in loss of life, property, and economy.

Natural disasters can cause massive losses and may affect a large population and geographical area. With the advancement of meteorological science, it is now possible to forecast certain natural disasters with varying precision; however, it is still not possible to completely avoid their effects on life and property. Natural disasters may cost billions of dollars and cripple economies. Natural disasters may jeopardize the survival of organizations. The following are some of the natural threats that should be considered when preparing a security management plan:

- Fires
- Floods
- Earthquakes
- Volcanoes
- Hurricanes

Fires

Organizations need to build a security management plan that helps them effectively handle fire incidents. The security management plan should include the following measures:

- Emergency exit doors to provide a way out for employees, important systems, and files
- Fire extinguishers at different points on the organization's premises to minimize the extent of the fire or to completely extinguish the fire
- Free space around the premises to allow fire engines and firefighters to operate freely
- Provisions for backups of all important data and documents at a third-party site

Floods

Floods often hit areas where there are rivers or lakes or where the drainage facilities are poor. The security management plan should include the following measures:

- The organization should build its structures in a secured location where flooding problems are minimal. Before building on a site, the organization should check for the possibility of flooding in that area.
- The organization should avoid storing important documents, data, and valuable property on the ground floor. This can help prevent damage to important assets during a flood.
- The organization can develop proper drainage facilities to reduce the incidence of most flooding problems. Floods are generally caused by poor drainage facilities.

Earthquakes

Earthquakes can lead to the destruction of an organization's valuable assets. Earthquakes can take place any time without a warning, making planning and precaution the only ways to protect life and property and to minimize damage. A security management plan should include the following measures:

- Before building on a site, the organization should study the geographical location to discover the frequency of earthquakes in that area.
- The organization needs to provide proper emergency exit facilities for employees and valuable assets during an earthquake.
- The organization should maintain a backup of all important resources and data at a different location in case of an earthquake.
- The organization should maintain emergency phone numbers and have a safe evacuation plan.
- If the building is in an earthquake-prone area, it should incorporate all necessary structural elements to minimize damage during an earthquake.

Man-Made Threats as Part of a Security Management Plan

Man-made disasters generally occur due to intervention, ignorance, or malicious intentions. In intentional threats, individuals with the intent to damage an organization or personnel opt for different methods and techniques. Individuals without any malicious intentions unknowingly cause disasters. Man-made disasters can range from events such as system crashes to terrorism.

Man-made attacks are classified into the following general categories:

- Human error
- Intentional attacks

Human Error

Disasters caused by human error are those that are mostly the result of errors in carrying out certain operations or processes, ignorance, or negligence. Disasters caused by human error include the following:

- Accidents
- Power outages
- Telecommunication outages
- System or network crashes

Accidents An accident may be the result of a person's inexperience or carelessness, or it may be the result of equipment malfunction. The following are some examples of accidents:

- A user uses a system and accidentally modifies or deletes data
- A user deletes data that are linked to data in another file, making the other file inoperable
- A user shuts down a system while critical operations are running

The security management plan should consider the following measures:

- Store a backup of all important data
- Keep backup systems on hand to replace any damaged systems
- Train personnel in the proper use of systems or equipment
- Prepare a checklist regarding the typical mistakes that personnel make

Power Outages Power outages are caused by an interruption in the power supply. Power outages can be short term or long term. The following are human errors involved in power outages:

- Mechanical failure that includes failure at the power station, damage of a power line, or a short circuit
- Overuse of power by the organization

The security management plan should include the following measures:

- Have a regular backup of data and systems to avoid any loss of data
- Make use of power generators to minimize data losses and system crashes
- Implement measures to prevent any fluctuations of power that may result in system crashes
- Do not use more power than necessary, and do not overload the power infrastructure

Telecommunication Outages Telecommunication outages disrupt communications, making it more difficult for the organization to handle emergencies. These types of outages include failure of Internet connections; communication stations, such as radio and television; and other communication media.
Telecommunication outages can occur due to the following:

- Mechanical failure caused by faulty equipment or machinery
- Human error

The security management plan should include the following measures:

- Make use of emergency alarms or signals to communicate about threat situations
- Make use of risk management techniques to reduce the impact of outages

System or Network Crashes When a system or network crashes, it stops responding to other parts of the system or network. A system or network crash can be caused by the following:

- Application errors
- Power outages
- Threats from the external and internal environment
- User actions
- Hardware faults

The security management plan should include the following measures:

- Make sure there is a continuous power supply to all critical systems.
- All systems should be protected by an effective antivirus tool.
- Users should only be allowed to perform the actions necessary to do their work.

Intentional Attacks

Intentional disasters refer to incidents when a person attempts to damage an organization or person for financial gain or revenge. The following are some human intentions that can harm or damage an organization or personnel:

- Terrorism
- Hacking
- Data theft

Intentional attacks such as terrorism and hacking are generally used as tools to achieve socioeconomic objectives, whereas financial gain is a prime objective in cases involving data theft. Organizations can overcome these attacks by means of awareness, vigilance, and proper preparedness for a timely response.

Terrorism Terrorism can damage a country socially and economically. The main intentions of terrorism are loss of life and disturbing a country's financial system. The security management plan should include the following measures:

- Have a security system and perform security checks to allow only authorized personnel into the building.
- Install an emergency alarm signal to alert employees and security forces in case of any terrorist actions in the organization.
- Deploy security personnel outside the building to combat any terrorist action outside the building.

- Monitor the Web sites that employees access to make sure they are not visiting terrorism sites.
- Place security cameras at different places all over the building to provide the most coverage.

Hacking Attackers hack systems and networks to illegally gain information or to cause damage to an organization or personnel. Hacking involves infringement on the privacy of others or damage to computer-based property such as files, Web pages, and software. The security management plan should include the following measures:

- Provide proper authentication to the organization's data and Web sites so that only authorized users and employees have access.
- Perform regular audits on system logs, user accounts, and passwords.
- Use a variety of antihacking tools.
- Disable any unused network services or services with known vulnerabilities.
- Install up-to-date security updates and patches.
- Place valuable information in a secured place to which third parties do not have access.

Data Theft Attackers acquire an organization's valuable data for their own profit. Attackers illegally copy information from either a business or an individual. Stolen information typically includes user information such as passwords, Social Security numbers, credit card information, and other personal information, as well as confidential corporate information.

The security management plan should include the following measures:

- Prevent data from unnecessarily flowing out of the organization.
- Allow personnel to access only the data they need to do their jobs.
- Maintain strong password protection on important data to prevent illegitimate access.
- Do not store passwords and other personal data on paper in unsecured areas, such as on a user's desk or in a trash bin.
- Make use of different encryption tools to make data unreadable to outsiders.

Chapter Summary

- A disaster is a natural or human-caused incident that negatively affects organizations or the environment.
- *Disaster recovery* involves the processes, policies, and procedures necessary for the recovery of operations and the continuation of the critical functions of an organization after a disaster.
- Business continuity is the ability of an organization to keep the business running after a disaster.
- A disaster recovery plan enables an organization to analyze and identify different ways to handle a disaster.
- Business continuity is not implemented at the time of a disaster, as it refers to activities performed daily to maintain service, consistency, and recoverability.
- A security management plan enables an organization to effectively manage security issues.
- Natural threats typically come without much warning, giving organizations little time to deploy security measures.
- Man-made disasters are caused by intervention, ignorance, or malicious intent.
- Power outages are caused by interruptions in the power supply.

Review Questions

1. Define disaster recovery.

2. List the responsibilities of a disaster recovery team.

3. Explain the different phases of disaster recovery.

4. List the best practices for disaster recovery.

5. Define business continuity. Discuss different factors that affect business continuity.

6. Describe the difference between disaster recovery and business continuity.

7. Describe the purpose of a security management plan.

8. Describe what should be included in a security management plan to deal with fire incidents.

_____

_____

_____

_____

9. Describe what should be included in a security management plan to deal with earthquake incidents.

_____

_____

_____

_____

10. Describe the different components of a security management plan to deal with telecommunication outages.

_____

_____

_____

_____

Hands-On Projects

1. Navigate to Chapter 1 of the Student Resource Center. Open data_recovery.pdf. Read the following sections:

   - 1.1 Introduction
   - 1.2 Reasons for Disaster Recovery
   - 1.5 Business Continuity Planning

2. Navigate to Chapter 1 of the Student Resource Center. Open Disaster Recovery Plans.pdf. Read the following sections:

   - Chapter 1: Introduction
   - Chapter 2: Research Background Information
   - Chapter 3: The Disaster Recovery Plan

3. Navigate to Chapter 1 of the Student Resource Center. Open Disaster Recovery Plan-part. pdf. Read the following sections:

   - 1. Notification Process
   - 1.2. System Unavailability Notification
   - 2. Recovery Process

4. Navigate to Chapter 1 of the Student Resource Center. Open Disaster Recovery Best Practices.pdf. Read the following sections:

   - 1 Executive Summary
   - 2 Disaster Recovery Planning
   - 3 Disaster Recovery Phases
   - 4 The Disaster Recovery Plan Document

5. Navigate to Chapter 1 of the Student Resource Center. Open chapter-13.pdf. Read the following sections:

   - Introduction
   - Road Accidents and Stampede

6. Navigate to Chapter 1 of the Student Resource Center. Open doc12973-7a.pdf. Read the following sections:

   - Natural Disasters
   - Volcanic Eruptions

7. Navigate to Chapter 1 of the Student Resource Center. Open txt-sini.pdf. Read the following sections:

   - Principal Causes of Disasters
   - Disaster Plan

Chapter 2

Laws and Acts

Objectives

After completing this chapter, you should be able to:

- Understand various laws related to disaster recovery

Key Terms

Civil law a set of rules that the state has established for itself, generally through common usage (common law), judicial decision, or statutory legislation, dealing with the private rights of individuals; in civil cases the defendant is never incarcerated and never executed, but if found liable, is usually fined for the damage caused by his or her action.

Criminal law a set of rules and statutes that specifically defines conduct prohibited by the state to protect public safety and welfare; in criminal prosecutions, the defendant is presumed innocent, and the state must prove beyond a reasonable doubt that he or she has indeed violated the law. The defendant, if found guilty, is usually punished by incarceration, fines paid to the government, or, in capital cases, execution.

Introduction to Laws and Acts

Local, state, and federal governments develop and implement a complex variety of laws and regulations related to disasters, regulating land use, building practices, emergency response planning, and other actions. These laws define government and private liability during the process of disaster recovery. Generally, laws can be put into two categories:

1. *Civil law*: A set of rules that the state has established for itself, generally through common usage (common law), judicial decision, or statutory legislation, dealing with the private rights of individuals. In civil cases the defendant is never incarcerated and never executed, but if found liable, is usually fined for the damage caused by his or her action.

2. *Criminal law*: A set of rules and statutes that specifically defines conduct prohibited by the state to protect public safety and welfare. In criminal prosecutions, the defendant is presumed

innocent, and the state must prove beyond a reasonable doubt that he or she has indeed violated the law. The defendant, if found guilty, is usually punished by incarceration, fines paid to the government, or, in capital cases, execution.

Every business is governed by laws that dictate how it must conduct itself in the normal course of business. For a publicly traded company, regulations are likely to include financial reporting and corporate governance rules intended to protect investors. In the case of a disaster, the burden of the proof is on the company to prove that all reasonable measures had been taken to mitigate the harm caused by the disaster. Courts evaluate liability through the following:

- Probability of loss
- Magnitude of damage
- Balance against the cost of prevention

This chapter familiarizes you with the laws and regulations relevant to disaster recovery, and serves as a reference for the full text of some of these laws and regulations.

Types of Relevant Acts

Acts that influence disaster recovery policies, practices, and standards include the following:

- Business contingency planning acts
- Liability acts
- Life/safety acts
- Risk-reduction acts
- Security acts
- Vital records acts

United States of America Laws and Acts

Sarbanes-Oxley Act of 2002[1]

The Sarbanes-Oxley Act introduced significant legislative changes to financial practice and corporate governance regulation. It has the following stated objective: "To protect investors by improving the accuracy and reliability of corporate disclosures made pursuant to the securities laws."

All companies must comply with this act as of 2005. It is organized into eleven titles, although sections 302, 401, 404, 409, 802, and 906 are the most significant for disaster recovery. In addition, the act also created a public company accounting board. This is a very high profile act, so any company must be extremely careful to comply with it.

The act covers financial reporting to the Securities and Exchange Commission (SEC) and states that auditors must keep every document regarding clients for at least seven years.

Foreign Corrupt Practices Act (FCPA)[2]

U.S. firms seeking to do business in foreign markets must be familiar with the FCPA. In general, the FCPA prohibits corrupt payments made to foreign officials for the purpose of obtaining or maintaining business. In addition, other statutes such as the mail and wire fraud statutes, 18 U.S.C. § 1341, 1343, and the Travel Act, 18 U.S.C. § 1952, which provides for federal prosecution of violations of state commercial bribery statutes, may also apply to such conduct.

The Department of Justice is the chief enforcement agency, with a lesser role played by the Securities and Exchange Commission (SEC). The Office of General Counsel of the Department of Commerce also answers general questions from U.S. exporters concerning the FCPA's basic requirements and constraints.

Enforcement

The Department of Justice is responsible for all criminal enforcement and for civil enforcement of the antibribery provisions with respect to domestic concerns as well as foreign companies and nationals. The SEC is responsible for the civil enforcement of the antibribery provisions with respect to issuers.

Antibribery Provisions

The FCPA makes it unlawful to bribe foreign government officials to obtain or retain business. With respect to the basic prohibition, there are five elements that must be met to constitute a violation of the act. These are described below.

Who The FCPA potentially applies to any individual, firm, officer, director, employee, or agent of a firm and any stockholder acting on behalf of a firm. Individuals and firms may also be penalized if they order, authorize, or assist someone else to violate the antibribery provisions or if they conspire to violate those provisions.

Under the FCPA, U.S. jurisdiction over corrupt payments made to foreign officials depends upon whether the violator is an issuer, a domestic concern, or a foreign national or business.

An issuer is a corporation that has issued securities that have been registered in the United States or who are required to file periodic reports with the SEC. A domestic concern is any individual who is a citizen, national, or resident of the United States, or any corporation, partnership, association, joint-stock company, business trust, unincorporated organization, or sole proprietorship that has its principal place of business in the United States, or that is organized under the laws of a state, territory, possession, or commonwealth of the United States.

Issuers and domestic concerns may be held liable under the FCPA under either territorial or nationality jurisdiction principles. For acts taken within the territory of the United States, issuers and domestic concerns are liable if they take an act in furtherance of a corrupt payment made to a foreign official using the U.S. mails or other means or instrumentalities of interstate commerce. Such means or instrumentalities include telephone calls, fax transmissions, wire transfers, and interstate or international travel. In addition, issuers and domestic concerns may be held liable for any act in furtherance of a corrupt payment taken outside the United States. Thus, a U.S. company or national may be held liable for a corrupt payment authorized by employees or agents operating entirely outside the United States, using money from foreign bank accounts, and without any involvement by personnel located within the United States.

Prior to 1998, foreign companies, with the exception of those who qualified as issuers, and foreign nationals were not covered by the FCPA. The 1998 amendments expanded the FCPA to assert territorial jurisdiction over foreign companies and nationals. A foreign company or person is now subject to the FCPA if it causes, directly or through agents, an act in furtherance of the corrupt payment to take place within the territory of the United States. There is, however, no requirement that such act make use of the U.S. mails or other means or instrumentalities of interstate commerce.

Finally, U.S. parent corporations may be held liable for the acts of foreign subsidiaries where they authorize, direct, or control the activity in question, as can U.S. citizens or residents, themselves domestic concerns, who were employed by or acting on behalf of such foreign-incorporated subsidiaries.

Corrupt Intent The person making or authorizing the payment must have a corrupt intent, and the payment must be intended to induce the recipient to misuse his or her official position to direct business wrongfully to the payer or to any other person. The FCPA does not require that a corrupt act succeeds in its purpose. The offer or promise of a corrupt payment can constitute a violation of the statute. The FCPA prohibits any corrupt payment intended to influence any act or decision of a foreign official in his or her official capacity, to induce the official to do or omit any act in violation of his or her lawful duty, to obtain any improper advantage, or to induce a foreign official to use his or her influence improperly to affect or influence any act or decision.

Payment The FCPA prohibits paying, offering, promising to pay (or authorizing to pay or offer) money or anything of value.

Recipient The prohibition extends only to corrupt payments made to a foreign official, a foreign political party or party official, or any candidate for foreign political office. A foreign official means any officer or employee of a foreign government, a public international organization, or any department or agency thereof, or any person acting in an official capacity.

The FCPA applies to payments to any public official, regardless of rank or position. The FCPA focuses on the purpose of the payment instead of the particular duties of the official receiving the payment, offer, or promise of payment, and there are exceptions to the antibribery provision for "facilitating payments for routine governmental action."

Business Purpose Test The FCPA prohibits payments made in order to assist firms in obtaining or retaining business for or with, or directing business to, any person. The Department of Justice interprets "obtaining or retaining business" broadly, such that the phrase encompasses more than the mere award or renewal of a contract. It should be noted that the business to be obtained or retained does not need to be with a foreign government or foreign government instrumentality.

Sanctions Against Bribery

Criminal The following criminal penalties may be imposed for violations of the FCPA's antibribery provisions:

- Corporations and other business entities are subject to a fine of up to $2,000,000.
- Officers, directors, stockholders, employees, and agents are subject to a fine of up to $100,000 and imprisonment for up to five years.

Moreover, under the Alternative Fines Act, these fines may be actually quite higher—the actual fine may be up to twice the benefit that the defendant sought to obtain by making the corrupt payment. Fines imposed on individuals may not be paid by their employer or principal.

Civil The attorney general or the SEC, as appropriate, may bring a civil action for a fine of up to $10,000 against any firm as well as any officer, director, employee, or agent of a firm, or stockholder acting on behalf of the firm, who violates the antibribery provisions. In addition, in an SEC enforcement action, the court may impose an additional fine not to exceed the following:

- The gross amount of the pecuniary gain to the defendant as a result of the violation
- A specified dollar limitation

The specified dollar limitations are based on the egregiousness of the violation, ranging from $5,000 to $100,000 for a natural person and $50,000 to $500,000 for any other person.

The attorney general or the SEC, as appropriate, may also bring a civil action to enjoin any act or practice of a firm whenever it appears that the firm (or an officer, director, employee, agent, or stockholder acting on behalf of the firm) is in violation (or about to be) of the antibribery provisions.

Other Governmental Action Under guidelines issued by the Office of Management and Budget, a person or firm found in violation of the FCPA may be barred from doing business with the federal government. Indictment alone can lead to suspension of the right to do business with the government. The president has directed that no executive agency shall allow any party to participate in any procurement or nonprocurement activity if any agency has debarred, suspended, or otherwise excluded that party from participation in a procurement or nonprocurement activity.

In addition, a person or firm found guilty of violating the FCPA may be ruled ineligible to receive export licenses; the SEC may suspend or bar persons from the securities business and impose civil penalties on persons in the securities business for violations of the FCPA; the Commodity Futures Trading Commission and the Overseas Private Investment Corporation both provide for possible suspension or debarment from the agency programs for violation of the FCPA; and a payment made to a foreign government official that is unlawful under the FCPA cannot be deducted under the tax laws as a business expense.

Private Cause of Action Conduct that violates the antibribery provisions of the FCPA may also give rise to a private cause of action for treble damages under the Racketeer Influenced and Corrupt Organizations Act (RICO), or to actions under other federal or state laws. For example, an action might be brought under RICO by a competitor who alleges that the bribery caused the defendant to win a foreign contract.

Health Care: HIPAA Regulations[3,4]

Public Law 104-191 of the 104th Congress has the following stated purpose:

To amend the Internal Revenue Code of 1986 to improve portability and continuity of health insurance coverage in the group and individual markets; to combat waste, fraud, and abuse in health insurance and health care delivery; to promote the use of medical savings accounts; to improve access to the long-term care services and coverage; to simplify the administration of the health insurance; and for other purposes.

HIPAA Privacy and Disclosures in Emergency Situations

The HIPAA Privacy Rule allows the patient's information to be shared to assist in disaster relief efforts and to assist patients in receiving the care they need. Providers and health plans covered by the HIPAA Privacy Rule can share the patient's information in the following ways:

- *Treatment*: Health care providers can share patient information as necessary to provide treatment. Treatment includes the following:

  - Sharing information with other providers (including hospitals and clinics)

  - Referring patients for treatment (including linking patients with the available providers in areas where the patients have relocated)

  - Coordinating patient's care with others (such as emergency relief workers or others that can help patients obtain the appropriate health services)

  Providers can also share the patient's information to the extent necessary to seek payment for these health care services.

- *Notification*: Health care providers can share the patient's information as necessary to identify, locate, and notify family members, guardians, or anyone else responsible for the individual's care of the individual's location, general condition, or death. The health care provider should get verbal permission from individuals, when possible; however, if the individual is incapacitated or not available, providers may share information for these purposes if, in their professional judgment, doing so is in the patient's best interest.

  Thus, when necessary, the hospital may notify the police, the press, or the public at large to the extent necessary to help locate, identify, or otherwise notify the family members and others as to the location and general condition of their loved ones.

  In addition, when a health care provider is sharing information with disaster relief organizations that, like the American Red Cross, are authorized by law or by their charters to assist in disaster relief efforts, it is unnecessary to obtain the patient's permission to share the information if doing so would interfere with the organization's ability to respond to the emergency.

- *Imminent danger*: Providers can share the patient's information with anyone as necessary to prevent or lessen a serious and imminent threat to the health and safety of a person or the public, consistent with applicable law and the provider's standards of ethical conduct.

- *Facility directory*: Health care facilities maintaining a directory of patients can tell people who call or ask about individuals whether the individual is at the facility, his or her location in the facility, and his or her general condition.

The HIPAA Privacy Rule does not apply to disclosures if they are not made by entities covered by the Privacy Rule. Thus, for instance, the HIPAA Privacy Rule does not restrict the American Red Cross from sharing a patient's information.

Financial Institutions: Financial Modernization Act of 1999[5]

The Financial Modernization Act of 1999, also known as the Gramm-Leach-Bliley Act or GLB Act, includes provisions to protect consumers' personal financial information held by financial institutions. There are three main parts to the act's privacy requirements:

1. The Financial Privacy Rule

2. The Safeguards Rule

3. Pretexting provisions

The GLB Act gives authority to eight federal agencies and the states to administer and enforce the Financial Privacy Rule and the Safeguards Rule. These two regulations apply to financial institutions, which include not only banks, securities firms, and insurance companies, but also companies providing many other types of financial products and services to consumers. These services include the following:

- Lending, brokering, or servicing any type of consumer loan

- Transferring or safeguarding money

- Preparing individual tax returns

- Providing financial advice or credit counseling

- Providing residential real estate settlement services

- Collecting consumer debts

The Financial Privacy Rule governs the collection and disclosure of customers' personal financial information by financial institutions. It also applies to companies who receive such information, whether or not they are financial institutions.

The Safeguards Rule requires all financial institutions to design, implement, and maintain safeguards to protect the customer's information. The Safeguards Rule applies not only to the financial institutions that collect information from their own customers, but also to those that receive customer information from other financial institutions.

The pretexting provisions of the GLB Act protect consumers from individuals and companies that obtain their personal financial information under false pretenses, a practice known as pretexting.

Flood Disaster Protection Act of 1973[6]

The act's stated purpose is as follows:

To expand the national flood insurance program by substantially increasing the limits of the coverage and total amount of insurance authorized to be outstanding and by requiring known flood-prone communities to participate in the program, and for other purposes.[7]

Findings and Declaration of Purpose

SEC.2. (a) The Congress finds that—

- (1) annual losses throughout the Nation from floods and mudslides are increasing at an alarming rate, largely as a result of the accelerating development of, and concentration of population in, areas of flood and mudslide hazards;
- (2) the availability of Federal loans, grants, guaranties, insurance, and other forms of financial assistance are often the determining factors in the utilization of land and the location and construction of public and of private industrial, commercial, and residential facilities;
- (3) property acquired or constructed with grants or other Federal assistance may be exposed to risk of loss through floods, thus frustrating the purpose for which such assistance was extended;
- (4) Federal instrumentalities insure or otherwise provide financial protection to banking and credit institutions whose assets include a substantial number of mortgage loans and other indebtedness secured by property exposed to loss and damage from floods and mudslides;
- (5) the Nation cannot afford the tragic losses of life caused annually by flood occurrences, nor the increasing losses of property suffered by flood victims, most of whom are still inadequately compensated despite the provision of costly disaster relief benefits; and
- (6) it is in the public interest for persons already living in flood-prone areas to have both an opportunity to purchase flood insurance and access to more adequate limits of coverage, so that they will be indemnified for their losses in the event of future flood disasters.

SEC.2. (b) The purpose of this Act, therefore, is to—

- (1) substantially increase the limits of coverage authorized under the national flood insurance program;
- (2) provide for the expeditious identification of, and the dissemination of information concerning, flood-prone areas;
- (3) require State or local communities, as a condition of future Federal financial assistance, to participate in the flood insurance program and to adopt adequate flood plan ordinances with effective enforcement provisions consistent with Federal standards to reduce or avoid future flood losses; and
- (4) require the purchase of flood insurance by property owners who are being assisted by Federal programs or by federally supervised, regulated, or insured agencies or institutions in the acquisition or improvement of land or facilities located or to be located in identified areas having special flood hazards.

Robert T. Stafford Disaster Relief and Emergency Assistance Act[8]

Robert T. Stafford Disaster Relief and Emergency Assistance Act, also known as the Stafford Act, is amended by Public Law 106-390, October 30, 2000.[9]

SEC. 101. (b) It is the intent of the Congress, by this Act, to provide an orderly and continuing means of assistance by the Federal Government to State and local governments in carrying out their responsibilities to alleviate the suffering and damage which result from such disasters by—

- (1) revising and broadening the scope of existing disaster relief programs;

- (2) encouraging the development of comprehensive disaster preparedness and assistance plans, programs, capabilities, and organizations by the States and by local governments;

- (3) achieving greater coordination and responsiveness of disaster preparedness and relief programs;

- (4) encouraging individuals, States, and local governments to protect themselves by obtaining insurance coverage to supplement or replace governmental assistance;

- (5) encouraging hazard mitigation measures to reduce losses from disasters, including development of land use and construction regulations; and

- (6) providing Federal assistance programs for both public and private losses sustained in disasters

Overview of the Stafford Act[10]

The Stafford Act authorizes the president to issue major disaster declarations that authorize federal agencies to provide assistance to states overwhelmed by disasters. Through executive orders, the president has delegated to the Federal Emergency Management Agency (FEMA), within the Department of Homeland Security (DHS), responsibility for administering the major provisions of the Stafford Act. Assistance authorized by the statute is available to individuals, families, state and local governments, and certain nonprofit organizations.

Activities undertaken under authority of the Stafford Act are provided through funds appropriated to the Disaster Relief Fund (DRF). Federal assistance supported by DRF money is used by states, localities, and certain nonprofit organizations to provide mass care, restore damaged or destroyed facilities, clear debris, and aid individuals and families with uninsured needs, among other activities.

Presidential Declarations

Under Stafford Act authority, five types of actions may be taken, summarized as follows:

1. *Major disaster*: The president issues a major disaster declaration after receiving a request from the governor of the affected state. Major disaster declarations may be issued after a natural catastrophe or, "regardless of cause, fire, flood, or explosion." A declaration authorizes DHS to administer various federal disaster assistance programs for victims of the declared disasters. Each major disaster declaration specifies the type of incident covered, the time period covered, the types of disaster assistance available, the counties affected by the declaration, and the name of the federal coordinating officer.

2. *Emergency*: The declaration process for emergencies is similar to that used for major disasters; the president may, however, issue an emergency declaration without a gubernatorial request if primary responsibility rests with the federal government. An emergency declaration may be issued on "any occasion or instance" in which the president determines that federal assistance is required. Under an emergency declaration, the federal government funds and undertakes emergency response activities, debris removal, and individual assistance and housing programs. DRF expenditures for an emergency are limited to $5 million per declaration unless the president determines that there is a continuing need; Congress must be notified if the $5 million ceiling is breached.

3. *Fire suppression*: The Secretary of DHS is authorized to provide fire suppression assistance to supplement the resources of communities when fires threaten such destruction as would warrant a major disaster declaration.

4. *Defense emergency*: Upon request from the governor of an affected state, the president may authorize the Department of Defense (DOD) to carry out emergency work for a period not to exceed 10 days. DOD emergency work is limited to work essential for the preservation of life and property.

5. *Predeclaration activities*: When a situation threatens human health and safety, and a disaster is imminent but not yet declared, the Secretary of DHS may place agency employees on alert. DHS monitors the status of the situation, communicates with state emergency officials on potential assistance requirements, and deploys teams and resources to maximize the speed and effectiveness of the anticipated federal response and, when necessary, performs preparedness and preliminary damage assessment activities.

In considering a gubernatorial request for disaster relief, the president evaluates a number of factors, including the cause of the catastrophe, damages, needs, certification by state officials that state and local governments will comply with cost sharing and other requirements, and official requests for assistance. FEMA has established thresholds that are considered by the president and DHS officials in the process of determining whether a major disaster is to be declared. Neither the Stafford Act nor implementing regulations provide for a Congressional role in the declaration process.

Types of Assistance and Eligibility

FEMA has established three major categories of aid under the Stafford Act—individual and household, public, and hazard mitigation assistance. The persons and organizations eligible for assistance authorized by the Stafford Act may be summarized as follows:

1. *Individuals and households*: Immediate temporary shelter; cash grants (maximum of approximately $25,000, adjusted for inflation) for uninsured emergency personal needs; temporary housing assistance (rental and mortgage payments), generally for 18 months; home repair grants; unemployment assistance due to the disaster; debris removal from private property when deemed in the public interest; emergency food supplies; legal aid for low-income individuals; and crisis counseling

2. *State, tribal, and local governments and certain private nonprofit organizations*: Repair, reconstruction, or replacement of infrastructure and recreational facilities; emergency protective measures, emergency communications, and transportation systems; and loans to replace lost revenue or meet federal cost-sharing requirements

3. *State governments*: Hazard mitigation assistance to reduce future disaster losses

CAN-SPAM Act of 2003[11]

Public Law 108–187

Section 1: Short Title

This Act may be cited as the "Controlling the Assault of Non-Solicited Pornography and Marketing Act of 2003," or the "CAN-SPAM Act of 2003."

Section 2: Congressional Findings and Policy

(a) Findings.—The Congress finds the following:

(1) Electronic mail has become an important and popular means of communication, relied on by millions of Americans on a daily basis for personal and commercial purposes. Its low cost and global reach make it convenient and efficient, and offer unique opportunities for the development and growth of frictionless commerce.

(2) The convenience and efficiency of electronic mail are threatened by the extremely rapid growth in the volume of unsolicited commercial electronic mail. Unsolicited commercial electronic mail is currently estimated to account for over half of all electronic mail traffic, up from an estimated 7% in 2001, and the volume continues to rise. Most of these messages are fraudulent or deceptive in one or more respects.

(3) The receipt of unsolicited commercial electronic mail may result in costs to recipients who cannot refuse to accept such mail and who incur costs for the storage of such mail, or for the time spent accessing, reviewing, and discarding such mail, or for both.

(4) The receipt of a large number of unwanted messages also decreases the convenience of electronic mail and creates a risk that wanted electronic mail messages, both commercial and noncommercial, will be lost, overlooked, or discarded amidst the larger volume of unwanted messages, thus reducing the reliability and usefulness of electronic mail to the recipient.

(5) Some commercial electronic mail contains material that many recipients may consider vulgar or pornographic in nature.

(6) The growth in unsolicited commercial electronic mail imposes significant monetary costs on providers of Internet access services, businesses, and educational and nonprofit institutions that

carry and receive such mail, as there is a finite volume of mail that such providers, businesses, and institutions can handle without further investment in infrastructure.

(7) Many senders of unsolicited commercial electronic mail purposefully disguise the source of such mail.

(8) Many senders of unsolicited commercial electronic mail purposefully include misleading information in the messages' subject lines in order to induce the recipients to view the messages.

(9) While some senders of commercial electronic mail messages provide simple and reliable ways for recipients to reject (or "opt-out" of) receipt of commercial electronic mail from such senders in the future, other senders provide no such "opt-out" mechanism, or refuse to honor the requests of recipients not to receive electronic mail from such senders in the future, or both.

(10) Many senders of bulk unsolicited commercial electronic mail use computer programs to gather large numbers of electronic mail addresses on an automated basis from Internet Web sites or online services where users must post their addresses in order to make full use of the Web site or service.

(11) Many States have enacted legislation intended to regulate or reduce unsolicited commercial electronic mail, but these statutes impose different standards and requirements. As a result, they do not appear to have been successful in addressing the problems associated with unsolicited commercial electronic mail, in part because, since an electronic mail address does not specify a geographic location, it can be extremely difficult for law-abiding businesses to know with which of these disparate statutes they are required to comply.

(12) The problems associated with the rapid growth and abuse of unsolicited commercial electronic mail cannot be solved by Federal legislation alone. The development and adoption of technological approaches and the pursuit of cooperative efforts with other countries will be necessary as well.

(b) Congressional Determination of Public Policy.—On the basis of the findings in subsection (a), the Congress determines that—

(1) there is a substantial government interest in regulation of commercial electronic mail on a nationwide basis;

(2) senders of commercial electronic mail should not mislead recipients as to the source or content of such mail; and

(3) recipients of commercial electronic mail have a right to decline to receive additional commercial electronic mail from the same source.

Requirements for Commercial E-Mailers[12]

The CAN-SPAM Act of 2003 establishes requirements for those who send commercial e-mail, spells out penalties for spammers and companies whose products are advertised in spam if they violate the law, and gives consumers the right to ask e-mailers to stop spamming them.

The law covers e-mail whose primary purpose is advertising or promoting a commercial product or service, including content on a Web site. A "transactional or relationship message" e-mail that facilitates an agreed-upon transaction or updates a customer in an existing business relationship may not contain false or misleading routing information, but otherwise is exempt from most provisions of the CAN-SPAM Act.

The Federal Trade Commission (FTC) is authorized to enforce the CAN-SPAM Act. CAN-SPAM also gives the Department of Justice (DOJ) the authority to enforce its criminal sanctions. Other federal and state agencies can enforce the law against organizations under their jurisdiction, and companies that provide Internet access may sue violators as well.

The following are the law's main provisions:

- *Bans false or misleading header information*: Any e-mail's From header, To header, and routing information must be accurate, and the person who initiated the e-mail must be identified.

- *Prohibits deceptive subject lines*: The subject line cannot mislead the recipient about the contents or subject matter of the message.

- *Requires an opt-out method*: There must be a return e-mail address or another Internet-based response mechanism that allows a recipient to request that no future e-mail messages be sent to that e-mail address, and those requests must be honored. There may be a menu of choices allowing a recipient to opt out of certain types of messages, but there must also be an option to end any commercial messages from the sender.

- *Requires that commercial e-mail be identified as an advertisement and include the sender's valid physical postal address*: The message must contain clear and conspicuous notice that the message is an advertisement or solicitation and that the recipient can opt out of receiving more commercial e-mails from the sender. It also must include the sender's valid physical postal address.

Penalties

Each violation of the above provisions is subject to fines of up to $11,000. Deceptive commercial e-mail also is subject to laws banning false or misleading advertising.

Additional fines are provided for commercial e-mailers who not only violate the rules described above, but also do the following:

- Harvest e-mail addresses from Web sites or Web services that have published a notice prohibiting the transfer of e-mail addresses for the purpose of sending e-mail

- Generate e-mail addresses using a dictionary attack, combining names, letters, or numbers into multiple permutations

- Use scripts or other automated ways to register for multiple e-mail or user accounts to send commercial e-mail

- Relay e-mails through a computer or network without permission—for example, by taking advantage of open relays or open proxies without authorization

The law allows the DOJ to seek criminal penalties, including imprisonment, for commercial e-mailers who do or conspire to do the following:

- Use another computer without authorization and send commercial e-mail from or through it

- Use a computer to relay or retransmit multiple commercial e-mail messages to deceive or mislead recipients or an Internet access service about the origin of the message

- Falsify header information in multiple e-mail messages and initiate the transmission of such messages

- Register for multiple e-mail accounts or domain names using information that falsifies the identity of the actual registrant

- Falsely represent themselves as owners of the multiple Internet Protocol addresses that are used to send commercial e-mail messages

Financial Institutions Reform, Recovery, and Enforcement Act of 1989[13]

SEC. 951. CIVIL PENALTIES

(a) IN GENERAL—

Whoever violates any provision of law to which this section is made applicable by subsection (c) of this section shall be subject to a civil penalty in an amount assessed by the court in a civil action under this section.

(b) MAXIMUM AMOUNT OF PENALTY—

(1) GENERALLY—

The amount of the civil penalty shall not exceed $1,000,000.

(2) SPECIAL RULE FOR CONTINUING VIOLATIONS—

In the case of a continuing violation, the amount of the civil penalty may exceed the amount described in paragraph (1) but may not exceed the lesser of $1,000,000 per day or $5,000,000.

(3) SPECIAL RULE FOR VIOLATIONS CREATING GAIN OR LOSS—

(A) If any person derives pecuniary gain from the violation, or if the violation results in pecuniary loss to a person other than the violator, the amount of the civil penalty may exceed the amounts described in paragraphs (1) and (2) but may not exceed the amount of such gain or loss.

(B) As used in this paragraph, the term "person" includes the Bank Insurance Fund, the Savings Association Insurance Fund and after the merger of such funds, the Deposit Insurance Fund, and the National Credit Union Share Insurance Fund.

(c) VIOLATIONS TO WHICH PENALTY IS APPLICABLE

This section applies to a violation of, or a conspiracy to violate—

(1) section 215, 656, 657, 1005, 1006, 1007, 1014, or 1344 of Title 18; or

(2) section 287, 1001, 1032, 1341 or 1343 of Title 18 affecting a federally insured financial institution.

This section shall apply to violations occurring on or after August 10, 1984.

(d) ATTORNEY GENERAL TO BRING ACTION—

A civil action to recover a civil penalty under this section shall be commenced by the Attorney General.

(e) BURDEN OF PROOF—

In a civil action to recover a civil penalty under this section, the Attorney General must establish the right to recovery by a preponderance of the evidence.

(f) ADMINISTRATIVE SUBPOENAS—

(1)IN GENERAL—

For the purpose of conducting a civil investigation in contemplation of a civil proceeding under this section, the Attorney General may—

(A) administer oaths and affirmations;

(B) take evidence; and

(C) by subpoena, summon witnesses and require the production of any books, papers, correspondence, memoranda, or other records which the Attorney General deems relevant or material to the inquiry. Such subpoena may require the attendance of witnesses and the production of any such records from any place in the United States at any place in the United States designated by the Attorney General.

(2) PROCEDURES APPLICABLE

The same procedures and limitations as are provided with respect to civil investigative demands in subsections (g), (h), and (j) of section 1968 of Title 18 apply with respect to a subpoena issued under this subsection. Process required by such subsections to be served upon the custodian shall be served on the Attorney General. Failure to comply with an order of the court to enforce such subpoena shall be punishable as contempt.

(3) LIMITATION—

In the case of a subpoena for which the return date is less than 5 days of service, no person shall be found in contempt for failure to comply by the return date if such person files a petition under paragraph (2) not later than 5 days after the date of service.

- (g) STATUTE OF LIMITATIONS—

A civil action under this section may not be commenced later than 10 years after the cause of action accrues.

Computer Security Act of 1987[14]

SEC. 2 PURPOSE

(a) IN GENERAL.-The Congress declares that improving the security and privacy of sensitive information in Federal computer systems is in the public interest, and hereby creates a means for establishing minimum acceptable security practices for such systems, without limiting the scope of security measures already planned or in use.

(b) SPECIFIC PURPOSES.-The purposes of this Act are—

1. by amending the Act of March 3, 1901, to assign to the National Bureau of Standards responsibility for developing standards and guidelines for Federal computer systems, including responsibility for developing standards and guidelines needed to assure the cost-effective security and privacy of sensitive information in Federal computer systems, drawing on the technical advice and assistance (including work products) of the National Security Agency, where appropriate;

2. to provide for promulgation of such standards and guidelines by amending section 111(d) of the Federal Property and Administrative Services Act of 1949;

3. to require establishment of security plans by all operators of Federal computer systems that contain sensitive information; and

4. to require mandatory periodic training for all persons involved in management, use, or operation of Federal computer systems that contain sensitive information.

Computer Fraud and Abuse Act of 1986[15]

Section 1030. Fraud and related activity in connection with computers

(a) Whoever—

1. knowingly accesses a computer without authorization or exceeds authorized access, and by means of such conduct obtains information that has been determined by the United States Government pursuant to an Executive order or statute to require protection against unauthorized disclosure for reasons of national defense or foreign relations, or any restricted data, as defined in paragraph r. of section 11 of the Atomic Energy Act of 1954, with the intent or reason to believe that such information so obtained is to be used to the injury of the United States, or to the advantage of any foreign nation;

2. intentionally accesses a computer without authorization or exceeds authorized access, and thereby obtains information contained in a financial record of a financial institution, or of a card issuer as defined in section 1602(n) of title 15, or contained in a file of a consumer reporting agency on a consumer, as such terms are defined in the Fair Credit Reporting Act (15 U.S.C. 1681 et seq.);

3. intentionally, without authorization to access any nonpublic computer of a department or agency of the United States, accesses such a computer of that department or agency that is exclusively for the use of the Government of the United States or, in the case of a computer not exclusively for such use, is used by or for the Government of the United States and such conduct affects the use of the Government's operation of such computer;

4. knowingly and with intent to defraud, accesses a Federal interest computer without authorization, or exceeds authorized access, and by means of such conduct furthers the intended fraud and obtains anything of value, unless the object of the fraud and the thing obtained consists only of the use of the computer;

5. intentionally accesses a Federal interest computer without authorization and by means of one or more instances of such conduct alters, damages, or destroys information in any such Federal interest computer, or prevents authorized use of any such computer or information, and thereby—

   (A) causes loss to one or more others of a value aggregating $1,000 or more during any one year period; or;

   (B) modifies or impairs, or potentially modifies or impairs the medical examination, medical diagnosis, medical treatment, or medical care of one or more individuals; or

6. knowingly and with intent to defraud traffics (as defined in section 1029) in any password or similar information through which a computer may be accessed without authorization, if—

   (A) such trafficking affects interstate or foreign commerce; or

   (B) such computer is used by or for the Government of the United States; shall be punished as provided in subsection (c) of this section.

(b) Whoever attempts to commit an offense under subsection (a) of this section shall be punished as provided in subsection (c) of this section.

(c) The punishment for an offense under subsection (a) or (b) of this section is—

(1)(A) a fine under this title or imprisonment for not more than ten years, or both, in the case of an offense under subsection (a)(1) of this section which does not occur after a conviction for another offense under such subsection, or an attempt to commit an offense punishable under this subparagraph; and

(B) a fine under this title or imprisonment for not more than twenty years, or both, in the case of an offense under subsection (a)(1) of this section which occurs after a conviction for another offense under such subsection, or an attempt to commit an offense punishable under this subparagraph; and

(2)(A) a fine under this title or imprisonment for not more than one year, or both, in the case of an offense under subsection (a)(2), (a)(3), or (a)(6) of this section which does not occur after a conviction for another offense under such subsection, or an attempt to commit an offense punishable under this subparagraph; and

(B) a fine under this title or imprisonment for not more than ten years, or both, in the case of an offense under subsection (a)(2), (a)(3) or (a)(6) of this section which occurs after a conviction for another offense under such subsection, or an attempt to commit an offense punishable under this subparagraph; and

(3)(A) a fine under this title or imprisonment for not more than five years, or both, in the case of an offense under subsection (a)(4) or (a)(5) of this section which does not occur after a conviction for another offense under such subsection, or an attempt to commit an offense punishable under this subparagraph; and

(3)(B) a fine under this title or imprisonment for not more than ten years, or both, in the case of an offense under subsection (a)(4) or (a)(5) of this section which occurs after a conviction for another offense under such subsection, or an attempt to commit an offense punishable under this subparagraph.

(d) The United States Secret Service shall, in addition to any other agency having such authority, have the authority to investigate offenses under this section. Such authority of the United States Secret Service shall be exercised in accordance with an agreement which shall be entered into by the Secretary of the Treasury and the Attorney General.

Federal Financial Institutions Examination Council (FFIEC)[16]

The FFIEC is a formal interagency body empowered to prescribe uniform principles, standards, and report forms for the federal examination of financial institutions by the Board of Governors of the Federal Reserve System, the Federal Deposit Insurance Corporation (FDIC), the National Credit Union Administration (NCUA), the Office of the Comptroller of the Currency (OCC), and the Office of Thrift Supervision (OTS), and to make recommendations to promote uniformity in the supervision of financial institutions.

Federal Reserve System

The Federal Reserve System is the central bank of the United States. It was founded by Congress in 1913 to provide the nation with a safer, more flexible, and more stable monetary and financial system. Over the years, its role in banking and the economy has expanded.

Today, the Federal Reserve's duties fall into four general areas:

1. Conducting the nation's monetary policy by influencing the monetary and credit conditions in the economy in pursuit of maximum employment, stable prices, and moderate long-term interest rates

2. Supervising and regulating banking institutions to ensure the safety and soundness of the nation's banking and financial system, and to protect the credit rights of consumers

3. Maintaining the stability of the financial system and containing systemic risk that may arise in financial markets

4. Providing financial services to depository institutions, the U.S. government, and foreign official institutions, including playing a major role in operating the nation's payments system

Federal Deposit Insurance Corporation (FDIC)[17]

The Federal Deposit Insurance Corporation (FDIC) preserves and promotes public confidence in the U.S. financial system through the following:

- Insuring deposits in banks and thrift institutions for at least $100,000

- Identifying, monitoring, and addressing risks to the deposit insurance funds

- Limiting the effect on the economy and the financial system when a bank or thrift institution fails

An independent agency of the federal government, the FDIC was created in 1933 in response to the thousands of bank failures that occurred in the 1920s and early 1930s. Since the start of FDIC insurance on January 1, 1934, no depositor has lost a single cent of insured funds as a result of a failure.

The FDIC receives no congressional appropriations—it is funded by premiums that banks and thrift institutions pay for deposit insurance coverage and from earnings on investments in U.S. Treasury securities. With an insurance fund totaling more than $49 billion, the FDIC insures more than $3 trillion of deposits in U.S. banks and thrifts—deposits in virtually every bank and thrift in the country.

Savings, checking, and other deposit accounts, when combined, are generally insured to $250,000 per depositor in each bank or thrift the FDIC insures. Deposits held in different categories of ownership—such as single or joint accounts—may be separately insured. Also, the FDIC generally provides separate coverage for retirement accounts, such as individual retirement accounts (IRAs) and Keoghs, insured up to $250,000. The FDIC insures deposits only. It does not insure securities, mutual funds, or similar types of investments that banks and thrift institutions may offer.

The FDIC directly examines and supervises about 5,250 banks and savings banks, more than half of the institutions in the banking system. Banks can be chartered by the states or by the federal government. Banks chartered by states also have the choice of whether to join the Federal Reserve System. The FDIC is the primary federal regulator of banks that are chartered by states that do not join the Federal Reserve System. In addition, the FDIC is the backup supervisor for the remaining insured banks and thrift institutions.

To protect insured depositors, the FDIC responds immediately when a bank or thrift institution fails. Institutions generally are closed by their chartering authority—the state regulator, the Office of the Comptroller of the Currency, or the Office of Thrift Supervision. The FDIC has several options for resolving institution failures, but the one most used is to sell deposits and loans of the failed institution to another institution. Customers of the failed institution automatically become customers of the assuming institution. Most of the time, the transition is seamless from the customer's point of view.

The FDIC is managed by a five-person Board of Directors, all of whom are appointed by the president and confirmed by the Senate, with no more than three being from the same political party.

National Credit Union Administration (NCUA)[18]

The National Credit Union Administration (NCUA) is the federal agency that charters and supervises federal credit unions and insures savings in federal and most state-chartered credit unions across the country through the National Credit Union Share Insurance Fund (NCUSIF), a federal fund backed by the full faith and credit of the U.S. government.

The 1970s brought major changes in the products offered by financial institutions and credit unions found they too needed to expand their services. In 1977, legislation expanded services available to credit union members, including share certificates and mortgage lending. In 1979, a three-member board replaced the NCUA administrator. That same year Congress created the Central Liquidity Facility, the credit union lender of last resort. The 1970s were years of tremendous growth in credit unions. The number of credit union members more than doubled and assets in credit unions tripled to over $65 billion.

Deregulation, increased flexibility in merger and field-of-membership criteria, and expanded member services characterized the 1980s. High interest rates and unemployment in the early 1980s brought supervisory changes and insurance losses. With the Share Insurance Fund experiencing stress, the credit union community called on Congress to approve a plan to recapitalize the Fund.

In 1985, federally insured credit unions recapitalized the NCUSIF by depositing 1% of their shares into the Share Insurance Fund. Backed by the "full faith and credit of the United States Government," the fully capitalized National Credit Union Share Insurance Fund has "fail safe" features. Since recapitalization, the NCUA Board has only charged credit unions one premium when the Fund dropped to a 1.23% equity level in 1991.

During the 1990s and into the 21st century, credit unions have been healthy and growing. Credit union failures remain low, and the Share Insurance Fund maintains a healthy equity level.

Office of the Comptroller of the Currency (OCC)[19]

The Office of the Comptroller of the Currency (OCC) charters, regulates, and supervises all national banks. It also supervises the federal branches and agencies of foreign banks. Headquartered in Washington, D.C., the OCC has four district offices plus an office in London to supervise the international activities of national banks.

The OCC was established in 1863 as a bureau of the U.S. Department of the Treasury. The OCC is headed by the comptroller, who is appointed by the president, with the advice and consent of the Senate, for a five-year term. The comptroller also serves as a director of the Federal Deposit Insurance Corporation (FDIC) and a director of the Neighborhood Reinvestment Corporation.

The OCC's nationwide staff of examiners conducts on-site reviews of national banks and provides sustained supervision of bank operations. The agency issues rules, legal interpretations, and corporate decisions concerning banking, bank investments, bank community development activities, and other aspects of bank operations.

National bank examiners supervise domestic and international activities of national banks and perform corporate analyses. Examiners analyze a bank's loan and investment portfolios, funds management, capital, earnings, liquidity, sensitivity to market risk, and compliance with consumer banking laws, including the Community Reinvestment Act. They review the bank's internal controls, internal and external audits, and compliance with the law. They also evaluate bank management's ability to identify and control risk.

In regulating national banks, the OCC has the power to do the following:

- Examine the banks.

- Approve or deny applications for new charters, branches, capital, or other changes in corporate or banking structure.

- Take supervisory actions against banks that do not comply with laws and regulations or that otherwise engage in unsound banking practices. The agency can remove officers and directors, negotiate agreements to change banking practices, and issue cease-and-desist orders as well as civil money penalties.

- Issue rules and regulations governing bank investments, lending, and other practices.

Objectives The OCC's activities are predicated on four objectives that support the OCC's mission to ensure a stable and competitive national banking system. The following are the four objectives:

1. To ensure the safety and soundness of the national banking system

2. To foster competition by allowing banks to offer new products and services

3. To improve the efficiency and effectiveness of OCC supervision, including reducing regulatory burden

4. To ensure fair and equal access to financial services for all Americans

Office of Thrift Supervision (OTS)[20]

The Office of Thrift Supervision (OTS) is the primary federal regulator of federally chartered and state-chartered savings associations, their subsidiaries, and their registered savings and loan holding companies. OTS was established as a bureau of the U.S. Department of the Treasury on August 9, 1989, and has four regional offices located in Jersey City, Atlanta, Dallas, and San Francisco. OTS is funded by assessments and fees levied on the industry it regulates.

Canadian Laws and Acts

Personal Information Protection and Electronic Documents Act (PIPEDA)[21]

The Personal Information Protection and Electronic Documents Act (PIPEDA) is federal legislation passed in 2001 and fully implemented on January 1, 2004. Increasingly, organizations and businesses rely on personal information to connect with their customers and members. Respecting and protecting customers' and members' privacy is part of good customer and member relations.

The stated purpose of the Act is "to establish, in an era in which technology increasingly facilitates the circulation and exchange of information, rules to govern the collection, use and disclosure of personal information in a manner that recognizes the right of privacy of individuals with respect to their personal information and the need of organizations to collect, use or disclose personal information for purposes that a reasonable person would consider appropriate in the circumstances."

PIPEDA requires Canadians to:

- Obtain the clear consent of an individual before collecting, using, or disclosing personal information about that individual

- Use the information only for the purposes consented to

- Protect the information from unauthorized access and use

- Keep the information up to date and correctly filed so that decisions are based on correct information

- Destroy information when it is no longer needed for the original purpose

- Implement accountability mechanisms in their organizations to ensure compliance with the above

What Is Personal Information?

The act aims to protect information about an individual, including information such as:

- Age, name, income, ethnic origin, religion, and blood type

- Opinions, evaluations, comments, social status, and disciplinary actions

- Credit records, employment history, and medical records

Personal information does not include the name, title, business address, or telephone number of an employee of an organization. For many organizations, this means that the information collected to establish eligibility for membership, programs, donor histories, personnel files of staff, and volunteers may be considered personal information.

Principles of PIPEDA

The act is based on the following ten principles that are applied to an organization's activities:

- *Accountability*: An organization is responsible for the personal information under its control and shall designate an individual who is responsible for the organization's compliance. This chief privacy officer will understand the policies and procedures, and deal with complaints.

- *Identifying purposes*: The purposes for which the information is collected should be identified on or at the time of collection. Organizations should develop "purpose statements."

- *Consent*: The knowledge and consent of the individual are required for collection, use, or disclosure of personal information in a commercial activity. Consent can be expressed or implied. Some examples of expressed consent are:

  - An individual completes and signs a form giving consent to the collection of information for specified purposes, its use, and if it is to be disclosed.

  - A check-off box allows individuals to request their personal information not be given.

- *Limiting collection*: Information is to be collected for specific purposes and can only be used for those purposes. Information cannot be collected by misleading or deceiving individuals about the purpose for which it is intended.

- *Limiting use, disclosure, and retention of personal information*: Organizations can only use, disclose, and retain personal information for the specific purposes it was collected for and must not retain it longer than needed for those specific purposes.

- *Accuracy*: Personal information shall be accurate, complete, and up to date.

- *Safeguards*: The organization must protect personal information against loss or theft as well as unauthorized access, disclosure, copying, use, or modification. The level of security should be appropriate to the sensitivity of the information. People with access should sign confidentiality agreements. The organization should ensure the security of its computers and paper files.

- *Openness*: The organization's privacy policies must be readily available to anyone.

- *Individual access*: Individuals have the right to know what personal information about them has been collected, how it is being used, and to whom it has been disclosed, and to challenge the accuracy and completeness and have errors corrected.

- *Challenging compliance*: Individuals should be able to address any challenges concerning compliance to the organization's chief privacy officer.

European Laws and Acts

U.K.: The Civil Contingencies Act[22]

The Civil Contingencies Act, and accompanying nonlegislative measures, delivers a single framework for civil protection in the event of a major emergency in the United Kingdom. The act is separated into two parts: local arrangements for civil protection (Part 1) and emergency powers (Part 2).

Part 1

Part 1 of the act and supporting regulations establish a clear set of roles and responsibilities for those involved in emergency preparation and response at the local level. The act divides local responders into two categories, imposing a different set of duties on each.

Category 1 includes organizations at the core of the response to most emergencies, such as emergency services, local authorities, and NHS bodies. Category 1 responders are subject to the full set of civil protection duties. They are required to do the following:

- Assess the risk of emergencies occurring and use this to inform contingency planning
- Put in place emergency plans
- Put in place business continuity management arrangements
- Put in place arrangements to make information available to the public about civil protection matters and maintain arrangements to warn, inform, and advise the public in the event of an emergency
- Share information with other local responders to enhance coordination
- Cooperate with other local responders to enhance coordination and efficiency
- Provide advice and assistance to businesses and voluntary organizations about business continuity management (local authorities only)

Category 2 organizations, such as health and safety executives and transport and utility companies, are cooperating bodies less likely to be involved in the heart of planning work but will be heavily involved in incidents that affect their sector. Category 2 responders have a lesser set of duties—cooperating and sharing relevant information with other Category 1 and 2 responders.

Category 1 and 2 organizations will come together to form local resilience forums (based on police areas), which will help coordination and cooperation between responders at the local level.

Part 2

Part 2 of the act updates the 1920 Emergency Powers Act to reflect the developments in the intervening years and the current and future risk profile. It allows for the making of temporary special legislation (emergency regulations) to help deal with the most serious of emergencies. The use of emergency powers is a last-resort option, and planning arrangements at the local level should not assume that emergency powers will be made available. Their use is subject to a robust set of safeguards; they can only be deployed in exceptional circumstances.

U.K.: Data Protection Act 1998[23]

The Data Protection Act 1998 gives legal rights to individuals (data subjects) with respect to personal data processed about them by others. The act promotes a culture of openness and fairness in those who process personal data (data controllers).

According to the act, U.K. citizens have the right to:

- Ask any data controller if it holds personal information
- Ask what the information is used for
- Ask to be given a copy of the information held
- Ask whether the data controller discloses the information to others and if so to whom
- Ask the data controller to correct, erase, or destroy any incorrect data
- Ask the data controller not to use personal information for direct marketing purposes
- Ask the data controller to stop processing that causes unwarranted damage or distress
- Seek compensation if the data controller has failed to uphold this act

EU: Directive 2002/58/EC[24]

Directive 2002/58/EC forms part of the Telecoms Package, a legislative framework designed to regulate the electronic communications sector and replace the existing regulations governing the telecommunications sector.

This directive tackles a number of issues of varying degrees of sensitivity, such as the retention of connection data by the member states for police surveillance purposes (data retention), the sending of unsolicited electronic messages, the use of cookies, and the inclusion of personal data in public directories.

- *Confidentiality of communications*: The directive reiterates the basic principle that member states must, through national legislation, ensure the confidentiality of communications made over a public electronic communications network. They must in particular prohibit the listening into, tapping, and storage of communications by persons other than users without the consent of the users concerned.
- *Data retention*: On the sensitive issue of data retention, the directive stipulates that member states may withdraw the protection of data only to allow criminal investigations or to safeguard national security,

defense, and public security. Such action may be taken only where it constitutes a "necessary, appropriate and proportionate measure within a democratic society."

- *Unsolicited electronic messages (spam)*: The directive takes an "opt-in" approach to unsolicited commercial electronic communications: users must have given their prior consent before such messages are addressed to them. This opt-in system also covers SMS text messages and other electronic messages received on any fixed or mobile terminal.

- *Cookies*: Cookies are hidden information exchanged between an Internet user and a Web server, and are stored in a file on the user's hard disk. Their original purpose was to retain information between sessions. They are also a useful and much-decried tool for monitoring a user's activity. The directive stipulates that users should have the opportunity to refuse to have a cookie or similar device stored on their terminal equipment. To that end, users must also be provided with clear and precise information on the purposes and role of cookies.

- *Public directories*: European citizens will have to give prior consent in order for their telephone numbers (landline or mobile), e-mail addresses, and postal addresses to appear in public directories.

EU: Directive 95/46/EC[25]

The directive contains definitions of basic terms pertaining to the field of personal data. It stipulates rules on collection, storage, and disclosure of personal data. It also determines rules and conditions of lawful personal data processing and rights of data subjects.

Article 1

In accordance with this directive, member states shall protect the fundamental rights and freedoms of natural persons and in particular their right to privacy with respect to the processing of personal data.

Article 2

For the purposes of this directive, "personal data" shall mean any information relating to an identified or identifiable natural person ("data subject"); an identifiable person is one who can be identified, directly or indirectly, in particular by reference to an identification number or to one or more factors specific to his or her physical, physiological, mental, economic, cultural, or social identity.

Article 6

Member states shall provide that personal data must be:

- Processed fairly and lawfully
- Collected for specified, explicit, and legitimate purposes and not further processed in a way incompatible with those purposes. Further processing of data for historical, statistical, or scientific purposes shall not be considered as incompatible provided that member states provide appropriate safeguards.
- Adequate, relevant, and not excessive in relation to the purposes for which they are collected and/or further processed
- Accurate and, where necessary, kept up to date; every reasonable step must be taken to ensure that data that are inaccurate or incomplete, having regard to the purposes for which they were collected or for which they are further processed, are erased or rectified
- Kept in a form that permits identification of data subjects for no longer than is necessary for the purposes for which the data were collected or for which they are further processed. Member states shall lay down appropriate safeguards for personal data stored for longer periods for historical, statistical, or scientific use.

EU: Financial Groups Directive (FGD)[26]

The Financial Groups Directive, referenced as 2002/87/EC, has resulted in two main areas of change:

1. First, the directive requires supervisors and groups to measure the prudential soundness of groups with significant business in both the banking/investment and the insurance sectors. This helps them better assess whether the group is a prudential source of weakness to the individual firms within in it. The directive

also makes some progress toward consistency of treatment between the sectors by amending the respective banking/investment and insurance sectoral group directives.

2. The directive also introduces new requirements for conglomerates with non-EEA parents, as well as non-EEA banking and investment groups (as a result of an amendment to the Banking Consolidation Directive). For each of these third-country groups, EEA authorities must work together as appropriate to determine whether the group is subject to equivalent groupwide supervision in its home country. Where this is not the case, the FGD/BCD requires that organizations undertake worldwide group supervision themselves or apply other methods that achieve the objectives of the relevant directive.

The Foundation of Personal Data Security Law: OECD Principles

The OECD Principles state that "personal data should be protected by reasonable security safeguards against such risks as loss of unauthorized access, destruction, use, modification, or disclosure of data."

Purpose Specification Principle

When personal data are collected in a justice system, the system's purpose should be specified in writing, not later than at the time of data collection. The subsequent use must be limited to the fulfillment of those stated purposes (or other compatible purposes that are specified on each occasion of change of purpose). As well, the personal data collected should be pertinent to the stated purposes for which the information is to be used.

The purpose statements also need to address various third-party and private-sector partnerships or relationships where personal data are or will be disclosed.

For example, each component of a justice system (law enforcement/investigative systems, prosecutorial systems, defense systems, court systems, correction systems, and probation and parole systems) has a set of stated purposes for collecting information. These purposes need to be articulated and harmonized prior to the technology design and prior to the outset of data collection. With an integrated system, data can be easily reused in the future. However, the purposes for collection, by each component of a justice system, should be relatively stable.

Generally, the purpose statements should directly relate to the mandate of the relevant sector of the justice system. For example, the purpose of law enforcement agencies for collecting personal information is to investigate (suspected) criminal activity to bring suspects to trial, whereas the purpose of the court system is to process cases, provide accurate and complete information for judicial decisions, and produce dispositions for complete criminal history records. The purposes of these systems should be harmonized to provide a privacy framework governing collection, use, and reuse of personal information.

Collection Limitation Principle

There should be some limits placed on the collection of personal data. Personal data should be obtained by lawful and fair means and, where appropriate, with the knowledge or consent of the data subject. It is important to remember that the knowledge and consent rights of individuals will vary depending on their relationship (e.g., suspect, offender, victim, witness, juror, offender's family) to the justice system.

A test of relevance should also be applied (e.g., by an independent third party or as authorized in legislation) when collecting personal data on individuals without their knowledge or consent, or when the individual is not charged with a crime, i.e., under investigation, or when an investigative body is information gathering.

This principle differentiates between the knowledge and consent rights of an offender, arrestee, victim, witness, juror, offender's family, or victim's family. Special consideration must be made to limit collection of personal information on victims, witnesses, and jurors (e.g., to test their credibility). For suspects or accused persons, although broader, the collection limits should be set by the legislative framework and legal precedent. However, obtaining a person's consent to collect their personal information is generally not applicable during case investigation or prosecution.

The collector of personal information varies. In the criminal justice system, the collector is generally law enforcement. In the civil justice system, it is the court. In the criminal justice system, personal information is collected by the investigative arm on suspects and those associated with the suspects, including victims, witnesses, and family members. In addition, most parts of the justice system collect personal information on offenders and those convicted, if only as a result of the actions, utterances, and changing condition of the convicted offender. As well, personal information is generated by the workings of the justice system itself as the offender moves through the various components of the justice system.

Data Quality Principle

Personal information, to the extent necessary for stated purposes, should be accurate, complete, current, and verified. This normally assumes that the person has some means of accessing the information to ensure it is accurate and up to date.

However, in the justice system other methods are needed to ensure that the data held are accurate and up to date. Those methods can involve passive data analysis, including cross-referencing, that identifies anomalies, plus authorized human correction that could involve the data subject. Separate from privacy concerns, data management and record retention need to be addressed as part of data quality. Inaccurate personal information can have a devastating impact on the person and the integrity of proceedings within the justice system. The accountability for data quality lies with the system's information steward.

Use Limitation Principle

Personal data should not be used or disclosed for purposes other than those specified in accordance with the purpose specification principle except:

- With the consent of the data subject
- By the authority of law
- For the safety of the community, including victims and witnesses

Generally, personal information should be retained as necessary, but its use must be limited to its original purpose for collection. Use limitation, generally, is more applicable where information is disclosed outside the justice system where issues of safety, risk, and the right to know by victims are factors applied in the use limitation principle. Within the criminal justice system, with the purpose for collection stipulated in the collection limitation principle, the use limitation principle is also applicable under the exception of the authority of law, and in an integrated justice system, where various components' system use purposes have been harmonized.

A general pattern of the use of personal information suggests that within the justice system, use is determined by access authorization and by assuming the doctrine of consistent use. Compilations of legal data prepared by the private sector may result in unintended consequences for citizens exercising their right to participate in the judicial system. For example, it is not uncommon for rental or housing associations to develop databases of persons who have filed an unlawful detainer claim. These legal actions are likely to be based on a valid claim by the renter or home owner, i.e., for lack of repair. The information in the database, however, follows an individual forever and may result in denial of housing.

A third area of concern is information sharing between "closed record" states and "open record" states, where the information not available to the public in the closed record state becomes publicly available once it is shared with the open record state. This type of availability has created a market for private information gatherers to use justice system access in one state to provide nonaccessible information to parties in their home state.

These types of data gathering have privacy implications that need to be addressed up front in integrated justice systems. Managing the sale and access to justice information may be difficult given the legislative framework in some states. Ideally, the sale of information in bulk should be limited to recognized justice system purposes, and contracts for the sale of bulk information should require compliance with privacy principles.

Through a privacy impact assessment, a justice system can be reviewed by the government for the impacts of information-handling practices. Ongoing reviews are necessary as future changes increase the ability to gather and use information and as market forces control these processes.

Security Safeguards Principle

Reasonable security safeguards against risks should protect personal data against loss or unauthorized access, destruction, use, modification, or disclosure of data. These safeguards should be provided according to the sensitivity of the information and risks to all involved parties. This principle recognizes that personal information collected by the justice system is highly sensitive and a natural target for compromise.

Openness Principle

There should be a general policy of openness about developments, practices, and policies with respect to the management of personal data (apart from the actual data). Openness includes public access to the management practices of the data, except where it directly relates to an investigation or a pending or open case, or where it involves safety concerns and other factors that a government determines as necessary exemptions. Barring these exceptions, the public should be able to establish the existence and nature of personal data (apart from the actual data), and the main purposes of the data's use, as well as the identity and office of the data controller responsible for that data.

In an investigation or prosecution of an offense, established precedent and evidentiary rules will determine the openness principle or exceptions to it.

The openness principle also requires clear communication to affected individuals where justice records are requested, sold, or released to third parties. The public should be informed of when information is sold in bulk for commercial purposes.

Individual Participation Principle

Given the unique environment of the justice system. an individual, or an agent for an individual or for victims and witnesses, should have the right, except as it would compromise an investigation, case, or court proceeding:

- To obtain confirmation of whether or not the data collector has data relating to him or her
- To have communicated to him or her data relating to him or her
  - Within a reasonable time
  - At a charge, if any, that is not excessive
  - In a reasonable manner
  - In a form that is readily intelligible to him or her
- To be given reasons if a request is denied and to be able to challenge such denial
- To challenge data relating to him or her and, if the challenge is successful, to have the data erased, rectified, completed, or amended
- To provide an annotation to data where an organization decides not to amend information as requested by an individual or an agent for an individual or for victims and witnesses

Accountability Principle

Accountability should be established within each information system to ensure the development and compliance with procedures that give effect to the principles stated above. The accountable party (information steward) is an individual or a body that must preserve the meaning and integrity of the other design principles and assess their effectiveness throughout the operation of the integrated system. Roles and responsibilities of the information steward should be established by the system's key partners at the development stages of an integrated justice information system.

The accountability principle is the "due process" mechanism of the privacy design principles. An individual or his or her proxy should be able to challenge the system's compliance with any one of the privacy design principles through administrative procedures designed, implemented, and enforced by the information steward. The information steward should assure that procedures are in places that guarantee a timely, fair response to inquiries.[27]

Dutch Personal Data Protection Act

Article 2

1. This Act applies to the fully or partly automated processing of personal data, and the no automated processing of personal data entered in a file or intended to be entered therein.

2. This Act does not apply to the processing of personal data:

   a. in the course of a purely personal or household activity;

   b. by or on behalf of the intelligence or security services referred to in the Intelligence and Security Services Act;

   c. for the purposes of implementing the police tasks defined in Article 2 of the Police Act 1993;

   d. governed by or under the Municipal Database (Personal Records) Act;

   e. for the purposes of implementing the Judicial Documentation Act;

   f. for the purposes of implementing the Electoral Provisions Act;

3. This Act does not apply to the processing of personal data by the armed forces where Our Defense Minister so decides with a view to deploying or making available the armed forces to maintain or promote

the international legal order. Such a decision shall be communicated to the Data Protection Commission as quickly as possible.

Article 3

1. This Act does not apply to the processing of personal data for exclusively journalistic, artistic or literary purposes, except where otherwise provided in this Chapter and in Articles 6 to 11, 13 to 15, 25, and 49.

2. The prohibition on processing personal data referred to in Article 16 does not apply where this is necessary for the purposes referred to under (1).

Article 4

1. This Act applies to the processing of personal data carried out in the context of the activities of an establishment of a responsible party in the Netherlands.

2. This Act applies to the processing of personal data by or for responsible parties who are not established in the European Union, whereby use is made of automated or nonautomated means situated in the Netherlands, unless these means are used only for forwarding personal data.

3. The responsible parties referred to under (2) are prohibited from processing personal data, unless they designate a person or body in the Netherlands to act on their behalf in accordance with the provisions of this Act. For the purposes of application of this Act and the provisions based upon it, the said person or body shall be deemed to be the responsible party.

Article 5

1. In the case that the data subjects are minors and have not yet reached the age of sixteen, or have been placed under legal restraint or the care of a mentor, instead of the consent of the data subjects, that of their legal representative is required.

   The data subjects or their legal representative may withdraw consent at any time.

Article 6

Personal data shall be processed in accordance with the law and in a proper and careful manner.

Article 7

Personal data shall be collected for specific, explicitly defined, and legitimate purposes.

Article 8

Personal data may only be processed where:

   a. the data subject has unambiguously given his consent for the processing;

   b. the processing is necessary for the performance of a contract to which the data subject is party, or for actions to be carried out at the request of the data subject and which are necessary for the conclusion of a contract;

   c. the processing is necessary in order to comply with a legal obligation to which the responsible party is subject;

   d. the processing is necessary in order to protect a vital interest of the data subject;

   e. the processing is necessary for the proper performance of a public law duty by the administrative body concerned or by the administrative body to which the data are provided, or

   f. the processing is necessary for upholding the legitimate interests of the responsible party or of a third party, to whom the data are supplied, except where the interests or fundamental rights and freedoms of the data subject, in particular the right to protection of individual privacy, prevail.

Article 9

1. Personal data shall not be further processed in a way incompatible with the purposes for which they have been obtained.

2. For the purposes of assessing whether processing is incompatible, as referred to under (1), the responsible party shall in any case take account of the following:

   a. the relationship between the purpose of the intended processing and the purpose for which the data have been obtained;

   b. the nature of the data concerned;

   c. the consequences of the intended processing for the data subject;

   d. the manner in which the data have been obtained, and

   e. the extent to which appropriate guarantees have been put in place with respect to the data subject.

3. The further processing of personal data for historical, statistical, or scientific purposes shall not be regarded as incompatible where the responsible party has made the necessary arrangements to ensure that the further processing is carried out solely for these specific purposes.

4. The processing of personal data shall not take place where this is precluded by an obligation of confidentiality by virtue of office, profession, or legal provision.

Article 10

1. Personal data shall not be kept in a form which allows the data subject to be identified for any longer than is necessary for achieving the purposes for which they were collected or subsequently processed.

2. Personal data may be kept for longer than provided under (1), where this is for historical, statistical, or scientific purposes, and where the responsible party has made the necessary arrangements to ensure that the data concerned are used solely for these specific purposes.

Article 11

1. Personal data shall only be processed where, given the purposes for which they are collected or subsequently processed, they are adequate, relevant, and not excessive.

2. The responsible party shall take the necessary steps to ensure that personal data, given the purposes for which they are collected or subsequently processed, are correct and accurate.

Article 12

1. Anyone acting under the authority of the responsible party or the processor, as well as the processor himself, where they have access to personal data, shall only process such data on the orders of the responsible party, except where otherwise required by law.

2. The persons referred to under (1), who are not subject to an obligation of confidentiality by virtue of office, profession, or legal provision, are required to treat as confidential the personal data which comes to their knowledge, except where the communication of such data is required by a legal provision or the proper performance of their duties. Article 272(2) of the Penal Code is not applicable.

Article 13

The responsible party shall implement appropriate technical and organizational measures to secure personal data against loss or against any form of unlawful processing. These measures shall guarantee an appropriate level of security, taking into account the state of the art and the costs of implementation, and having regard to the risks associated with the processing and the nature of the data to be protected. These measures shall also aim at preventing unnecessary collection and further processing of personal data.

Article 14

1. Where responsible parties have personal data processed for their purposes by a processor, these responsible parties shall make sure that the processor provides adequate guarantees concerning the technical and organizational security measures for the processing to be carried out. The responsible parties shall make sure that these measures are complied with.

2. The carrying out of processing by a processor shall be governed by an agreement or another legal act whereby an obligation is created between the processor and the responsible party.

3. The responsible party shall make sure that the processor:

   a. processes the personal data in accordance with Article 12(l) and

   b. complies with the obligations incumbent upon the responsible party under Article 13.

4. Where the processor is established in another country of the European Union, the responsible party shall make sure that the processor complies with the laws of that other country, notwithstanding the provisions of (3)(b).

5. With a view to the keeping of proof, the parts of the agreement or legal act relating to personal data protection and the security measures referred to in Article 13, shall be set down in writing or in another equivalent form.

Article 15

The responsible party shall make sure that the obligations referred to in Articles 6 to 12 and 14(2) and (5) of this Chapter are complied with.

Article 16

It is prohibited to process personal data concerning a person's religion or philosophy of life, race, political persuasion, health and sexual life, or personal data concerning trade union membership, except as otherwise provided in this Section. This prohibition also applies to personal data concerning a person's criminal behavior, or unlawful or objectionable conduct connected with a ban imposed with regard to such conduct.

Article 17

1. The prohibition on processing personal data concerning a person's religion or philosophy of life, as referred to in Article 16, does not apply where the processing is carried out by:

   a. church associations, independent sections thereof or other associations founded on spiritual principles, provided that the data concerns persons belonging thereto;

   b. institutions founded on religious or philosophical principles, provided that this is necessary to the aims of the institutions and for the achievement of their principles, or

   c. other institutions provided that this is necessary to the spiritual welfare of the data subjects, unless they have indicated their objection thereto in writing.

2. In the cases referred to under (1)(a), the prohibition also does not apply to personal data concerning the religion or philosophy of life of family members of the data subjects provided that:

   a. the association concerned maintains regular contacts with these family members in connection with its aims, and

   b. the family members have not indicated any objection thereto in writing.

3. In the cases referred to under (1) and (2), no personal data may be supplied to third parties without the consent of the data subject.

Article 18

1. The prohibition on processing personal data concerning a person's race, as referred to in Article 16, does not apply where the processing is carried out:

   a. with a view to identifying data subjects and only where this is essential for that purpose;

   b. for the purpose of assigning a preferential status to persons from a particular ethnic or cultural minority group with a view to eradicating or reducing actual inequalities, provided that:

      i this is necessary for that purpose;

      ii the data only relate to the country of birth of the data subjects, their parents or grandparents, or to other criteria laid down by law, allowing an objective determination whether a person belongs to a minority group as referred to under (b), and

      iii the data subjects have not indicated any objection thereto in writing.

Article 19

1. The prohibition on processing personal data concerning a person's political persuasion, as referred to in Article 16, does not apply where the processing is carried out:

    a. by institutions founded on political principles with respect to their members or employees or other persons belonging to the institution, provided that this is necessary to the aims of the institutions and for the achievement of their principles, or

    b. with a view to the requirements concerning political persuasion that can reasonably be applied in connection with the performance of duties in administrative and advisory bodies.

2. In the cases referred to under (1)(a), no personal data may be supplied to third parties without the consent of the data subject.

Article 20

1. The prohibition on processing personal data concerning a person's trade union membership, as referred to in Article 16, does not apply where the processing is carried out by the trade union concerned or the trade union federation to which this trade union belongs, provided that this is necessary to the aims of the trade union or trade union federation;

2. In the cases referred to under (1), no personal data may be supplied to third parties without the consent of the data subject.

Article 21

1. The prohibition on processing personal data concerning a person's health, as referred to in Article 16, does not apply where the processing is carried out by:

    a. medical professionals, health care institutions or facilities or social services, provided that this is necessary for the proper treatment and care of the data subject, or for the administration of the institution or professional practice concerned;

    b. insurance companies as referred to in Article 1(1)(h) of the Insurance Supervision Act 1993, insurance companies as referred to in Article 1(c) of the Funeral Insurance Supervision Act, and intermediaries and subagents as referred to in Article 1(b) and (c) of the Insurance Mediation Act, provided that this is necessary for:

        i   assessing the risk to be insured by the insurance company and the data subject has not indicated any objection thereto, or

        ii the performance of the insurance agreement;

    c. schools, provided that this is necessary with a view to providing special support for pupils or making special arrangements in connection with their state of health;

    d. institutions for probation, child protection or guardianship, provided that this is necessary for the performance of their legal duties;

    e. Our Minister of Justice, provided that this is necessary in connection with the implementation of prison sentences or detention measures, or

    f. administrative bodies, pension funds, employers or institutions working for them, provided that this is necessary for:

        i   the proper implementation of the provisions of laws, pension regulations, or collective agreements that create rights dependent on the state of health of the data subject, or

        ii the reintegration of or support for workers or persons entitled to benefit in connection with sickness or work incapacity.

2. In the cases referred to under (1), the data may only be processed by persons subject to an obligation of confidentiality by virtue of office, profession, or legal provision, or under an agreement. Where responsible parties personally process data and are not already subject to an obligation of confidentiality by virtue of office, profession, or legal provision, they are required to treat the data as confidential, except where they are required by law or in connection with their duties to communicate such data to other parties who are authorized to process such data in accordance with (1).

3. The prohibition on processing other personal data, as referred to in Article 16, does not apply where this is necessary to supplement the processing of personal data concerning a person's health, as referred to under (1)(a), with a view to the proper treatment or care of the data subject.

4. Personal data concerning inherited characteristics may only be processed, where this processing takes place with respect to the data subject from whom the data concerned have been obtained, unless:

   a. a serious medical interest prevails, or

   b. the processing is necessary for the purpose of scientific research or statistics.

   In the case referred to under (b), Article 23(l)(a) and (2) shall likewise be applicable.

5. More detailed rules may be issued by general administrative regulation concerning the application of (1)(b) and (e).

Article 22

1. The prohibition on processing personal data concerning a person's criminal behavior, as referred to in Article 16, does not apply where the processing is carried out by bodies, charged by law with applying criminal law and by responsible parties who have obtained these data in accordance with the Police Registers Act or the Judicial Documentation Act.

2. The prohibition does not apply to responsible parties who process these data for their own purposes with a view to:

   a. assessing an application by data subjects in order to make a decision about them or provide a service to them, or

   b. protecting their interests, provided that this concerns criminal offenses that have been or, as indicated by certain facts and circumstances, can be expected to be committed against them or against persons in their service.

3. The processing of these data concerning personnel in the service of the responsible party shall take place in accordance with the rules established in compliance with the procedure referred to in the Works Councils Act.

4. The prohibition does not apply where these data are processed for the account of third parties:

   a. by responsible parties acting in accordance with a license issued under the Private Security Organizations and Investigation Bureaus Act;

   b. where these third parties are legal persons forming part of the same group, as referred to in Article 2:24(b) of the Civil Code, or

   c. where appropriate and specific guarantees have been provided and the procedure referred to in Article 31 has been followed.

5. The prohibition on processing other personal data, as referred to in Article 16, does not apply where this is necessary to supplement the processing of data on criminal behavior, for the purposes for which these data are being processed.

6. The provisions of (2) to (5) are likewise applicable to personal data relating to a ban imposed by a court concerning unlawful or objectionable conduct.

7. Rules may be issued by general administrative regulation concerning the appropriate and specific guarantees referred to under (4)(c).

Article 23

1. Without prejudice to Articles 17 to 22, the prohibition on processing personal data referred to in Article 16 does not apply where:

   a. this is carried out with the express consent of the data subject;

   b. the data have manifestly been made public by the data subject;

   c. this is necessary for the establishment, exercise, or defense of a right in law;

    d. this is necessary to comply with an obligation of international public law, or

    e. this is necessary with a view to an important public interest, where appropriate guarantees have been put in place to protect individual privacy and this is provided for by law or else the Data Protection Commission has granted an exemption. When granting an exemption, the Commission can impose rules and restrictions.

2. The prohibition on the processing of personal data referred to in Article 16 for the purpose of scientific research or statistics does not apply where:

    a. the research serves a public interest,

    b. the processing is necessary for the research or statistics concerned,

    c. it appears to be impossible or would involve a disproportionate effort to ask for express consent, and

    d. sufficient guarantees are provided to ensure that the processing does not adversely affect the individual privacy of the data subject to a disproportionate extent.

3. Processing referred to under (1)(e) must be notified to the European Commission. This notification shall be made by Our Minister concerned where the processing is provided for by law. The Data Protection Commission shall make the notification in the case that it has granted an exemption for the processing.

Article 24

1. A number that is required by law for the purposes of identifying a person may only be used for the processing of personal data in execution of the said law or for purposes stipulated by the law.

2. Cases other than those referred to under (1) can be designated by general administrative regulation in which a number to be indicated in this connection, as referred to under (1), can be used. More detailed rules may be laid down in this connection concerning the use of such a number.[28]

Austrian Federal Act Concerning the Protection of Personal Data

Section 1: Fundamental Right to Data Protection

1. Everybody shall have the right to secrecy for the personal data concerning him, especially with regard to his private and family life, insofar as he has an interest deserving such protection. Such an interest is precluded when data cannot be subject to the right to secrecy due to their general availability or because they cannot be traced back to the data subject.

2. Insofar as personal data is not used in the vital interest of the data subject or with his consent, restrictions to the right to secrecy are only permitted to safeguard overriding legitimate interests of another, namely in case of an intervention by a public authority the restriction shall only be permitted based on laws necessary for the reasons stated in Art. 8, Para. 2 of the European Convention on Human Rights (Federal Law Gazette No. 210/1958). Such laws may provide for the use of data that deserve special protection only in order to safeguard substantial public interests and shall provide suitable safeguards for the protection of the data subjects' interest in secrecy. Even in the case of permitted restrictions the intervention with the fundamental right shall be carried out using only the least intrusive of all effective methods.

3. Everybody shall have, insofar as personal data concerning him are destined for automated processing or manual processing, i.e. in filing systems without automated processing, as provided for by law,

    a the right to obtain information as to who processes what data concerning him, where the data originated, for which purpose they are used, as well as to whom the data are transmitted;

    b the right to rectification of incorrect data and the right to erasure of illegally processed data.

4. Restrictions of the rights according to para. 3 are only permitted under the conditions laid out in para. 2.

5. The fundamental right to data protection, except the right to information, shall be asserted before the civil courts against organizations that are established according to private law, as long as they do not act in execution of laws. In all other cases the Data Protection Commission shall be competent to render the decision, unless an act of Parliament or a judicial decision is concerned.

Section 2: Legislative Power and Enforcement

1. The Federation shall have power to pass laws concerning the protection of personal data that are automatically processed.

2. The Federation shall have power to execute such federal laws. Insofar as such data are used by a State, on behalf of a State, by or on behalf of legal persons established by law within the powers of the States these Federal Acts shall be executed by the States unless the execution has been entrusted by federal law to the Data Protection Commission, the Data Protection Council, or the courts.

Section 3: Territorial Jurisdiction

1. The provisions of this Federal Act shall be applied to the use of personal data in Austria. This Federal Act shall also be applied to the use of data outside of Austria, insofar as the data is used in other Member States of the European Union for purposes of a main establishment or branch establishment (sect. 4 subpara. 15) in Austria of the controller (sect. 4 subpara. 4).

2. Deviating from para. 1 the law of the state where the controller has its seat applies, when a controller of the private sector (sect. 5 para. 3), whose seat is in another Member State of the European Union, uses personal data in Austria for a purpose that cannot be ascribed to any of the controller's establishments in Austria.

3. Furthermore, this law shall not be applied insofar as data are only transmitted through Austrian territory.

4. Legal provisions deviating from paras. 1 to 3 shall be permissible only in matters not subject to the jurisdiction of the European Union.

Section 5: Public and Private Sector

1. Data applications shall be imputed to the public sector according to this Federal Act if they are undertaken for purposes of a controller of the public sector (p. 2).

2. Public sector controllers are all those controllers who

   a. Are established according to public law legal structures, in particular also as an organ of a territorial corporate body, or

   b. As far as they execute laws despite having been incorporated according to private law.

3. Controllers not within the scope of para. 2 are considered controllers of the private sector according to this Federal Act.

Section 14: Data Security Measures

1. Measures to ensure data security shall be taken by all organizational units of a controller or processor that use data. Depending on the kind of data used as well as the extent and purpose of the use and considering the state of technical possibilities and economic justifiability it shall be ensured that the data are protected against accidental or intentional destruction or loss, that they are properly used and are not accessible to unauthorized persons.

2. In particular, the following measures are to be taken insofar as this is necessary with regard to the last sentence of para. 1:

   a. the distribution of functions between the organizational units as well as the operatives regarding the use of data shall be laid down expressly,

   b. the use of data must be tied to valid orders of the authorized organizational units or operatives,

   c. every operative is to be instructed about his duties according to this Federal Act and the internal data protection regulations, including data security regulations,

   d. the right of access to the premises of the data controller or processor is to be regulated,

   e. the right of access to data and programs is to be regulated as well as the protection of storage media against access and use by unauthorized persons,

   f. the right to operate the data processing equipment is to be laid down and every device is to be secured against unauthorized operation by taking precautions for the machines and programs used,

g. logs shall be kept in order that the processing steps that were actually performed, in particular modifications, consultations and transmissions, can be traced to the extent necessary with regard to their permissibility,

h. documentation shall be kept on the measures taken pursuant to subparas. 1 to 7 to facilitate control and conservation of evidence.

These measures must, taking into account the technological state of the art and the cost incurred in their execution, safeguard a level of data protection appropriate with regard to the risks arising from the use and the type of data to be protected.

3. Unregistered transmissions from data applications subject to an obligation to grant information pursuant to sect. 26 shall be logged in such a manner that the right of information can be granted to the subject pursuant to sect. 26. Transmissions provided for in the standard ordinance (sect. 17 para. 2 lit. 6) and the model ordinance (sect. 19 para. 2) do not require logging.

4. Logs and documentation data may not be used for purposes that are incompatible with the purpose of the collection - viz., monitoring the legitimacy of the use of the logged and documented data files. In particular, any further use for the purpose of supervising the data subjects whose data is contained in the logged data files, as well as for the purpose of monitoring the persons who have accessed the logged data files, or for any purpose other than checking access rights shall be considered incompatible, unless the data is used is for the purpose of preventing or prosecuting a crime according to sect. 278a StGB13 (criminal organization) or a crime punishable with a maximum sentence of more than five years imprisonment.

5. Unless expressly provided for otherwise by law, logs and documentation data shall be kept for three years. Deviations from this rule shall be permitted to the same extent that the logged or documented data files may legitimately be erased earlier or kept longer.

6. Data security regulations are to be issued and kept available in such a manner that the operatives can inform themselves about the regulations to which they are subject at any time.

Section 15: Confidentiality of Data

1. Controllers, processors and their operatives—these being the employees and persons comparable to employees—shall keep data from uses of data confidential that have been entrusted or made accessible to them solely for professional reasons, without prejudice to other professional obligations of confidentiality, unless a legitimate reason exists for the transmission of the entrusted or accessed data (confidentiality of data).

2. Operatives shall transmit data only if expressly ordered to do so by their employer. Controllers and processors shall oblige their operatives by contract, insofar as they are not already obliged by law, to transmit data from uses of data only if so ordered and to adhere to the confidentiality of data even after the end of their professional relationship with the controller or processor.

3. Controllers and processors may only issue orders for the transmission of data if this is permitted pursuant to the provisions of this Federal Act. They shall inform the operatives affected by these orders about the transmission orders in force and about the consequences of a violation of data confidentiality.

4. Without prejudice to the constitutional right to issue instructions, a refusal to follow an order to transmit data on the grounds that it violates the provisions of this Federal Act shall not be to the operatives' detriment.[29]

German Federal Data Protection Act

Section 1: Purpose and Scope

1. The purpose of this Act is to protect the individual against his right to privacy being impaired through the handling of his personal data.

2. This Act shall apply to the collection, processing, and use of personal data by

    1. public bodies of the Federation,

2. public bodies of the Lander insofar as data protection is not governed by Land legislation and insofar as they:

    a. execute federal law or

    b. act as bodies of the judicature and are not dealing with administrative matters,

3. private bodies insofar as they process or use data in or from data files in the normal course of business or for professional or commercial purposes.

    3. There shall be the following restrictions to the application of this Act:

        1. Sections 5 and 9 only of this Act shall apply to automated data files that are temporarily set up exclusively for reasons of processing and are automatically erased after processing.

        2. Sections 5, 9, 39, and 40 only of this Act shall apply to nonautomated data files in which the personal data are not intended for communication to third parties. Furthermore, the regulations on the processing and use of personal data in records shall apply to the data files of public bodies. If personal data are communicated in a particular case, the provisions of this Act shall apply without restriction.

4. Insofar as other legal provisions of the Federation are applicable to personal data, including their publication, such provisions shall take precedence over the provisions of this Act. This shall not affect the duty to observe the legal obligation of maintaining secrecy, or professional or special official confidentiality not based on legal provisions.

5. The provisions of this Act shall take precedence over those of the Administrative Procedures Act insofar as personal data are processed in ascertaining the facts.

Section 2: Public and Private Bodies

1. "Public bodies of the Federation" mean the authorities, the bodies of the judicature, and other public-law institutions of the Federation, of the federal corporations, establishments, and foundations under public law as well as of their associations irrespective of their legal structure. The enterprises established by law out of the Special Fund of the German Federal Postal Administration are to be considered as public bodies, as long as they have an exclusive right according to the Postal Administration Law or the Telecommunication Installations Act.

2. "Public bodies of the Lander" means the authorities, the bodies of the judicature and other public-law institutions of a Land, of a municipality, an association of municipalities or other legal persons under public law subject to Land supervision as well as of their associations irrespective of their legal structure.

3. Private-law associations of public bodies of the Federation and the Lander performing public administration duties shall be regarded as public bodies of the Federation, irrespective of private shareholdings, if

    1. they operate beyond the territory of a Land or

    2. the Federation possesses the absolute majority of shares or votes.

    Otherwise they shall be regarded as public bodies of the Lander.

4. "Private bodies" means natural or legal persons, companies and other private-law associations insofar as they are not covered by paragraphs 1 to 3 above. To the extent that a private body performs sovereign public administration duties, it shall be treated as a public body for the purposes of this Act.

Section 4: Admissibility of Data Processing and Use

1. The processing and use of personal data shall be admissible only if this Act or any other legal provision permits or prescribes them or if the data subject has consented.

2. When consent is obtained from the data subject, he shall be informed of the purpose of storage and of any envisaged communication of his data and, at his request, of the consequences of withholding consent. Consent shall be given in writing unless special circumstances warrant any other form. If consent is to be given together with other written declarations, the declaration of consent shall be made distinguishable in its appearance.

3. In the field of scientific research, a special circumstance pursuant to the second sentence of paragraph 2 above shall also be deemed to exist where the defined purpose of research would be impaired considerably

if consent were obtained in writing. In such case the information pursuant to the first sentence of paragraph 2 above and the reasons from which considerable impairment of the defined purpose of research would arise shall be recorded in writing.

Section 5: Confidentiality

Persons employed in data processing shall not process or use personal data without authorization (confidentiality). On taking up their duties such persons, insofar as they work for private bodies, shall be required to give an undertaking to maintain such confidentiality. This undertaking shall continue to be valid after termination of their activity.

Section 7: Compensation by Public Bodies

1. Where a public body causes harm to the data subject through automated processing of his personal data that is inadmissible or incorrect under the provisions of this Act or other data protection provisions, such body is obliged to compensate the data subject for the harm thus caused, irrespective of any fault.

2. In grave cases of violation of privacy, the data subject shall receive adequate pecuniary compensation for the immaterial harm caused.

3. The claims under paragraphs 1 and 2 above shall be limited to a total amount of DM 250,000. Where, due to the same occurrence, compensation has to be paid to several persons and exceeds the maximum amount of DM 250,000, the compensation paid to each of them shall be reduced in proportion to the maximum amount.

4. If, in the case of a data file, several bodies are entitled to store the data and the injured person is unable to ascertain the controller of the data file, each body shall be liable.

5. Where several parties are responsible they shall be jointly and severally liable.

6. Sections 254 and 852 of the Civil Code shall apply mutatis mutandis to contributory negligence on the part of the data subject and to statutory limitation.

7. Provisions according to which a party responsible is liable to a greater extent than under this provision or according to which another person is responsible for the harm shall remain unaffected.

8. Recourse may be had to ordinary courts of law.

Section 8: Compensation by Private Bodies

If a data subject asserts a claim against a private body for compensation because of automated data processing that is inadmissible or incorrect under this Act or other data protection provisions and if it is disputed whether the harm caused results from a circumstance for which the controller of the data file is responsible, the burden of proof shall rest with the controller of the data file.

Section 9: Technical and Organizational Measures

Public and private bodies processing personal data either on their own behalf or on behalf of others shall take the technical and organizational measures necessary to ensure the implementation of the provisions of this Act, in particular the requirements set out in the annex to this Act. Measures shall be required only if the effort involved is reasonable in relation to the desired level of protection.

Section 14: Storage, Modification, and Use of Data

1. The storage, modification, or use of personal data shall be admissible where it is necessary for the performance of the duties of the controller of the data file and if it serves the purposes for which the data were collected. If there has been no preceding collection, the data may be modified or used only for the purposes for which they were stored.

2. Storage, modification, or use for other purposes shall be admissible only if

   1. a legal provision prescribes or peremptorily presupposes this,

   2. the data subject has consented,

   3. it is evident that this is in the interest of the data subject and there is no reason to assume that he would withhold consent if he knew of such other purpose,

4. particulars supplied by the data subject have to be checked because there are actual indications that they are incorrect,

5. the data can be taken from generally accessible sources or the controller of the data file would be entitled to publish them, unless the data subject clearly has an overriding legitimate interest in excluding the change of purpose,

6. this is necessary to avert substantial detriment to the common weal or any other immediate threat to public safety,

7. this is necessary to prosecute criminal or administrative offences, to implement sentences or measures as defined in section 11 (1), No. 8 of the Penal Code or reformatory or disciplinary measures as defined in the Youth Courts Act, or to execute decisions imposing administrative fines,

8. this is necessary to avert a grave infringement of another person's rights, or

9. this is necessary for the conduct of scientific research; scientific interest in conduct of the research project substantially outweighs the interest of the data subject in excluding the change of purpose, and the research purpose cannot be attained by other means or can be attained thus only with disproportionate effort.

3. Processing or use for other purposes shall not be deemed to occur if this serves the exercise of powers of supervision or control, the execution of auditing or the conduct of organizational studies for the controller of the data file. This shall also apply to processing or use for training and examination purposes by the controller of the data file, unless the data subject has overriding legitimate interests.

4. Personal data stored exclusively for the purpose of monitoring data protection, safeguarding data, or ensuring proper operation of a data processing system may be used exclusively for such purposes.

Section 16: Communication of Data to Private Bodies

1. The communication of personal data to private bodies shall be admissible if

   1. this is necessary for the performance of the duties of the communicating body and the requirements of section 14 of this Act are met or

   2. the recipient credibly proves a justified interest in knowledge of the data to be communicated and the data subject does not have a legitimate interest in excluding their communication.

2. Responsibility for the admissibility of communication shall rest with the communicating body.

3. In cases of communication under paragraph 1, No. 2 above, the communicating body shall inform the data subject of the communication of his data. This shall not apply if it can be assumed that he will acquire knowledge of such communication in another manner or if such information would jeopardize public safety or otherwise be detrimental to the Federation or a Land.

4. The recipient may process or use the communicated data only for the purpose for which they were communicated to him. The communicating body shall point this out to the recipient. Processing or use for other purposes shall be admissible if communication under paragraph 1 above would be admissible and the communicating body has consented.

Section 24: Monitoring by the Federal Commissioner for Data Protection

1. The Federal Commissioner for Data Protection shall monitor compliance with the provisions of this Act and other data Protection provisions by public bodies of the Federation. Where personal data in records are processed or used, the Federal Commissioner shall monitor their collection, processing, or use if the data subject adequately indicates that his rights have been infringed in this respect or if the Federal Commissioner has in his possession adequate indications of such infringement.

2. Monitoring by the Federal Commissioner shall also extend to personal data subject to professional or special official secrecy, especially tax secrecy under section 30 of the Tax Code. In the case of the Federal Authorities within the meaning of section 2 para. (1) Sentence 2, the mail and telecommunication secrecy (Section 10 Basic Law) shall be restricted, as long as it is necessary for the exercise of supervision of the controller of the data file. Except as provided in No. 1 below, the right of monitoring shall not extend to the contents of posts and telecommunications. The following shall not be subject to monitoring by the Federal Commissioner:

1. personal data subject to monitoring by the commission set up under section 9 of the Act Implementing Article 10 of the Basic Law, unless the commission requests the Federal Commissioner to monitor compliance with data protection provisions in connection, with specific procedures or in specific areas and to report thereon exclusively to it, and

   a. personal data subject to privacy of posts and telecommunications under article 10 of the Basic Law,

   b. personal data subject to medical privacy, and

   c. personal data in personnel or vetting records.

   If the data subject objects in a particular case vis-à-vis the Federal Commissioner for Data Protection to the monitoring of data relating to him. Without prejudice to the Federal Commissioner's right of monitoring, the public body shall inform data subjects in a general form of their right of objection.

3. Federal courts shall be subject to monitoring by the Federal Commissioner only where they deal with administrative matters.

4. Public bodies of the Federation shall be obliged to support the Federal Commissioner and his assistants in the performance of their duties. In particular they shall be granted

   1. information in reply to their questions as well as the opportunity to inspect all documents and records, especially stored data and data processing programs, connected with the monitoring referred to in paragraph 1 above,

   2. access to all official premises at any time.

   The authorities referred to in sections 6 (2) and 19 (3) of this Act shall afford support exclusively to the Federal Commissioner himself and the assistants appointed by him in writing. The second sentence above shall not apply to such authorities where the supreme federal authority establishes in a particular case that such information or inspection would jeopardize the security of the Federation or a Land.

5. The Federal Commissioner shall inform the public body of the results of his monitoring. He may combine them with proposals for improving data protection, especially for rectifying irregularities discovered in the processing or use of personal data. Section 25 of this Act shall remain unaffected.

6. Paragraph 2 above shall apply mutatis mutandis to public bodies responsible for monitoring compliance with data protection provisions in the Lander.

Section 28: Storage, Communication, and Use of Data for Own Purposes

1. The storage, modification, or communication of personal data or their use as a means of fulfilling one's own business purposes shall be admissible

   1. in accordance with the purposes of a contract or a quasicontractual fiduciary relationship with the data subject,

   2. insofar as this is necessary to safeguard justified interests of the controller of the data file and there is no reason to assume that the data subject has an overriding legitimate interest in his data being excluded from processing or use,

   3. if the data can be taken from generally accessible sources or the controller of the data file would be entitled to publish them, unless the data subject clearly has an overriding legitimate interest in his data being excluded from processing or use,

   4. if this is necessary in the interest of the controller of the data file for the conduct of scientific research, if scientific interest in conduct of the research project substantially outweighs the interest of the data subject in excluding the change of purpose and if the research purpose cannot be attained by other means or can be attained thus only with disproportionate effort.

   The data must be obtained fairly and lawfully.

2. Communication or use shall also be admissible

   1. insofar as this is necessary to safeguard justified interests of a third party or public interests or

   2. if the data, compiled in lists or otherwise combined, concern members of a group of persons and are restricted to

      • the data subject's membership of this group of persons,

      • occupation or type of business,

- name,
- title,
- academic degrees,
- address,
- year of birth

And if there is no reason to assume that the data subject has a legitimate interest in his data being excluded from communication. In the cases under (b) above it can generally be assumed that such interest exists where data are to be communicated which were stored for the purposes of a contract or a quasi-contractual fiduciary relationship and which concern

- health matters,
- criminal offences,
- administrative offences,
- religious or political views and
- when communicated by the employer, to the legal status under labor law or if this is necessary in the interest of a research institute for the conduct of scientific research, if scientific interest in conduct of the research project substantially outweighs the interest of the data subject in excluding the change of purpose and if the research purpose cannot be attained by other means or can be attained thus only with disproportionate effort.

3. If the data subject objects vis-à-vis the controller of the data file to the use or communication of his data for purposes of advertising or of market or opinion research, use or communication for such purposes shall be inadmissible. Where the data subject objects vis-à-vis the recipient of data communicated under paragraph 2 above to processing or use for purposes of advertising or of market or opinion research, the recipient shall block the data for such purposes.

4. The recipient may process or use the communicated data for the purpose for which they were communicated to him. Processing or use for other purposes shall be admissible only if the requirements of paragraphs 1 and 2 above are met. The communicating body shall point this out to the recipient.

Section 29: Storage of Data in the Normal Course of Business for the Purpose of Communication

1. The storage or modification of personal data in the normal course of business for the purpose of communication shall be admissible if

   1. there is no reason to assume that the data subject has a legitimate interest in his data being excluded from storage or modification or

   2. the data can be taken from generally accessible sources or the controller of the data file would be entitled to publish them, unless the data subject clearly has an overriding legitimate interest in his data being excluded from use or processing.
   The second sentence of section 28 (1) of this Act shall apply.

2. Communication shall be admissible if

   a the recipient credibly proves a justified interest in knowledge of the data or

   b the data pursuant to Section 28 (2), No. 1 (b) of this Act have been compiled in lists or otherwise combined and are to be communicated for purposes of advertising or of market or opinion research and

   c there is no reason to assume that the data subject has a legitimate interest in his data being excluded from communication.
   The second sentence of Section 28 (2), No. 1 of this Act shall apply mutatis mutandis. In the case of communication under No. 1 (a) above, the reasons for the existence of a justified interest and the means of credibly presenting them shall be recorded by the communicating body. In the case of communication through automated retrieval, such recording shall be required of the recipient.

3. Section 28 (3) and (4) of this Act shall apply to the processing or use of communicated data.

Section 30: Storage of Data in the Normal Course of Business for the Purpose of Communication in Depersonalized Form

1. If personal data are stored in the normal course of business in order to communicate them in depersonalized form, the characteristics enabling information concerning personal or material circumstances to be attributed to an identified or identifiable individual shall be stored separately. Such characteristics may be combined with the information only where necessary for storage or scientific purposes.

2. The modification of personal data shall be admissible if

   1. there is no reason to assume that the data subject has a legitimate interest in his data being excluded from modification or

   2. the data can be taken from generally accessible sources or the controller of the data file would be entitled to publish them, unless the data subject clearly has an overriding legitimate interest in his data being excluded from modification.

3. Personal data shall be erased if their storage is inadmissible.

4. Sections 29, 33 to 35 of this Act shall not apply.

Section 32: Obligatory Registration

1. Bodies which in the normal course of business

   1. store personal data for the purpose of communication,

   2. store personal data for the purpose of depersonalized communication, or

   3. are commissioned to process or use personal data as a service enterprise

   As well as their branches and dependent offices shall notify the commencement and termination of their activities to the relevant supervisory authority within one month.

2. Upon registration, the following particulars shall be supplied for the register kept by the supervisory authority:

   1. name or title of the body,

   2. owners, managing boards, managing directors, or other lawfully, or Constitutionally appointed managers and the persons placed in charge of data processing,

   3. address,

   4. business purposes of the body and of data processing,

   5. name of the data protection officer,

   6. general description of the type of personal data stored. This information shall not be required in the case of paragraph 1, No. 3, above.

3. Upon registration, the following particulars that shall not be included in the register shall also be supplied:

   1. type of data processing systems used,

   2. in the event of regular communication of personal data, the recipients and type of data communicated.

4. Paragraph 1 above shall apply mutatis mutandis to the change of particulars supplied in accordance with paragraphs 2 and 3 above.

5. The supervisory authority may determine in a particular case which particulars have to be supplied in accordance with paragraph 2, Nos. 4 and 6, paragraph 3 and paragraph 4 above. The effort connected with the supply of these particulars must be in reasonable proportion to their significance for monitoring by the supervisory authority.

Section 33: Notification of the Data Subject

1. If personal data are stored for the first time for one's own purposes, the data subject shall be notified of such storage and of the type of data. If personal data are stored in the normal course of business for the purpose of communication, the data subject shall be notified of their initial communication and of the type of data communicated.

2. Notification shall not be required if

    1. the data subject has received knowledge by other means of the storage or communication of the data,

    2. the data are stored merely because they may not be erased due to legal, statutory, or contractual provisions on their preservation or exclusively serve purposes of data security or data protection control,

    3. the data must be kept secret in accordance with a legal provision or by virtue of their nature, in particular on account of an overriding legal interest of a third party,

    4. the relevant public body has stated to the controller of the data file that publication of the data would jeopardize public safety or order or would otherwise be detrimental to the Federation or a Land,

    5. the data are stored in a data file which is kept only temporarily and is erased within three months of being set up,

    6. the data are stored for one's own purposes

        a. are taken from generally accessible sources or

        b. notification would considerably impair the business purposes of the controller of the data file, unless the interest in notification outweighs such impairment, or

    7. the data are stored in the normal course of business for the purpose of communication and

        a. are taken from generally accessible sources insofar as they relate to those persons who published these data or

        b. the data are compiled in lists or otherwise combined (section 29 (2), No. 1 (b) of this Act).

Section 35: Correction, Erasure, and Blocking of Data

1. Incorrect personal data shall be corrected.

2. Apart from the cases mentioned in paragraph 3, Nos. 1 and 2, below, personal data may be erased at any time. They shall be erased if

    1. their storage is inadmissible,

    2. they relate to health matters, criminal offences, administrative offences as well as religious or political views and the controller of the data file cannot prove that they are correct,

    3. they are processed for one's own purposes, as soon as knowledge of them is no longer needed for fulfilling the purpose for which they are stored, or

    4. they are processed in the normal course of business for the purpose of communication and an examination five calendar years after their first being stored shows that further storage is not necessary.

3. Instead of erasure, personal data shall be blocked insofar as

    1. in the case of paragraph 2, No. 3 or 4 above, preservation periods prescribed by law, statutes, or contracts rule out any erasure,

    2. there is reason to assume that erasure would impair legitimate interests of the data subject, or

    3. erasure is not possible or is only possible with disproportionate effort due to the specific type of storage.

4. Personal data shall also be blocked if the data subject disputes that they are correct and it cannot be ascertained whether they are correct or incorrect.

5. Where they are stored in the normal course of business for the purpose of communication, personal data which are incorrect or whose correctness is disputed need not be corrected, blocked, or erased except in the cases mentioned in paragraph 2, No. 2 above, if they are taken from generally accessible sources and are stored for documentation purposes. At the request of the data subject, his counterstatement shall be added to the data for the duration of their storage. The data may not be communicated without this counterstatement.

6. If necessary to protect legitimate interests of the data subject, the correction of incorrect data, the blocking of disputed data, and the erasure or blocking of data due to inadmissible storage shall be notified to the bodies to which these data are transmitted for storage within the framework of regular data communication.

7. Blocked data may be communicated or used without the consent of the data subject only if

   1. this is indispensable for scientific purposes, for use as evidence, or for other reasons in the overriding interests of the controller of the data file or a third party and

   2. communication or use of the data for this purpose would be admissible if they were not blocked.

Section 36: Appointment of a Data Protection Officer

1. Private bodies which process personal data automatically and regularly employ at least five permanent employees for this purpose shall appoint in writing a data protection officer within one month of the commencement of their activities. The same shall apply where personal data are processed by other means and at least 20 persons are permanently employed for this purpose.

2. Only persons who possess the specialized knowledge and demonstrate the reliability necessary for the performance of the duties concerned may be appointed data protection officer.

3. The data protection officer shall be directly subordinate to the owner, managing board, managing director, or other lawfully or Constitutionally appointed manager. He shall be free to use his specialized knowledge in the area of data protection at his own discretion. He shall suffer no disadvantage through the performance of his duties. The appointment of a data protection officer may only be revoked at the request of the supervisory authority or by section 626 of the Civil Code being applied mutatis mutandis.

4. The data protection officer shall be bound to maintain secrecy on the identity of the data subject and on circumstances permitting conclusions to be drawn about the data subject, unless he is released from this obligation by the data subject.

5. The private body shall support the data protection officer in the performance of his duties and in particular, to the extent needed for such performance, make available assistants as well as premises, furnishings, equipment, and other resources.

Section 37: Duties of the Data Protection Officer

1. The data protection officer shall be responsible for ensuring that this Act and other provisions concerning data protection are observed. For this purpose he may apply to the supervisory authority in cases of doubt. In particular he shall

   1. monitor the proper use of data processing programs with the aid of which personal data are to be processed; for this purpose he shall be informed in good time of projects for automatic processing of personal data;

   2. take suitable steps to familiarize the persons employed in the processing of personal data with the provisions of this Act and other provisions concerning data protection, with particular reference to the situation prevailing in this area and the special data protection requirements arising therefrom;

   3. assist and advise in the selection of persons to be employed in the processing of personal data.

2. The data protection officer shall receive from the private body a list on

   1. data processing systems used,

   2. designation and type of data files,

   3. type of data stored,

   4. business purposes, the fulfillments of which necessitate knowledge of these data,

   5. their regular recipients,

   6. groups of persons entitled to access or persons exclusively entitled to access.

3. Paragraph 2, Nos. 2 to 6 above shall not apply to data files that are kept only temporarily and are erased within three months of being set up.

Section 38: Supervisory Authority

1. The supervisory authority shall check in a particular case that this Act and other data protection provisions governing the processing or use of personal data in or from data files are observed if it possesses sufficient indications that any such provision has been violated by private bodies, especially if the data subject himself submits evidence to this effect.

2. If personal data are in the normal course of business

   1. stored for the purpose of communication,

   2. stored for the purpose of depersonalized communication or

   3. processed by service enterprises commissioned to do so,

   The supervisory authority shall monitor observance of this Act or other data protection provisions governing the processing or use of personal data in or from data files. The supervisory authority shall keep a register in accordance with section 32 (2) of this Act. The register shall be open to inspection by any person.

3. The bodies subject to monitoring and the persons responsible for their management shall provide the supervisory authority on request and without delay with the information necessary for the performance of its duties. A person obliged to provide information may refuse to do so where he would expose himself or one of the persons designated in section 383 (1), Nos. 1 to 3, of the Code of Civil Procedure to the danger of criminal prosecution or of proceedings under the Administrative Offenses Act. This shall be pointed out to the person obliged to provide information.

4. The persons appointed by the supervisory authority to exercise monitoring shall be authorized, insofar as necessary for the performance of the duties of the supervisory authority, to enter the property and premises of the body during business hours and to carry out checks and inspections there. They may inspect business documents, especially the list under section 37 (2) of this Act as well as the stored personal data and the data processing programs. Section 24 (6) of this Act shall apply mutatis mutandis. The person obliged to provide information shall permit such measures.

5. To guarantee data protection under this Act and other data protection provisions governing the processing or use of personal data in or from data files, the supervisory authority may instruct that, within the scope of the requirements set out in section 9 of this Act, measures be taken to rectify technical or organizational irregularities discovered. In the event of grave irregularities of this kind, especially where they are connected with a specific impairment of privacy, the supervisory authority may prohibit the use of particular procedures if the irregularities are not rectified within a reasonable period contrary to the instruction pursuant to the first sentence above and despite the imposition of a fine. The supervisory authority may demand the dismissal of the data protection officer if he does not possess the specialized knowledge and demonstrate the reliability necessary for the performance of his duties.

6. The Land governments or the bodies authorized by them shall designate the supervisory authorities responsible for monitoring the implementation of data protection within the area of application of this Part.

7. The Industrial Code shall continue to apply to commercial firms subject to the provisions of this Part.

Section 39: Limited Use of Personal Data Subject to Professional or Special Official Secrecy

1. Personal data that are subject to professional or special official secrecy and that have been supplied by the body bound to secrecy in the performance of its professional or official duties may be processed or used by the controller of the data file only for the purpose for which he has received them. In the event of communication to a private body, the body bound to secrecy must give its consent.

2. The data may be processed or used for another purpose only if the change of purpose is permitted by special legislation.

Section 40: Processing and Use of Personal Data by Research Institutes

1. Personal data collected or stored for scientific research purposes may be processed or used only for such purposes.

2. The communication of personal data to other than public bodies for scientific research purposes shall be admissible only if these undertake not to process or use the communicated data for other purposes and to comply with the provisions of paragraph 3 below.

3. The personal data shall be depersonalized as soon as the research purpose permits this. Until such time the characteristics enabling information concerning personal or material circumstances to be attributed to an identified or identifiable individual shall be stored separately. They may be combined with the information only to the extent required by the research purpose.

4. Bodies conducting scientific research may publish personal data only if

   1. the data subject has consented or

   2. this is indispensable for the presentation of research findings on contemporary events.

Section 43: Criminal Offenses

1. Anyone who, without authorization,

   1. stores, modifies, or communicates,

   2. makes available for automatic retrieval, or

   3. retrieves or obtains for himself or for others from data files

   Any personal data protected by this Act that are not common knowledge shall be punished by imprisonment for up to one year or by a fine.

2. Likewise punishable shall be anyone who

   1. obtains by means of incorrect information the communication of personal data protected by this Act which are not common knowledge,

   2. contrary to the first sentence of section 16 (4), the first sentence of section 28 (4), also in conjunction with section 29 (3), the first sentence of section 39 (1) or section 40 (1) of this Act, uses the communicated data for other purposes by transmitting them to third parties, or

   3. contrary to the second sentence of section 30 (1) of this Act, combines the characteristics mentioned in the first sentence of section 30 (1) with the information or, contrary to the third sentence of section 40 (3), combines the characteristics mentioned in the second sentence of section 40 (3) with the information.

3. Where the offender commits the offence in exchange for payment or with the intention of enriching himself or another person or of harming another person, he shall be liable to imprisonment for up to two years or to a fine.

4. Such offenses shall be prosecuted only if a complaint is filed.

Section 44: Administrative Offenses

1. An administrative offense shall be deemed to have been committed by anyone who, whether intentionally or through negligence,

   1. contrary to the third or fourth sentence of section 29 (2) of this Act, fails to record the reasons described there or the means of credibly presenting them,

   2. contrary to section 32 (1), also in conjunction with section 32 (4) of this Act, fails to submit a notification or fails to do so within the prescribed time limit or, contrary to section 32 (2), also in conjunction with section 32 (4) of this Act, falls, when registering, to provide the required particulars or to provide correct or complete particulars,

   3. contrary to section 33 (1) of this Act, fails to notify the data subject or fails to do so correctly or completely,

   4. contrary to the third sentence of section 35 (5) of this Act, communicates data without a counterstatement,

   5. contrary to section 36 (1) of this Act, fails to appoint a data protection officer or fails to do so within the prescribed time limit,

   6. contrary to the first sentence of section 38 (3) of this Act, fails to provide information or fails to do so correctly, completely, or within the prescribed time limit or, contrary to the fourth sentence of section 38 (4) of this Act, refuses to grant access to property or premises, or refuses to permit checks or inspections or the inspection of business documents, or

7. fails to comply with an executable instruction under the first sentence of section 38 (5) of this Act.

2. Such administrative offences shall be punishable by a fine of up to DM 50,000.

Annex to the First Sentence of Section 9 of This Act

Where personal data are processed automatically, measures suited to the type of personal data to be protected shall be taken

1. to prevent unauthorized persons from gaining access to data processing systems with which personal data are processed (access control);

2. to prevent storage media from being read, copied, modified, or removed without authorization (storage media control);

3. to prevent unauthorized input into the memory and the unauthorized examination, modification, or erasure of stored personal data (memory control);

4. to prevent data processing systems from being used by unauthorized persons with the aid of data transmission facilities (user control);

5. to ensure that persons entitled to use a data processing system have access only to the data to which they have a right of access (access control);

6. to ensure that it is possible to check and establish to which bodies personal data can be communicated by means of data transmission facilities (communication control);

7. to ensure that it is possible to check and establish which personal data have been input into data processing systems by whom and at what time (input control);

8. to ensure that, in the case of commissioned processing of personal data, the data are processed strictly in accordance with the instructions of the principal (job control);

9. to prevent data from being read, copied, modified, or erased without authorization during the transmission of personal data or the transport of storage media (transfer control);

10. to arrange the internal organization of authorities or enterprises in such a way that it meets the specific requirements of data protection (organizational control).

Australian Laws and Acts

Health Records and Information Privacy Act (HRIP)[30]

The HRIP Act governs the handling of health information in both the public and private sectors in New South Wales. This includes hospitals (public and private), doctors, and other health care organizations. It also includes all other organizations that have any type of health information, including such places as a university that undertakes research or a gymnasium that records information about a person's health and injuries.

The HRIP Act contains 15 health privacy principles (HPPs) outlining how health information must be collected, stored, used, and disclosed. The health privacy principles can be grouped into seven main headings:

- Collection
- Storage
- Access and accuracy
- Use
- Disclosure
- Identifiers and anonymity
- Transferals and linkage

These are legal obligations that must be followed, although the HRIP Act provides for a number of legal exemptions from these principles. The HRIP Act also sets out how to handle complaints regarding the handling of health information.

Financial Transactions Reporting (FTR) Act 1988[31]

Australia's anti–money laundering program places obligations on financial institutions and other financial intermediaries. Those obligations are contained in the Financial Transaction Reporting Act 1988 (the FTR Act). The FTR Act requires cash dealers, as defined in the act, to report to the Director of AUSTRAC (Australian Transaction Reports and Analysis Centre):

- Suspicious transactions
- Cash transactions of AUS $10,000 or more or the foreign currency equivalent
- International funds transfer instructions

The FTR Act also requires cash dealers to verify the identity of persons who are signatories to accounts, and also prohibits accounts being opened or operated under a false name.

Cash dealers as defined in the FTR Act include the following:

- Banks, building societies, and credit unions
- Financial corporations
- Insurance companies and insurance intermediaries
- Securities dealers and futures brokers
- Cash carriers
- Managers and trustees of unit trusts
- Firms that deal in travelers checks, money orders, and the like
- Persons who collect, hold, exchange, or remit currency on behalf of other persons
- Currency and bullion dealers
- Casinos and gambling houses
- Totalisators

The legislation provides penalties for avoiding the reporting requirements and presenting false or incomplete information. It also has penalties for persons who facilitate or assist in these activities.

The reporting and identification requirements, backed by penalties for offenses, provide a strong deterrent to money launderers and facilitators of money laundering. These provisions increase the level of risk associated with abuse of the Australian financial system by tax evaders and organized crime groups. It also adds to their costs of doing business and, in particular, in laundering their illicit profits.

The legislation also sets a standard that must be met by cash dealers. Failure to meet the standard places the cash dealer at risk of being used in the process of money laundering and thus subject to consequential penalties when detected. Penalties include pecuniary penalties and imprisonment.

Spam Act 2003

The Spam Act 2003 prohibits the sending of spam, which is identified as a commercial electronic message sent without the consent of the addressee via e-mail, short message service (SMS), multimedia message service (MMS), or instant messaging.

Chapter Summary

- Public safety is a major responsibility of local, state, and federal governments.
- A variety of laws define government and private liability in the process of disaster recovery.
- The Sarbanes-Oxley Act introduced significant legislative changes to financial practice and corporate governance regulation.
- In Australia, the Spam Act 2003 prohibits the sending of spam, which is identified as a commercial electronic message sent without the consent of the addressee via e-mail, short message service (SMS), multimedia message service (MMS), or instant messaging.

Review Questions

1. What is the Sarbanes-Oxley Act?

_____

_____

_____

_____

2. What is the FCPA?

_____

_____

_____

_____

3. What is HIPAA?

_____

_____

_____

_____

_____

4. What is the Gramm-Leach-Bliley Act?

_____

_____

_____

_____

_____

5. What is the Flood Disaster Prevention Act of 1973?

_____

_____

_____

_____

_____

6. What is PIPEDA?

_____

_____

_____

_____

7. What is the Data Protection Act of 1998?

_____

_____

_____

_____

8. What are the OECD Principles of Corporate Governance?

_____

_____

_____

_____

9. What is the FTR Act of 1988?

_____

_____

_____

_____

Hands-On Projects

1. Read about several U.S. laws and acts.

   ▪ Navigate to Chapter 2 of the Student Resource Center.

   ▪ Open 01ccma.pdf and read the content.

2. Read about the Data Protection Act of 1998.

   ▪ Navigate to Chapter 2 of the Student Resource Center.

   ▪ Open data_protection_-_when_and_how_to_complain.pdf and read the content.

3. Read about the Sarbanes-Oxley Act.

   ▪ Navigate to Chapter 2 of the Student Resource Center.

   ▪ Open Zhang_Ivy_Economic_Consequences_of_S_O.pdf and read the content.

   ▪ 3-68

Endnotes

[1] http://www.sarbanes-oxley-forum.com/
[2] http://www.usdoj.gov/
[3] http://www.cms.hhs.gov/
[4] http://www.hhs.gov/
[5] http://www.ftc.gov/
[6] http://www.fdic.gov/
[7] http://www.fdic.gov/regulations/laws/rules/6500-3600.html.
[8] http://www.fema.gov/
[9] http://www.fema.gov/pdf/about/stafford_act.pdf.
[10] http://fpc.state.gov/
[11] http://www.google.com/url?sa=t&source=web&ct=res&cd=5&ved=0CCAQFjAE&url=http%3A%2F%2Ffrwebgate.access.gpo.gov%2Fcgibin%2Fgetdoc.cgi%3Fdbname%3D108_cong_public_laws%26docid%3Df%3Apubl187.108.pdf&ei=XN4nS7inM9SWlAfGrIipDQ&usg=AFQjCNEXwLhZeBD_o5G0mrHO7AsiEiFmGQ&sig2=X4ziBrmpb0Br95j83aSmBg.
[12] http://www.ftc.gov/
[13] http://www.fdic.gov/regulations/laws/rules/8000-3100.html.
[14] http://epic.org/
[15] http://www.cnrc.navy.mil/sandiego/Security_Notice/Computer_Fraud_and_Abuse_Act/computer_fraud_and_abuse_act.htm.
[16] http://www.ffiec.gov/
[17] http://www.federalreserve.gov/
[18] http://www.ncua.gov
[19] http://www.occ.treas.gov/
[20] http://www.ots.treas.gov/
[21] http://www.omafra.gov.on.ca/
[22] http://www.cabinetoffice.gov.uk/
[23] http://www.ne-derbyshire.gov.uk/

[24]http://europa.eu/
[25]http://www.giodo.gov.pl/
[26]http://www.fsa.gov.uk/
[27]http://www.dutchdpa.nl/indexen/en_ind_wetten_wbp_wbp.shtml
[28]http://www.ris.bka.gv.at/Dokumente/Erv/ERV_1999_1_165/ERV_1999_1_165.html.
[29]http://www.bdd.de/Download/bdsg_eng.pdf
[30]http://www.lawlink.nsw.gov.au/
[31]Source: http://www.austrac.gov.au/

Chapter 3

Disaster Recovery Planning and Implementation

Objectives

After completing this chapter, you should be able to:

- Secure computer systems
- Develop, test, and implement a disaster recovery plan

Key Terms

Degaussing   the process of thoroughly deleting data from magnetic media

Functional verification   a process in which a tester creates conditions to which a security measure should respond and then notes the effects of that measure

Introduction to Disaster Recovery Planning and Implementation

When a disaster strikes, there is little time to react. The longer it takes to get critical systems up and running, the greater the potential loss. It is extremely important to be prepared to take action immediately. Therefore, the first steps in disaster recovery are planning and prevention. This chapter teaches you about system security, in order to prevent disasters in the first place, and planning for disaster recovery.

Aspects of Security

There are five primary aspects of security:

1. *Confidentiality*: Confidentiality is the prevention of unauthorized access, disclosure, and use of information. Loss of confidential information may lead to both tangible and intangible losses.

2. *Integrity*: This refers to the reliability and trustworthiness of information, and the quality of a system itself. Integrity means that there has been no unauthorized data manipulation and that the information received is the same as the information sent. Loss of information integrity could be a result of intentional attack or an error in the underlying information processing and communication system.

3. *Availability*: Availability is the ability to access necessary services and resources. This is, of course, critical for organizations that depend on these services and resources.

4. *Authentication*: Authentication provides the ability to confirm the identity of a person or the origin of an artifact, or to ensure that a computer program is a trusted one. Access control systems use various authentication mechanisms including passwords and biometrics.

5. *Nonrepudiation*: This guarantees that the sender has sent the message and the receiver has received the message, eliminating the possibility of denial on both ends. This is achieved through the use of digital signatures, time stamps, and confirmation services.

Application Security

In addition to the previously mentioned primary aspects of security, the following factors are critical for application security:

- *Access control*: Access to an application requires certain rights. Access control ensures that in the event of a disaster, investigators can determine who accessed the application. Methods of managing access control include:
  - Read, write, and execute permissions
  - Role-based access control performed by the administrator
  - Control access depending on the IP address
  - Control access based on the object level

- *Authorization*: Who is authorized to do what, when, and how

- *Confidentiality/privacy*: Often, sensitive data is treated the same as other data, which leads to threats related to confidentiality and privacy. Applications should be developed to keep confidential and private information secret.

- *Encryption*: Encryption changes data, preventing, attackers from reading the data after intercepting them. In order to read the data, the recipient must know the decryption procedure. Encryption algorithms can be asymmetric or symmetric. Asymmetric algorithms use separate keys for encryption and decryption, while symmetric algorithms use a single key for both encryption and decryption.

- *Segregation of data and privileges*: Data should be segregated through access control mechanisms. Only components that require access to the data should have access. Centralizing sensitive data helps the application designer better organize security functionality.

- *Error-handling*: Error-handling refers to the behavior of an application when something unexpected occurs. Error-handling components include:
  - Defining the type of error, such as processing error, runtime error, violation of security, or bug in a program
  - Defining the severity level of an error
  - Auditing different logging components, such as files, e-mail messages, or SMS messages
  - Responding to the error in ways such as issuing a warning, stopping the component's activities, restarting the service, shutting down the application, and informing the administrator

- *Testing for security*: Security measures must be tested to confirm their effectiveness. The most common method is **functional verification**, in which the tester creates conditions to which a security measure should respond and then notes the effects of that measure.

Security Issues with Commercial Off-The-Shelf (COTS) Products

By using commercial off-the-shelf (COTS) products, an organization can save the time and effort of creating their own programs and services by purchasing these products from a third-party vendor. This can speed up and reduce the cost of system construction, but it can also introduce the following issues:

- *Integration*: COTS products must be integrated with existing systems and may contain incompatibilities with existing programs and services.

- *Dependency on the third-party vendor*: Because COTS products require little effort by the organization, it becomes increasingly dependent on the third-party vendor. This can cause a risk if the vendor goes out of business or fails to produce products that meet the organization's changing requirements.

- *Failure to meet individual requirements*: Because COTS products are designed for general use, they may not meet all of the organization's specific requirements. Organizations then have to give up some of their requirements or build new products in addition to the COTS products.

- *Threats of failure*: If the COTS products do not perform as expected, projects may turn out poorly or fail entirely.

Database Security

Confidentiality, integrity, and availability, known as the *Information Security Triad*, are the most important elements of all information security. Databases implement various design and logical components to achieve these security elements.

System and Object Privileges

A particular user can connect to a database when the system grants the user the necessary privileges, or authorizations, to do so. There are several types of privileges, including the following:

- *System privileges*: System privileges permit the user to implement a systemwide action. Administrators and system developers are usually the only ones allowed to access system privilege configuration and information.

- *Schema object privileges*: Through schema object privileges, users are assigned privileges to a particular object or piece of data. Schema object privileges provide table security to data manipulation language (DML) and data dictionary language (DDL) operations. These privileges can only be granted by the object owner or the administrator. The owner can also give permission to a user, so that the user can give access to others.

Managing System and Object Privileges

The user must provide an authentic username and password to access the database or specific database tables. The following are different ways to manage these privileges:

- *Role-based privilege management*: Roles can be assigned to a single person or to a group of people. The following are some types of roles:

  - *Database roles*: Database roles can be used to provide privileges relating to accessing and modifying data in the database. These roles are assigned to users based on their job functions.

  - *Global roles*: A global role applies to an entire database.

  - *Enterprise roles*: These roles are assigned to enterprise users who have global roles on multiple databases.

  - *Secure application roles*: With secure application roles, users can be prevented from bypassing security measures in order to access data.

- *Managing privileges using stored procedures*: Users can be prevented from performing operations on the database by using stored procedures.

- *Managing privileges using network facilities*: Database roles can help manage and administer privileges from external services for all network resources.

- *Managing privileges by providing access to views*: Users can be given access to a particular view of a table, thus eliminating the possibility of accessing the entire table.

Row-Level Security

Access to particular rows of a table gives users the information they need without showing them information they should not see. Ways to achieve row-level security include the following:

- *Complex and dynamic views*: An application designer defines complex views by making user security tables. These security tables are then joined with the application tables depending on the application user's username.
- *Virtual private database*: In a virtual private database, or VPD, the users create row-level security by performing query modification based on a security policy.
- *Label-based access control*: In this type of access control, organizations provide sensitivity labels to data rows, and restrict and control the access to data based on those labels.

Encrypting Data on the Server

Encryption makes data unusable by unauthorized users. There are many industry standard encryption algorithms, including Data Encryption Standard (DES) and the more secure Triple DES (3DES) and Advanced Encryption Standard (AES)

Database Integrity Mechanisms

Database integrity ensures that the data present in a database are accurate and consistent.

System Availability Factors

Data must be accessible to authorized users at all times. System availability depends on the following factors:

- *Storage quotas*: The administrator should maintain a policy limiting each user to a specific amount of disk space in the database.
- *Resource limits*: Users should be restricted to only the resources necessary for their jobs.
- *Hot backups*: The administrator should always maintain a backup of critical data in case of an unexpected data loss or application error.
- *Resistance to attack*: Developers should write software based on secure coding standards.
- *Secure configuration*: Administrators should configure systems to prevent as many known vulnerabilities as possible.

Database Security Checklist

The following is a checklist for ensuring database security:

- Build a baseline for future database security by assessing the present level of security.
- Regularly check the database for vulnerabilities. Types of database vulnerabilities include the following:
  - *Vendor bugs* are any buffer overflow or programming errors caused when the user executes commands. These bugs can usually be eliminated by applying patches.
  - *Poor database architecture* can cause security issues. These vulnerabilities are difficult to fix because they require major reworking by the vendor.
  - Database security can be compromised if the database is configured incorrectly. This vulnerability is called a *misconfiguration*.
  - *Incorrect usage* is when attackers can use developer tools to break into a system.
- Regularly assess the database permissions granted to users.
- Apply patches to the database regularly.
- Perform frequent audits to test the accuracy of the security policies and discover any irregularities.

- Use security auditing tools to monitor and record the functions of the database and alerts in the case of undesired actions. Use an alert system that provides real-time security awareness.

- If the security audits do not succeed in securing the database, encryption is the most effective tool to protect critical data.

- Change default passwords immediately, and regularly change all passwords.

- Disable any user accounts that are not in use.

Distributed System Security

A distributed system is a collection of processors connected through a communication network. These systems make use of both local and remote resources, and can be used for:

- Resource sharing
- Increased computation speed
- Increased reliability through redundancy
- Communication

Distributed systems have four layers: host, infrastructure, application, and service. All of these layers must be secured.

1. Host-based vulnerabilities

   - *Malware*: Malware is software intended to perform undesired activities, often without the user's knowledge. Malware includes viruses, rootkits, Trojans, and other unwanted software.

   - *Eavesdropping*: Electronic eavesdropping is the use of an electronic device to monitor communications without the consent of the involved parties. A person can eavesdrop over almost any communication medium, including telephone lines, e-mail, and instant messaging.

   - *Resource starvation*: Here, the attacker consumes a particular resource until it is exhausted. For example, an attacker can continuously issue requests to a Web site to create shopping carts or users.

   - *Privilege escalation*: This is any attack that gives a user unauthorized access to resources.

2. Infrastructure-level vulnerabilities

   - *Network-level threats and vulnerabilities*: Common vulnerabilities at the network level include poor installation settings and outdated security patches. Network-level attacks include spoofing, denial of service (DoS), and packet sniffing.

   - *Grid computing threats and vulnerabilities*: Grid computing threats are related to many computers acting together to solve a single problem. Administrators must ensure that all computers in the grid are secure.

   - *Storage threats and vulnerabilities*: Storage devices must be protected from unauthorized external access using security software.

3. Application-level vulnerabilities

   - Individual applications are prone to different vulnerabilities, such as viruses, Trojans, and buffer overflows.

4. Service-level vulnerabilities

   - *Service-level threats and vulnerabilities*: These include software service-level problems, software error events such as memory errors, buffer overflows due to poor programming, and critical errors caused by improper implementation of software systems.

   - *Service-level security requirements*: Organizations should implement application service-level vulnerability assessment tests to detect software service-level vulnerabilities and software error events as part of an enterprise-level security test program. They should provide real-time assessment of software service-level problems, real-time software error events, and automatic alerts of critical errors.

   - *Service-level attacks*: Denial-of-service (DoS) and distributed denial-of-service (DDoS) attacks are the most common, followed by buffer overflow attacks, leading to systemwide compromise.

Firmware Security

Firmware is the fixed, small program that resides inside various electronic devices. This controls the basic, low-level operations in the device. Firmware is stored in computer chips such as ROM, PROM, and EPROM. Firmware security features include the following:

- *Power-on password*: Power-on password authentication is a form of preboot security. When the system is powered on, it tells the user to enter the stored password in order to continue with the boot process. When the password is entered incorrectly a certain number of times, the system is restarted. This is only effective on a single-user system, because the computer can only have one password.

- *Smart-card authentication*: With smart-card authentication, the user must provide the correct smart card and PIN to boot the system. That way, the user only needs to remember a small PIN instead of a strong password.

- *Embedded security chip authentication*: On computers that contain an embedded security chip, users are required to enter a key passphrase before the machine will boot. If the given key passphrase is authentic, the BIOS proceeds to boot the operating system. If the authentication is unsuccessful after a certain number of retries, the system halts or shuts down.

- *DriveLock hard drive protection*: DriveLock integrates with a power-on password and protects hard drive access with a password. DriveLock provides protection to a hard drive even if the hard drive is placed in another system.

- *Disk Sanitizer*: Information stored on a hard drive can still pose a security threat when the system is recycled or disposed. A data removal program, such as Disk Sanitizer, completely removes and destroys the data from the hard drive. That way, the data is impossible to retrieve, even using advanced tools.

Industrial Security

Industrial security is achieved through proper system design, effective monitoring, and comprehensive management of industrial functions. Measures taken for industrial security include the following:

- Make sure that security functions are working properly. Perform regular audits of these functions.
- Train employees about security measures. Employees should be able to handle sudden, undesired events.
- Clearly define the measures to be taken in the event of a disaster.
- Have specialized personnel for specific security functions.
- Protect important assets and documents in a secure location, such as a third-party site. Storing data off-site ensures that it will be available after even the most devastating disaster.

Vulnerabilities in Network Security Software and Services

Although network security software is used to protect the network from undesired events and threats, these programs contain their own vulnerabilities. The following are some common vulnerabilities in network security software:

- Firewalls
  - Misconfiguration
  - Trusting some IP addresses
  - Availability of extra and unnecessary services on the firewall
  - Unnecessarily opened TCP and UDP ports
- IPSec VPN
  - Most VPN servers can be fingerprinted by different fingerprinting methods
  - Insecure default settings
  - Insecure storage of authentication data by VPN clients
  - Offline password cracking

- Man-in-the-middle attacks
- Denial-of-service attacks
- Voice over IP (VoIP)
  - Low bandwidth
  - Minimal resources
  - Insufficient data verification
  - File/resource manipulation flaws
  - Authentication and certificate errors
  - Homogeneous network
  - Physical connection quality and packet collision

Remanence

Even after data are supposedly deleted from a medium, like a hard drive or memory card, a trace of the data usually remains. This is called remanence. There are two types of remanence: optical remanence and magnetic remanence.

1. In *optical remanence*, some information remains after data are removed from optical storage media, such as a CD-ROM or DVD-ROM. The best way to completely remove these data is to destroy the disc. Shredders strong enough to handle these discs are inexpensive and convenient.

2. *Magnetic remanence* is the residual magnetic information stored on hard drives, floppy disks, or magnetic tapes. This can be removed with a degausser device. **Degaussing** is the process of thoroughly deleting data from magnetic media.

When traces of data are present in storage devices, there is always a threat of those data being recovered by a third party. This leads to data theft and loss of valuable information such as passwords and crucial files.

Disaster Recovery Plan (DRP)

A disaster recovery plan, or DRP, aids and supports an organization in restoring information technology functions after a disaster. The DRP describes the framework and procedures to be followed in the case of a disaster. The DRP should address the following areas:

- *Prevention (predisaster)*: The organization should first secure vulnerable systems, protect systems containing important data, and train the disaster recovery team. This planning will make it significantly easier to quickly recover from a disaster.

- *Continuity (during a disaster)*: In this phase, the primary objective is to maintain and continue the critical operations that allow the organization to function properly. It includes maintaining the critical systems and resources, as well as moving systems and resources to secondary sites during a disaster.

- *Recovery (postdisaster)*: This phase includes restoring all systems and resources to their regular and fully operational state. All systems and resources present at secondary locations are brought back to the original site.

The main objectives of the DRP are as follows:

- Reducing the disruptions to normal operations
- Building alternate means of operation
- Educating the disaster recovery team about the emergency procedures
- Minimizing the system's downtime and recovery time
- Reducing the potential losses of core assets
- Defining clear procedures, reducing the need to make on-the-spot decisions
- Simulating several disaster recovery scenarios
- Ensuring system dependability before storing backups

When developing a DRP, an organization should be sure to meet these points:

- Defining the DRP's structure, elements, and phases
- Training personnel effectively
- Testing the DRP to be sure it functions properly
- Preparing an emergency response team to handle the disaster situation immediately
- Backing up data off-site
- Ensuring backup computers can handle the increased data load
- Circulating a contact list of all relevant staff
- Defining a prearranged disaster recovery site

Business Impact Analysis (BIA)

Organizations should perform a business impact analysis, or BIA, to identify the business and operational impact of a disaster. It should include the time frames within which systems must be restored and the time required to recover these systems. The BIA's objectives are as follows:

- Identifying the full business process
- Determining all potential financial, legal, and regulatory impacts
- Setting up time frames for recovery of all business-related processes
- Defining the key inner and outer dealings and dependencies of each process
- Identifying the required resources for all processes to recover and their related recovery time frames
- Training personnel in the recovery process
- Making management aware of the continuity plans

Table 3-1 shows a sample BIA form.

Business Impact Analysis	
Site Name:	System Name:
Date BIA Completed:	BIA Contact:
Assessment Date:	Functional Area:
System Information:	Information regarding the functions of the system and the system architecture.
Internal System Contacts	Responsibilities
Contact #1	Identify the personnel or offices in the organization that depend on or support the system.
Contact #2	
Contact #3	
External System Contacts	Responsibilities
Contact #1	Identify the individuals, positions, or offices outside the organization that depend on or support the system; specify their relationship to the system.
Contact #2	
Contact #3	
Hardware Resources	Identify the specific hardware used by the system.
Hardware	
Hardware	
Hardware	
Software Resources	Identify the software used by the system, including quantity and type.

Table 3-1   This is a sample business impact analysis form   *(continues)*

Software	
Software	
Software	
Critical Role	**Critical Resources**
Identify critical role	List the IT resources required for accomplishing the roles.
Identify critical role	
Identify critical role	

Table 3-1 This is a sample business impact analysis form *continued*

Disaster Recovery Roles and Responsibilities

When creating a disaster recovery plan, it is important to specify roles and responsibilities. Everyone involved in the plan should have a very clear idea of what is expected. The following sections detail the responsibilities of various personnel.

Operations Recovery Director

- Predisaster
  - Approving the final DRP and procedures
  - Maintaining the DRP and procedures
  - Conducting DR training
  - Authorizing the periodic testing of the DRP
- Postdisaster
  - Declaring the occurrence of a disaster
  - Defining the implementation of strategy if more than one strategy exists
  - Authorizing the travel and housing arrangements for team members
  - Managing and monitoring the overall recovery process
  - Providing updates on the status of disaster recovery efforts to the senior and user management
  - Coordinating media and press releases

Operations Recovery Manager and Teams

- Predisaster
  - Developing, maintaining, and updating the DRP
  - Appointing recovery personnel
  - Assigning parts of the DRP to the individual recovery teams and their members
  - Coordinating plan testing
  - Training disaster recovery team members on plan implementation
- Postdisaster
  - Obtaining the required approvals to activate the disaster recovery plan and the recovery teams
  - Informing all the recovery team leaders or alternates about the disaster declaration
  - Determining the degree of outage due to the disaster
  - Coordinating and summarizing the damage reports from all teams
  - Informing the organization's directors of the disaster's severity
  - Conducting briefings with all recovery teams
  - Coordinating all recovery teams
  - Requesting remote data backup, documentation, and required resources from the IT technical team

- Authorizing purchases and expenditures for required resources
- Reporting the recovery effort status to the operations recovery management director
- Coordinating media press releases

Facility Recovery Team

- Predisaster
  - Preparing the alternate site with hardware and supplies
  - Creating a complete layout and recovery procedure for the alternate site
- Postdisaster
  - Repairing and rebuilding the primary site

Network Recovery Team

- Predisaster
  - Installs networking equipment at the alternate site
- Postdisaster
  - Providing network connections at the alternate site
  - Restoring network connections at the primary site

Platform Recovery Team

- Predisaster
  - Maintaining lists of equipment needed in the restoration process
- Postdisaster
  - Installing hardware equipment
  - Restoring data and systems from remote backups

Application Recovery Team

- Predisaster
  - Testing applications for vulnerabilities
- Postdisaster
  - Restoring the database
  - Addressing specific application-related issues

Damage Assessment and Salvage Team

- Predisaster
  - Understanding the DR roles and responsibilities
  - Working closely with disaster recovery teams to minimize the occurrence of a disaster in the data center
  - Training employees to be well prepared in the case of emergencies
  - Participating in the DRP testing as needed
- Postdisaster
  - Determining damage and accessibility to the organization's resources
  - Determining the level of the damage to the data center in the organization
  - Assessing the need for physical security
  - Estimating the recovery time according to the damage assessment
  - Identifying the hardware and other equipment that can be repaired
  - Explaining to the disaster recovery team the extent of damages, estimated recovery time, physical safety, and repairable equipment

- Maintaining a repairable hardware and equipment log
- Coordinating with vendors and suppliers to restore, repair, or replace equipment
- Coordinating the transportation of salvaged equipment to a recovery site, if necessary
- Providing support to clean up the data center after a disaster

Physical Security Team

- Predisaster
  - Understanding the DR roles and responsibilities
  - Working closely with the DR team to ensure the physical safety of the existing systems and resources
  - Training employees
  - Becoming familiar with emergency contact numbers
  - Participating in DRP testing as needed
  - Maintaining the list of members allowed to enter the disaster site and recovery site
- Postdisaster
  - Assessing damage at the disaster site
  - Blocking the data center from illegal access
  - Scheduling security for transporting files, reports, and equipment
  - Providing assistance for investigations of the damaged site

Communications Teams

- Predisaster
  - Understanding DR roles and responsibilities
  - Working closely with the DR team to ensure the physical safety of existing systems and resources
  - Training employees
  - Participating in disaster recovery plan testing as required
  - Establishing and maintaining the communications equipment at the alternate site
- Postdisaster
  - Assessing communication equipment requirements by coordinating with other teams
  - Retrieving the communication configuration from off-site storage units
  - Planning, coordinating, and installing communication equipment at the alternate site
  - Planning, coordinating, and installing network cabling at the alternate site

Hardware Installation Teams

- Predisaster
  - Understanding the disaster recovery roles and responsibilities
  - Coordinating with the DR team to minimize the impact of a disaster in the data center
  - Training employees
  - Participating in DRP testing as needed
  - Maintaining the current system and LAN configuration in off-site storage
- Postdisaster
  - Verifying hardware requirements at the alternate location
  - Inspecting the alternate location for the required physical space
  - Notifying the alternate site of the impending occupancy
  - Interfacing with the IT technical and operation teams about the space configuration of the alternate location
  - Coordinating the transportation of repairable equipment to the alternate location

- Informing the administration team regarding the need for equipment repair and new equipment
- Ensuring the installation of temporary terminals connecting to the alternate location mainframe
- Planning and installing the hardware at the alternate location
- Planning, transporting, and installing hardware at the permanent location, when available
- Setting and operating a sign-in/sign-out method for all resources at the alternate location

IT Operations Teams

- Predisaster
  - Understanding disaster recovery roles and responsibilities
  - Coordinating with the DR team to ensure the physical safety of existing systems and resources
  - Training employees to be well prepared in case of emergencies
  - Ensuring complete backups as per the schedule
  - Ensuring backups are sent to the remote location as per the schedule
  - Participating in DRP testing as needed
- Postdisaster
  - Supporting the IT technical team as needed
  - Sending and receiving off-site storage containers
  - Ensuring backup tapes are sent to off-site storage
  - Maintaining a sign-in/sign-out method for all resources at the alternate location
  - Checking the alternate site's floor configuration to aid in the communication team's installation plans
  - Checking the security of the alternate location and its LAN network
  - Coordinating the transfer of systems, resources, and people to the alternate location

IT Technical Teams

- Predisaster
  - Understanding the disaster recovery roles and responsibilities
  - Working closely with disaster recovery teams to minimize the occurrence of a disaster in the data center
  - Training employees
  - Participating in DRP testing as needed
- Postdisaster
  - Restoring system resources from the backup media
  - Initializing new tapes as required in the DR process
  - Conducting backups at the remote location
  - Testing and verifying operating systems
  - Modifying the LAN configuration to connect with the alternate location's configuration

Administration Teams

- Predisaster
  - Understanding disaster recovery roles and responsibilities
  - Training employees
  - Ensuring the maintenance of the required business interruption insurance
  - Ensuring the adequate availability of emergency funds throughout the DR process
  - Assessing the alternative communication required if telephone services become unavailable
  - Participating in DRP testing as needed

- Postdisaster
    - Preparing, coordinating, and obtaining proper sanctions for all procurement requests
    - Maintaining logs of all procurements in process and scheduled deliveries
    - Processing the payment requests for all invoices related to the recovery procedure
    - Arranging travel and lodging for the recovery teams
    - Providing alternative communications for recovery team members if normal telephone service is not available
    - Performing provisional clerical and managerial duties as needed by the DR teams

Disaster Recovery Planning Steps

When putting together a disaster recovery plan, an organization should follow these steps:

1. *Identify and assess the risks*: Identify and list serious incidents that can affect the normal operations of the organization. Prioritize the list according to severity level.

2. *Prioritize business processes*: In case resources are limited, use those resources efficiently to provide an effective disaster recovery plan. Prioritize the business processes that are:
    - Most essential to the organization's mission
    - Most and least needed during a disaster

3. *Prioritize technology services*: After determining critical business processes, map the processes to the technology components that make those processes possible. This information is useful in identifying critical technology environment components and prioritizing each component accordingly.

4. *Define recovery strategy*: The recovery time objective (RTO) is the acceptable amount of time for returning the services or information availability to an organization after a disaster occurs. The recovery point objective (RPO) is the amount of data loss that can be considered acceptable when a disaster occurs. Implementing RTO and RPO for each critical information system helps in developing a plan that reflects the priorities of the organization. They also function as tools to check the success of the chosen strategies when a disaster recovery plan is tested.

5. *Secure facilities*: Having efficient technology facilities is useful when a disaster strikes. The technology facilities should be constructed so that they are secured and protected from any disruptive events. There are many inexpensive facility tools that can be used to minimize disaster situations, including electrical surge protectors, power conditioning units, and fire suppression systems.

6. *Identify alternate sites*: Maintain an alternate site for temporarily relocating required systems and resources. This site should be able to function when the primary location cannot. The alternate site should contain accurate and current technology environment documentation.

7. *Use redundancy and failover*: An extensive variety of technology solutions can be used for maintaining application and data continuity when a disaster occurs. Combining these technologies with a strategy of geographically dispersed technology resources will help in protecting data.

8. *Document the plan*: The disaster recovery plan should be documented in sequential milestones to allow the organization to return to normal operations. The first milestone should document the process of dealing with the immediate aftermath of the disaster. This includes notifying key employees, emergency services, and others who are required to respond to the disaster. The plan should then include resuming the operation of the technology services based on the business process priorities. The roles and responsibilities of all individuals should be described in the plan. The disaster recovery team should be able to access the plan even if the primary site is unavailable. Store multiple copies of the plan off-site.

9. *Test the plan*: Perform regular tests on the disaster recovery plan in order to ensure its effectiveness. The tests should be performed on the complete plan process. A useful testing technique is to develop a test scenario based on a disaster situation. After completing the testing, review the results with the team members to determine any possible improvements and update the plan accordingly.

10. *Update the recovery plan*: To make the disaster recovery plan effective, keep it up to date and applicable to current technology and business processes. Changes made to the plan should be communicated to all personnel affected by those changes.

Disaster Preparedness

To be adequately prepared for a disaster, it is essential to determine and assign responsibilities. The following are steps an organization should take:

1. Include the role names and the responsibilities of each role in the disaster recovery plan.
2. The person in charge should make policy decisions.
3. The person in charge should make critical IT-related decisions only after consulting with IT personnel.
4. Offer disaster recovery training for key (or all) staff members.
5. Set up a clear chain of command.

Strategies used in disaster preparedness include:

- Storing important data off-site and including information on how to access those data in the disaster recovery plan
- Maintaining hard copies of important data (including the disaster recovery plan)
- Maintaining current information regarding contacts and system resources
- Employing malware removal programs
- Utilizing and frequently examining devices such as UPS, fire and smoke sensors and alarms, and antitheft systems
- Updating compliance assessments (such as for Sarbanes-Oxley) whenever changes are made to the IT infrastructure
- Documenting all preventive measures in the disaster recovery plan
- Maintaining backup servers at various locations
- Conducting training sessions

Profiles

As part of disaster recovery planning, it is important to keep profiles of operations, applications, and inventory.

Operations Profile

The operations profile gives an overview of operations, governance and accountability, decision makers, and who is responsible for each part of the DRP. The profile contains the following parts:

- *System description*: This describes the system architecture and its key functionality. It provides details of the operating environment, physical location, user groups, and partnerships with external organizations and interfacing systems. It also describes the technical considerations that relate to the recovery point, such as backup and storage measures.
- *Governance and accountability*: Organizations should set a clear chain of command to avoid any disruptions in the plan. The disaster recovery officer is responsible for ensuring people's safety and implementing the procedures mentioned in the DRP. Figure 3-1 shows a sample diagram of governance and accountability.
- *Roles and responsibilities*: Organizations need to identify the roles needed to respond to a disaster. The DRP establishes several teams, each one assigned to participate in recovering separate operations. Members of the team are also in charge of daily operations system maintenance. Organizations can use a table like Table 3-2 to keep track of roles and responsibilities.

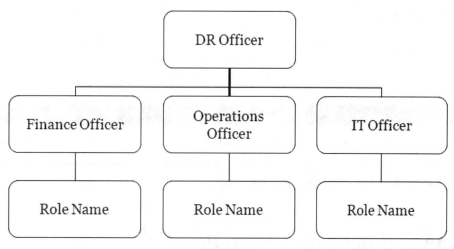

Figure 3-1   This is a sample chart of governance and accountability.

Role	Telephone Number	Organization	Area of Responsibility

Table 3-2   Organizations can use a table like this to keep track of roles and responsibilities

Application Profiles

It is important to keep profiles of all systems, including both priority systems and nonpriority systems. For priority systems, organizations should include both the RPO and RTO. Table 3-3 is a sample of a table that can be used to keep track of priority systems, and Table 3-4 is a sample of a table that can be used for other systems.

System	Critical Periods	RPO	RTO	Owner
Payroll	End of month	7 days	1 day	
Oracle	End of week	2 days	1 day	

Table 3-3   This is an example table for keeping track of priority systems

Name	Critical	Asset	Manufacturer	Job Run
Name of system	Yes/No	Yes/No	Manufacturer name	Daily/Weekly

Table 3-4   A table like this can be used to keep track of all other systems

Inventory Profile

Organizations should keep an inventory of all physical items that should be restored or replaced in the event of a disaster. Table 3-5 is an example of a table used to keep this inventory.

Manufacturer	Description	Model	Serial #	Own/Lease	Comments

Table 3-5   **This is an example of an inventory of physical items**

Notification and Activation Procedures

Organizations should activate the DRP if the system is unavailable for an extended period of time or if the facility is damaged and unavailable. When activating the plan, they should follow these steps:

1. The disaster recovery manager decides to invoke the DRP. If it is during normal business hours, deploy the emergency evacuation plan if necessary. If it is during off hours, notify the facilities manager about the situation. Contact emergency services if the situation warrants. The facilities manager and disaster recovery manager will evaluate the situation when it is safe to do so.

2. The disaster recovery manager contacts the disaster recovery site providers and gives the required level of information.

3. The disaster recovery manager contacts the necessary third-party recovery teams.

4. The disaster recovery manager contacts the operations managers.

5. The operations managers contact their individual teams, who are given their responsibilities.

6. The disaster recovery manager contacts the human resources manager.

7. The human resources manager contacts all personnel who are needed in the DRP to inform them of the invocation and instruct them to stand by for further instructions.

8. The disaster recovery manager contacts the public relations manager. The public relations manager is responsible for notifying clients, board members, stakeholders, and the media.

9. The disaster recovery manager provides directions and a map to the disaster recovery site to everyone who must be there.

10. The recovery team will familiarize itself with the disaster recovery site and begin the process of recovering the system.

Damage Assessment Procedure

The damage assessment procedure should include the following steps:

1. Determining the cause of the disruption

2. Estimating the affected physical space

3. Estimating the time required to repair services to normal operation

4. Evaluating the status of the equipment functionality and inventory

5. Reducing the additional disruption or damage

Response Checklist

Organizations should maintain a checklist of what must be done to effectively manage a disaster situation. This checklist ensures that all relevant activities have been performed within the required time frame. The checklist should include each activity, who is responsible for that activity, and when that activity should be carried out. Table 3-6 shows an example response checklist, and Table 3-7 shows a follow-up checklist for after the disaster has been handled.

Ref	Activity	Responsibility	Time Frame	Signoff
1	If there is a loss of site, coordinate with the business continuity plan team.		Immediate	
2	If there is loss of site, coordinate activities with the building officer to gain access to facilities.		Immediate	
3	Conduct the initial assessment of the incident, determine the severity, and formulate a salvage operation.		Within X minutes of the incident	
4	Conduct team leaders meeting.		Within X minutes of the incident	
5	Announce activation of the disaster recovery plan to the team leaders.		Within X minutes of the incident	
6	Determine availability of: backup data for the recovery of systems; access to the data delivered prior to the incident; receiving and processing data by alternate means; redirecting service to the alternate site.		Within X minutes of the incident	
7	Contact backup facilities as necessary.		Within X minutes of the incident	
8	Communicate activation of the disaster recovery plan to the alternate sites.		Within X minutes of the incident	
9	Monitor and review the recovery procedures.		Continuously	
10	Contact vendors.		Within X minutes of the incident	

Table 3-6   This is a sample response checklist

Action	Yes/No
Obtain emergency cash for immediate supplies.	
Arrange for transportation to backup site and vice versa.	
Arrange for living quarters, if required.	
Arrange for eating establishments.	
Identify all personnel and their telephone numbers.	
Arrange for sending and receipt of mail.	
Arrange for office supplies.	
Buy or lease equipment, as required.	
Decide the sequence to start up applications.	
Identify number of workstations needed.	
Check that all data are taken to the backup location.	
Arrange for transportation of supplementary items required at backup location.	
Take directions and connect to the backup location.	
Bring technical documentation and procedural manuals.	
Ensure staff members understand their tasks.	
Inform insurance companies.	

Table 3-7   This is an example follow-up checklist

Objectives				
1				
2				
3				
Preconditions				
1				
2				
3				
Documentation				
1				
2				
3				
Ref	**Task**	**Performed By:**	**Time Frame**	**Signoff By:**
1		Minutes/Hours/Days		
2				
Objectives				
1				

Table 3-8 Use a table like this to record recovery procedures

Recovery Procedures

Organizations need to maintain detailed instructions for recovering all systems at the backup site. These instructions should include the tasks the disaster recovery personnel should follow to recover systems, applications, or infrastructure in the required time frame. These tasks should include hardware acquisition, software installation, and retrieving and loading backup tapes. Table 3-8 shows an example recovery procedure table.

Testing and Maintenance Procedures

The disaster recovery plan should be tested and maintained properly, ensuring that the document remains relevant and reliable in case of a disaster. The document owner is responsible for updating the plan to reflect the recovery steps, contact details, and references that change over time.

Testing consists of a combination of these approaches:

- Scenario testing, in which recovery procedures are tested based on a scenario to ensure that they remain relevant
- Transferring systems to an alternate site to ensure that systems can be reproduced within a particular time frame
- Structured walk-through, designed to expose errors or omissions without the planning and expenses associated with performing a full operations test

Organizations can use a table like Table 3-9 to keep track of testing tasks.

Organizations should maintain a schedule, like the one in Table 3-10, indicating when each section of the DRP should be tested.

After performing a test, the team should fill out a report, like the one in Table 3-11.

Alternate Site Requirements

When searching for a suitable alternate site, organizations need to make sure they have the necessary resources to provide continuity of operations. These resources may include the following:

- Office space
  - Identify access to the office space.
  - Identify how much workspace each staff member requires.

Ref	Task	Responsibility	Time Frame	Signoff
1	Determine the testing approach to be adopted.			
2	Conduct testing meeting with participants.			
3	Test the developed plans.			
4	Identify gaps/needs in the current plan.			
5	Incorporate changes into DRP.			
6	Publish and distribute the final copies.			

Table 3-9 A table like this one can be used to keep track of testing tasks

Section of Disaster Recovery Plan	Scheduled Testing Date

Table 3-10 A schedule like this indicates when each section of the DRP should be tested

Disaster Recovery Test Report	
Site Name:	System Name:
Customer:	Contact:
Test Date:	Functional Area:
Test Type: Walkthrough Partial Simulation Full Simulation	
Description and Scope of Test:	
Proposed Changes to Disaster Recovery Plan:	
Approval: Reviewed By:_____ Disaster Recovery Manager Approved By:_____ Customer (optional)	Date: _____ Date: _____

Table 3-11 After performing a test, record its results in a form like this one

- Identify room or space that can be allocated for meetings.
- Identify the space for storing folders, papers, or equipment.
- Identify facilities for storing cash, checkbooks, and other valuable items.
- Office equipment
  - Ensure that there are services to enable normal business functions, such as phone lines, Internet access, and fax machines.
  - If possible, assign phones with a direct-dial facility.
  - Identify the fax facilities.
  - Identify requirements for standard office supplies, such as paper, pens, and copying facilities.

- Computer equipment
  - Identify the computer equipment required by the organization.
  - Specify the number of computers that can run the necessary applications. Confirm who will set up these applications.
  - Discuss access to the LAN and how the organization will assign logons and passwords.
  - Identify the number and types of printers that will be made available.

Returning to Normal Operations

Organizations should outline the activities needed to restore system operations at the original site or, if necessary, a new site. There should be as little a gap as possible between systems operating at the alternate site and at the new one, much like the changeover between the original site and the alternate site. Organizations can use a table like Table 3-12 to show these steps.

Ref	Task	Performed By:	Time Frame	Signoff By:
1	Describe the steps to restore the system.		Minutes/Hours/Days	
2				
3				
4				
5				

Table 3-12   Use a table like this one to show the steps needed to restore the original site or to move operations to a new site

Next, organizations should outline the procedures for maintaining the systems at the alternate site and the original or new site simultaneously, before the procedures are entirely changed over to the new site. Table 3-13 shows an example of this outline.

Ref	Task	Performed By:	Time Frame	Signoff By:
1			Minutes/Hours/Days	
2				
3				
4				
5				

Table 3-13   Create an outline like this to show how the systems at the alternate site and the original or new site can operate concurrently

Finally, organizations should outline the procedures for deactivating the alternate location. These procedures should:

- Ensure that sensitive information is managed properly
- Ensure that materials and equipment are labeled, packaged, and shipped to the original or new site
- Instruct the team to return to the original location or report to the new one

Organizations can use a table like Table 3-14 to create a deactivation plan.

Ref	Task	Performed By:	Time Frame	Signoff By:
1			Minutes/Hours/Days	
2				
3				
4				
5				

Table 3-14   Create a deactivation plan to shut down the alternate site

Communications Plan

Organizations must describe the communication process in the event of a disaster situation. External communication is required to keep key stakeholders informed of the project status, issues, and risks. When communicating with employees, organizations should do the following:

- Provide employees with a safe alternate working environment.
- Ensure employees' safety.
- Provide complete information about the current problem and regular updates on the situation.
- Provide appropriate contact information to all employees.

When communicating with clients, organizations should do the following:

- Ensure clients' safety.
- Continue to provide clients with their expected level of service.
- Meet all financial, legal, and contractual obligations.
- Provide a single point of contact.

Table 3-15 is a template for a communications plan.

What	Audience	Frequency	Prepared By	Purpose	Media

Table 3-15   Keep a communications plan to make sure employees and clients stay informed

Disaster Recovery Planning in a Virtualized Environment

Server virtualization is an effective tool for disaster recovery planning. It is easy to deploy and integrate, and offers several advantages, such as the following:

- Lower cost than physical servers
- Minimizes hardware downtime
- Recovers data quickly

When implementing server virtualization, organizations should consider the following:

- *Data protection (backups)*: Installing a conventional backup agent on every virtual machine provides data protection similar to the physical server environment.
- *Recovery granularity*: Granular (file-level) restoring facilities can be obtained by implementing image-level backups. This deployment provides rapid recovery with a lower software cost.
- *Restore performance*: I/O performance is the most significant feature when performing backups and restoring virtual servers.
- *RTOs/RPOs*: When there are applications with less tolerance for downtime (RTO = 0), a failover component is necessary to fulfill the recovery requirements. Similarly, for applications with stringent recovery point objectives and less tolerance for data loss, a replication solution is required for protecting data according to the backup schedule.

Chapter Summary

- Confidentiality is maintained through user authentication and access control.
- Application security can be achieved by implementing security techniques and following security guidelines.

■ A distributed system is a collection of processors connected through a communication network.

■ Firmware is programming written to the read-only memory (ROM) of a various electronic devices.

■ Remanence is the residual representation of data that have been deleted.

■ A disaster recovery plan assists and supports organizations in restoring the information technology functions after a disaster.

■ Organizations perform BIA to identify the business's critical activities and the time frames within which systems must be restored when a disaster occurs.

■ To make a disaster recovery plan effective, organizations must keep it up to date and applicable to current technology and business processes.

■ The disaster recovery plan should be tested and maintained properly, ensuring that the document remains relevant and reliable.

■ During the implementation of the recovery process, it is important for the DR teams to communicate and work together.

■ Server virtualization is an effective tool for disaster recovery.

Review Questions

1. What are the aspects of information security?

_____

_____

_____

_____

2. What are the elements of application security?

_____

_____

_____

_____

3. What are the pros and cons of COTS software?

_____

_____

_____

_____

4. What are some database security issues?

_____

_____

_____

_____

5. What are the vulnerabilities of distributed systems?

_____

_____

_____

_____

6. What firmware security options are available?

_____

_____

_____

_____

7. What are the vulnerabilities in network security software?

_____

_____

_____

_____

8. What is remanence and how can it be overcome?

_____

_____

_____

_____

9. What makes an effective DRP?

_____

_____

_____

_____

10. What is a BIA?

_____

_____

_____

_____

11. What is an operations profile?

_____

_____

_____

_____

12. What are the requirements for an alternate site?

_____

_____

_____

_____

Hands-On Projects

HANDS-ON PROJECTS

1. Read about Internet security.

   ■ Navigate to Chapter 3 of the Student Resource Center.

   ■ Open Internet_Security.pdf and read the content.

2. Read about penetration testing.

   ■ Navigate to Chapter 3 of the Student Resource Center.

   ■ Open Netwk Vulnerability Test_wp.pdf and read the content.

3. Read about the evolution of security needs.

   ■ Navigate to Chapter 3 of the Student Resource Center.

   ■ Open Security.pdf and read the content.

4. Read about business continuity management.

   ■ Navigate to Chapter 3 of the Student Resource Center.

   ■ Open Business Continuity and Disaster Recovery Leaflet.pdf and read the content.

5. Read about disaster recovery planning.

   ■ Navigate to Chapter 3 of the Student Resource Center.

   ■ Open BCP.pdf and read the content.

6. Read about creating a backup plan.

   ■ Navigate to Chapter 3 of the Student Resource Center.

   ■ Open business_continuity.pdf and read the content.

7. Read about business continuity versus disaster recovery.

   ■ Navigate to Chapter 3 of the Student Resource Center.

   ■ Open Continuity.pdf and read the content.

Chapter 4

Business Continuity Management

Objectives

After completing this chapter, you should be able to:

- Build, manage, implement, and maintain a business continuity plan
- Understand the elements of business continuity management
- Develop business continuity strategies
- Develop a crisis communication plan
- Develop an emergency response plan
- Develop a contingency plan
- Utilize virtualization disaster recovery

Key Terms

Business impact analysis (BIA)   an essential function of a business continuity plan that includes analysis of vulnerabilities, risks, components critical to business functionality and/or survival, and a strategy for minimizing those discovered risks to keep the business operational during any critical disruption

Imaging   the process of creating a single file with the complete contents of a storage device

Load balancing   the process of sharing Web traffic across multiple servers

Recovery Point Objective (RPO)   the point in time to which an organization plans to recover its data after a disaster

Recovery Time Objective (RTO)   the maximum allowable time in which a business process must be restored after a disruption to avoid the negative consequences of a disaster or major disruption

Introduction to Business Continuity Management

Business continuity, or simply BC, is the ability of a business to continue operations with minimal disruption or downtime after a disaster. Business continuity management (BCM) is the process of managing risks and ensuring business continuity. This is an ongoing process with several different but complementary elements. This chapter introduces you to BCM and teaches you several forms of BCM, including business continuity plans, contingency plans, and virtualization data recovery.

Elements of Business Continuity Management

Business continuity management includes the following elements:

- *Risk mitigation plan*: By developing, implementing, and testing risk mitigation strategies, an organization is better protected from unexpected threats. There must be a detailed plan for risk identification, prioritization, monitoring, and mitigation. This allows the organization to systematically address potential risk events.

- *Business continuity plan*: Organizations should build comprehensive business continuity plans or BCPs. A BCP's main goal is to reduce losses to the organization, serve customers with minimal disruptions, and mitigate the negative effects of these disruptions on business operations.

- *Pandemic plan*: A pandemic can lead to human resource disruption, damaging the organization. It is necessary to prepare the company in case a health crisis causes organizational downtime.

- *Contingency plan*: BCM is, as a whole, preparing for unexpected events. Contingency planning includes preparing plans and strategies to effectively handle unexpected problems, emergencies, and catastrophic events.

- *Business recovery*: Business recovery involves restoring critical business functions within an acceptable time frame. Depending on the recovery strategies used, this can include temporary manual processing, recovery and operation on an alternate system, or relocation and recovery at an alternate site. This plan should consider aspects such as cost, acceptable outage time, and security.

- *Audits*: Organizations should perform regular audits on their business continuity processes. They should ensure they are well prepared and still appropriate to the changing business. Some aspects of the auditing process can be automated using audit management software.

Business Continuity Plan

Business continuity starts with a well-defined and well-documented business continuity plan that addresses all risks and secures systems vital to business operations. A BCP includes provisions for redundancies at all levels. That includes not just servers, storage, and networking equipment, but also other infrastructures such as air conditioning and power supplies.

The BCP should clearly lay out how to quickly recover from a disaster in order to reduce the disaster's impact. Figure 4-1 shows how the BCP is used to:

1. Understand the business

2. Build BCM strategies

3. Develop BCP response

4. Develop BCP culture

5. Exercise auditing and maintenance

A business continuity plan should address the following four components:

1. Readiness

2. Prevention

3. Response

4. Recovery/resumption

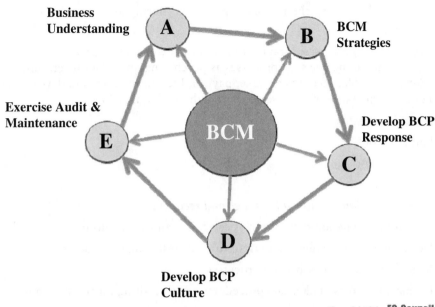

Figure 4-1   These are the five goals of a BCP.

Readiness

The readiness portion of the BCP covers preparatory steps and provides a strong foundation for the remainder of the BCP.

Assign Accountability

The senior leadership of the organization is responsible for creating, maintaining, testing, and implementing the BCP. All staff members must understand that the BCP is a high priority. It is also important that management at all levels understand their own level of accountability in the BCP.

- *Corporate policy*: The BCP should contain all steps to protect people, property, and business interests.
- *Ownership of systems, processes, and resources*: Organizations must clearly identify who is responsible for systems, resources, and key business processes.
- *Planning team*: A BCP team should be appointed to ensure widespread acceptance of the BCP.
- *Communicating the BCP*: The organization needs to communicate the BCP throughout all levels and departments of the organization. All employees should know the BCP structure and their roles within the plan.

Perform Risk Assessment

Risk assessment will identify and analyze the types of risk that can potentially impact the organization. Using existing information about known or anticipated risks, organizations should identify and review new risks that may impact the business and rate the likelihood of each risk. A risk assessment matrix mapping assets, vulnerabilities, probable threats, and risk mitigation methods can be used to identify risks and prioritize mitigation strategies.

Conduct a Business Impact Analysis (BIA)

After identifying the risks, the impact of an interruption in normal operations should be examined in a *business impact analysis (BIA)*. A BIA is an essential function of a business continuity plan that includes analysis of vulnerabilities, risks, components critical to business functionality and/or survival, and a strategy for minimizing those discovered risks to keep the business operational during any critical disruption. The following are the steps involved in a BIA:

1. *Identify critical processes*: Organizations must identify and document critical business processes. The document should include such processes as purchasing, manufacturing, supply chain, sales, distribution, accounts receivable, accounts payable, payroll, IT, and research and development. Organizations should assign the importance of these services as high, medium, or low.

2. *Assess crisis impact*:
   - Human cost
   - Financial cost
   - Reputation cost

3. *Determine maximum allowable outage and recovery time*:
   - Determine the period that a process can fail to function before the impact becomes unacceptable
   - Determine the acceptable amount of time for restoring the process
   - Identify and document backup processes
   - Evaluate the costs of alternate procedures versus waiting for the system to be restored

4. *Identify resources required for resumption and recovery*: These resources consist of personnel, technology, hardware and software, specialized equipment, and critical business records. Identifying, backing up, and storing critical business records in a secured location are important parts of an effective BCP.

Strategic Planning

Strategic planning addresses identification and implementation of:

- Methods to mitigate the risks and exposures identified in the BIA and risk assessment
- Plans and procedures to respond to any crisis

The BCP should contain multiple strategies to address different probable situations. It also addresses the duration of a business interruption and the extent of interruption. The strategies selected should be attainable, cost effective, likely to succeed, and relevant to the size and scope of the organization.

Crisis Management and Response Team Development

There must be a clear definition of the management structure. The team should contain representatives from human resources, information technology, security, legal, manufacturing, and other critical business support functions.

The crisis management team is supported by the required response teams, considering factors such as size and type, number of employees, and location. Response teams develop response plans to address the different aspects of a potential crisis, including site restoration, damage assessment, information technology, and administrative support. Response plans should be contained within the overall BCP.

Contact information for the personnel assigned to the crisis management and response teams should be included in the plan. Organizations should establish procedures to ensure that the information is kept up to date.

Prevention

Prevention includes limiting, preventing, or avoiding the impact of a crisis.

Compliance with Corporate Policy

Organizations should perform compliance audits on the BCP's policies and procedures. Any violations in the policy and procedures should be highlighted and corrected.

Mitigation Strategies

Cost-effective mitigation strategies should lessen the impact of a potential crisis. For example, a strong record management and technology disaster recovery program mitigates the loss of important data and documents.

Organizations must identify the different resources that contribute to the mitigation process. These resources, including the essential personnel and their roles and responsibilities, should be documented in the plan.

The resources that support the organization in mitigating the crisis should be monitored to ensure their availability and performance during the crisis. Some of these systems and resources include emergency equipment, local resources and vendors, system backups and off-site storage, and alternate worksites.

Avoidance, Deterrence, and Detection

The goal of avoidance is to prevent a crisis from happening in the first place by identifying, understanding, and addressing potential crises using risk assessment. Deterrence and detection can make a hostile action more difficult to carry out against the organization.

The facility security programs that support and enhance avoidance, deterrence, and detection are:

- *Architectural*: Natural or human-made barriers
- *Operational*: Security officers, employee security awareness programs, and protective security operations
- *Technological*: Intrusion detection, access control, recorded video surveillance, and package and baggage screening

Response

It is important to respond effectively, appropriately, and quickly during a crisis.

Recognize Potential Crises

- *Identify and recognize the danger signals*: A danger signal coupled with the likelihood of an event indicates an imminent crisis. Warning signs can include legislative changes, corporate policy changes, changes to the competitive environment, warnings of natural disasters, potential for civil or political instability, and changes to the supply-based environment.
- *Recognize and report potential crises*: Some departments or functions exist only to watch for the warning signs of an imminent crisis. The personnel employed in this department should be given proper training. A potential crisis should be communicated to all employees.

Notify the Teams

Once a potential crisis is recognized, the information should be given to the supervisor, a member of management, or whoever is responsible for crisis notification and management. Organizations must establish and document specific notification criteria, including who should be notified, when, and by whom.

Assess the Situation

Organizations must assess the problem and its severity at the beginning of the crisis. They should consider factors such as the size of the problem, its potential for escalation, and the impacts of the situation.

Declare a Crisis

Organizations must clearly define, document, and fit the specific parameters as to when a situation should be declared a crisis. The responsibilities for declaring a crisis should also be defined and assigned. Activities when declaring a crisis can include additional call notification, relocation, response-site and alternate-site activation, team deployment, emergency contract activation, and operational changes.

Execute the Plan

When developing the BCP, organizations should take into consideration the worst-case scenario and scale the response appropriately to match the actual crisis. When initiating a response, organizations should protect the following interests, with the most important listed first:

1. Secure personnel safety
2. Protect assets
3. Restore the critical business processes and systems
4. Reduce the length of business interruption
5. Prevent damage to the organization's reputation
6. Control media coverage
7. Maintain customer relations

Communications

- *Identifying the audiences*: The organization should identify the internal and external audiences to convey crisis and organizational response information to. It should divide the audiences into appropriate segments and communicate the required messages to each group.

- *Communicating with audiences*: These criteria should be taken into account in the crisis communications strategy:

  - Communications should be timely and honest.

  - Audiences should hear news directly from the organization before they hear it from any other source.

  - Communications should provide objective and subjective assessments.

  - All employees should be informed at approximately the same time.

  - Audiences should have the opportunity to ask questions, if possible.

  - The organization should provide regular updates and allow audiences to know when the next update will be issued.

- *Official spokesperson*: The organization should employ a single spokesperson to manage and disseminate crisis communications to the media and others. The personnel should be trained in media relations during a crisis.

Resource Management

The Human Element   Organizations should devise a system by which all personnel can be accounted for after the onset of a crisis. They should arrange for crisis counseling as necessary and provide financial support to victims. The payroll system should remain functional throughout the crisis.

Logistics   Logistical decisions made in advance impact the success and failure of a good BCP. Organizations must identify the primary crisis management center. This center is used for directing and overseeing crisis management activities. The organization should do the following:

- Set up alternate worksites during the recovery period.

- Examine the existing funding and insurance policies, and identify any additional funding and insurance.

- Establish critical vendor or service provider agreements, and maintain their contact information as part of the BCP.

- Make mutual aid agreements with other organizations to borrow required resources during a crisis.

Recovery and Resumption

Organizations should assess the damages once the crisis management team is activated. This damage assessment can be performed by the crisis management team or by a designated damage assessment team.

In the case of physical damage, the team is mobilized to the damaged site. The team makes an assessment of the extent of the damage and the time for which the facility will be nonfunctional. In case of less concrete damage to the business and information technology, the assessment is made as the crisis unfolds.

Resumption of Critical and Remaining Processes

When the extent of damage is known, organizations should determine and document the schedule for resumption. Prioritization should be based on the criticality of the process and other factors, including relationships to other processes, critical schedules, and regulatory requirements.

The resumption of the processes should be performed based on the prioritization schedule. The resumptions can take place at the alternate worksite. Organizations must make sure to document when the processes were resumed.

Once the critical processes have been resumed, the resumption of the remaining processes can be addressed. Where possible, the prioritization of these processes should be thoroughly documented in advance.

Return to Normal Operations

In this step, the organization is returned to normal, as well as possible. Each step of the process and all decisions should be carefully documented.

Implementing and Maintaining the Plan

The BCP is a living document that changes constantly to remain relevant and functional. It must be regularly tested, evaluated, and maintained. Employees must also be regularly trained to comply with the BCP.

Testing and Training

Organizations must train and educate the team members and the general employees to validate and enhance the BCP. Personnel should be trained regarding their individual responsibilities during a crisis. They should become familiar with the key components of the BCP and response plans. This training includes procedures for evacuation, check-in processes to account for employees, alternate worksite arrangements, and handling media inquiries.

Testing the BCP enables teams and employees to understand their roles and reveal any deficiencies in the BCP. Larger organizations may wish to establish a test team. Tests start relatively simple, with checklists and simple exercises. Eventually, tests become full-scale activations of the entire BCP, including the participation of public safety and emergency responders.

There are several different roles that test participants can fill, including the following:

- *Facilitators*: They posses all the knowledge about the test scenario and supervise the exercises. They introduce action messages simulating crisis situations and provide exercise oversight.

- *Controllers*: They introduce artificial stimuli at the direction of the facilitator. They make decisions during unanticipated actions or resource requirements. Controllers reduce damages by maintaining order.

- *Simulators*: They add realism to the scenario, portraying other companies, agencies, and organizations that interact with the participants.

- *Observers*: They are present to observe and document the performance. They should possess a strong knowledge about the subject matters and functions being evaluated. Observers evaluate the actions of the participants and the effectiveness of the BCP.

- *Participants*: They assume the crisis roles and perform actual or simulated activities appropriate to the type of exercise and scenario used.

Evaluation and Maintenance

Organizations should evaluate and review the BCP on a regular basis. In addition, they should conduct an evaluation after any of the following events:

- Risk assessment
- New regulatory requirements
- Occurrence of a crisis

After the review, organizations should modify any areas of the BCP that are shown to be insufficient. They should assign clear responsibility for BCP maintenance. Maintenance can be planned or unplanned and should reflect any changes in the operation of the organization that affect the BCP. The plan may need to be changed in the event of:

- Systems and application software changes
- Changes to the organization and its business processes
- Personnel changes (employees and contractors)
- Supplier changes
- Critical lessons learned from testing
- Issues discovered during the actual implementation of the plan in a crisis
- Changes to the external environment
- Other items noted during the review of the plan and identified during the risk assessment

Developing Business Continuity Strategies

Obtaining Management Approval

The easiest way to obtain management's approval is often to utilize an existing reporting process. That way, management is provided with regular status reports throughout the strategy development process. Senior management (particularly chief executive, financial, and operational officers) should review the developed strategies.

Preplanning

Organizations should review all the critical business processes and systems, **RTO** (**recovery time objective**: the maximum allowable time in which a business process must be restored after a disruption to avoid the negative consequences of a disaster or major disruption), **RPO** (**recovery point objective**: the point in time to which an organization plans to recover its data after a disaster), dependencies (such as vendors and suppliers), and the financial impact of prolonged outages. They should utilize the information in the business impact analysis (BIA) to ensure that new critical processes and systems are identified.

Continuity planners and business managers need to understand the potential impact of all relevant laws, industry regulations, and government codes, so it is necessary to determine who is responsible for maintaining current knowledge of these laws and regulations. Continuity planners and business managers must also be aware of the necessary types of audits and other reporting requirements.

Organizations must determine the worst-case scenario for which each strategy might apply and make sure there are strategies in place for new, emerging threats.

Planning and Development

Organizations must identify and incorporate risk mitigation strategies. They should identify vital records throughout the organization, including both electronic and paper, and make sure that a strategy exists for protecting these records. The BCP should include details of the backup and storage strategy for these vital records, such as location, method, and security.

Continuity planners should identify internal and external continuity resources. They should identify the available recovery alternatives available for each critical business function and assess the feasibility of using these alternatives.

Crisis Communication Plan

In addition to material damages, a crisis can harm an organization's reputation. Minimizing this damage requires a crisis communication plan. This plan offers several possible crisis scenarios and describes how to communicate with other persons and organizations during these scenarios. An efficient crisis communication plan should be flexible enough to adapt to specific situations as they unfold. The plan must be tested to ensure its effectiveness.

Preparing for a Crisis

The organization should first establish a crisis communication team. The team should meet regularly so that everyone is aware of his or her responsibilities. Next, the organization should show how to identify a crisis. It is important that any crisis be identified as early as possible.

Types of Crises

There are three types of crises:

- A sudden crisis is an immediate, unexpected crisis.
- A smoldering crisis begins small but grows larger. It is especially important to resolve these crises quickly.
- A bizarre crisis is unusual and unexpected.

Handling a Crisis

Once a crisis is indentified, organizations should take the following actions:

- Gather the facts.
- Convene the crisis communication team.

- Activate all relevant safety plans.
- Designate a command center and/or media center.
- Prepare a statement and background information.

Communication Guidelines

The following are some guidelines for communication concerning a crisis:

- Identify the stakeholders who should be informed about the situation.
- Have a single spokesperson to ensure a unified and consistent message to the public. The spokesperson should be informed of the latest developments.
- Provide guidance to the public in case of a health risk.
- Officials should develop simple messages for their stakeholders and the media. The messages should be delivered continuously and clearly.
- The crisis team should assess any possible tough questions that the media and public might ask.
- Communicate the facts of the crisis to the audience.
- Public affairs should control the flow of information by holding a series of press briefings.
- The spokesperson should keep records of all communications.
- Respond to the media quickly and fairly.

Emergency Response Plan

The emergency response plan describes the roles and operations of all units and personnel during an emergency. This plan should use a management system commonly known as the incident command system (ICS). ICS offers an organizational structure that assists in responding to all levels of emergencies, from simple to complex. It provides the flexibility to respond to an incident as its severity escalates.

The purpose of the ICS is to:

- Provide an organizational structure that grows quickly in response to the requirements of an emergency.
- Provide the incident commander (the designated person in charge of the emergency response) with the controls needed to direct and coordinate all operations and all agencies responding to the incident.
- Efficiently train employees on critical functions.
- Define staff positions who are responsible for managing a particular incident or incident level.

The emergency response plan should designate an emergency operations center (EOC). This is the centralized location for managing emergency operations.

There are three emergency severity levels:

1. *Level 1*: The emergency incident is managed without activating the EOC.
2. *Level 2*: This requires a multiunit response where the EOC is partially activated. Depending on the event, some EOC staff may be notified at the discretion of the incident commander.
3. *Level 3*: The emergency cannot be managed with normal resources. Additional personnel are requested to staff the EOC. In this level, a state of the disaster is declared.

Emergency Response Checklist

- Start a log of actions.
- Coordinate with emergency services.
- Identify any damage.
- Identify disrupted functions.
- Convene the response and recovery teams.
- Provide information to the staff.
- Decide on the course of action.

- Communicate decisions to staff and business partners.
- Provide public information to maintain reputation and business.
- Arrange a debriefing.
- Review the business continuity management plan.

Emergency Management Team (EMT)

In case of a major disaster, the emergency management team (EMT) will assemble and assess the situation. This team decides whether to implement the relevant business continuity plans. The BCP team leader will activate the plan once instructions are received from the operations manager of the emergency management team.

The BCP team leader will direct all ad hoc requests for decisions, assistance with facilities, acquiring outside services, etc., to the EMT through the operations manager. It will be the BCP team leader's responsibility to contact all the team members or their alternates and ensure that they convene at the emergency operations center.

Figure 4-2 shows the EMT's hierarchy.

Contingency Planning

A contingency plan, sometimes called a worst-case scenario plan or Plan B, helps sustain and recover vital corporate information after an emergency. IT contingency planning considers critical organizational assets, including business process continuity, organizational process continuity, and recovery planning. Recovery strategies and resources supporting the recovery must be in sync with one another.

Contingency planning includes the following plans:

- Business continuity plan (BCP), discussed earlier
- Business recovery plan (BRP), included in the BCP, outlining the restoration of business functions following an emergency
- Continuity of operations plan (COOP), helping to restore essential business functions at an alternate site temporarily
- Continuity of support plan/IT contingency plan, ensuring that services meet the needs of the IT system's users
- Crisis communication plan, outlining communication procedures

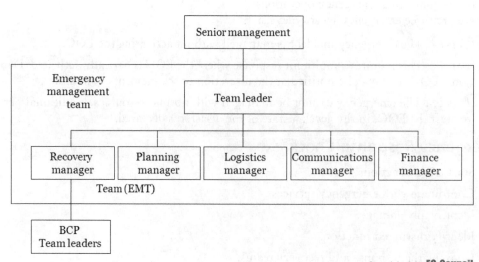

Figure 4-2   The EMT reports directly to senior management.

- Cyber-incident response plan, helping identify and mitigate malicious IT attacks
- Disaster recovery plan (DRP), part of the BCP explaining how to restore the operability of a system or facility
- Occupant emergency plan (OEP), addressing the procedures that should be carried out in situations that may jeopardize health and safety of personnel, the environment, or property

Contingency Planning and System Development

The system development life cycle (SDLC) is the process of developing an information system. This includes the following five phases, shown in Figure 4-3:

1. *Initiation*: The initiation phase includes determining the information system's goals and feasibility. The system's feasibility includes its system requirements and how well they match with operational processes. The requirements for a contingency plan should be analyzed based on the system's requirements and design.

2. *Development and acquisition*: Specific contingency plans can be incorporated as the concepts developed in the initiation phase are brought into the system design. The costs involved in modifying the system in the operation and maintenance phase can be minimized by robustness and redundancy in the system design.

3. *Implementation*: This phase involves testing the system as well as the contingency plan. The results must be documented after verifying the contingency plan.

4. *Operation and maintenance*: When the system is ready for operation, administrators should conduct a training and awareness program to familiarize users with the system and the contingency plan. Regular test runs should be conducted to verify the effectiveness of the contingency plan, and the plan should be updated based on the results of these tests.

5. *Disposal*: Legacy systems are replaced with newer systems in order to implement advanced applications. Until the new systems are tested, the older systems' contingency plans remain in effect. Some parts of the old systems can be used as spare parts for the new systems.

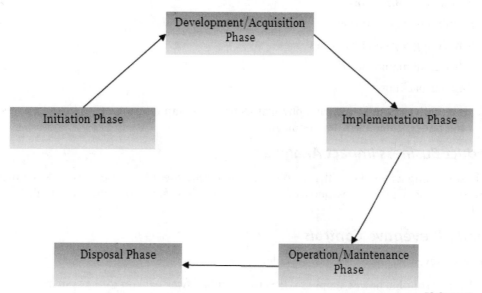

Figure 4-3   These are the five phases of the SDLC.

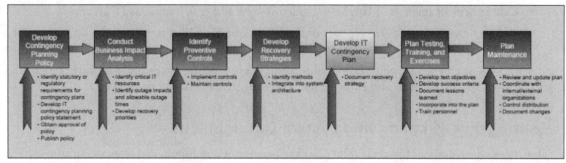

Source: http://www.nist.gov. Accessed 9/2009.

Figure 4-4 These are the steps of the IT contingency planning process.

IT Contingency Planning Process

Planning and maintaining an effective IT contingency plan includes the following steps, as shown in Figure 4-4:

1. Develop the contingency planning policy statement.

2. Conduct the business impact analysis (BIA).

3. Identify preventive controls.

4. Develop recovery strategies.

5. Develop an IT contingency plan.

6. Plan testing, training, and exercises.

7. Plan maintenance.

Develop the Contingency Planning Policy Statement

Developing a policy statement for the contingency plan ensures that it is both effective and easy to understand. The statement should clearly define the objectives of the contingency plan and everyone's responsibilities regarding the plan. Senior management should be involved in creating these definitions.

Key elements in the contingency planning policy statement include:

*   Roles and responsibilities

*   Scope

*   Resource requirements

*   Requirements for training

*   Scheduling tests and exercises

*   Scheduling maintenance

*   Regular backups

Representatives from IT security, physical security, human resources, and IT operations should be consulted during the policy statement's development.

Conduct Business Impact Analysis

The business impact analysis (BIA) involves documenting the information system's requirements and processes in order to anticipate the consequences of a disruption. The steps for conducting a BIA can be found earlier in this chapter.

Identify Preventive Controls

Common preventive measures may include:

*   Uninterruptible power supplies (UPS) to provide power backup to the system

*   Gas- or diesel-powered generators for backup power

*   Air-conditioning systems that continue to function after the failure of some components

- Fire suppression systems and fire/smoke detectors
- Water sensors in the computer room ceiling and floor
- Plastic tarps over IT equipment to protect them from water damage
- Heat-resistant and waterproof containers for backups and nonelectronic records
- Emergency master system shutdown switch
- Maintaining regular backups and storing backup media, nonelectronic records, and system documentation off-site
- Cryptographic key management and other access controls

Develop Recovery Strategies

Recovery strategies help in the quick restoration of IT operations after an emergency. These methods are covered in the following sections.

Backup Methods Critical data of the IT system should be backed up regularly, with more critical data backed up more frequently. Data can be backed up on a wide range of removable devices. Data storage facilities can also be located off-site, to protect them from threats facing the organization. Organizations should consider the following factors when choosing an off-site backup location:

- *Geographic area*: If the organization is affected by a local disaster, the storage facility should be far enough away that it will not be affected.
- *Accessibility*: Organizations should consider how long it would take to retrieve the backup from the remote site.
- *Security*: The storage facility should be secured from external and internal threats.
- *Environmental conditions*: The temperature of the storage facility, humidity controls, fire detection and prevention, and power management controls should be considered.
- *Cost*: Organizations should calculate the cost of operating the off-site backup facility and shipping the backups to the remote location.

Alternate Sites Contingency plans should consider an alternate site where the business functions of the organization can be carried out until the original facility returns to working order. It is important to prepare for long periods of time at the alternate site in the case of a major disaster.

There are three options available for an alternate site:

1. Site owned and operated by the organization
2. Site owned by an internal or external entity
3. Commercially leased facility

These alternate sites can be classified in terms of their operational readiness:

- *Cold*: Cold sites are cost-effective facilities with sufficient electrical power, air conditioning, and telecommunications to support a computer system. They do not actually house a computer system, so the computer and the necessary peripherals must be relocated to these sites after the disaster.
- *Warm*: These sites have the same conditions as cold sites, except they also contain part of the system's hardware and software. They are maintained in an operational condition to accommodate the disrupted system, so operations can resume quickly.
- *Hot*: Hot sites have similar computer systems already installed. Because of the computer systems, they are ready for operations as soon as the contingency plan is activated.
- *Mobile*: Mobile sites are facilities contained in a vehicle that can be driven to the alternate site. They house all the necessary equipment to meet the IT system requirements.
- *Mirrored*: Mirrored sites are built, maintained, and operated by the organization. They are identical to the primary sites that house the same equipment and facilities as the primary site. Data is stored simultaneously in the primary site and mirrored site.

Mirrored sites and hot sites are expensive but offer complete, fast recovery. Cold sites, though inexpensive, may take a longer time for recovery.

Equipment Replacement IT systems have to be quickly replaced if they are damaged in a disaster. Three basic strategies help in replacing the equipment:

1. *Vendor agreements*: Service-level agreements (SLAs) are made with hardware, software, and support vendors when the equipment is purchased and as the contingency plans are being developed. These agreements should specify how long it would take for the vendors to fix the affected systems or even replace them in the case of a disaster.

2. *Equipment inventory*: Required equipment should be purchased in advance and stored in an alternate site. The drawback of this plan is that the equipment could become obsolete, making it necessary to buy every new piece of equipment twice.

3. *Existing compatible equipment*: Equipment present at a hot site or compatible equipment from a different organization could be used.

Roles and Responsibilities Disaster recovery (DR) teams should be trained to implement the recovery strategies and contingency plans. These teams are responsible for bringing the IT system back to normal operations. Each team is led by a team leader, who directs the team members to their specific responsibilities and ensures that the team is coordinating with other teams while working on the contingency plan. The team leader is also responsible for decision making.

Cost Considerations The contingency planning coordinator ensures that the plan is implemented effectively, the personnel are trained, and a sufficient budget is allotted. The coordinator should ensure that the costs for equipment replacement, shipping, training programs, backup options, selection of alternate sites, and other resources are within the budget constraints.

Plan Testing, Training, and Exercises

The contingency plan (see IT Contingency Plan Development below) must be tested for its effectiveness. These tests will reveal any flaws in the plan and give the recovery teams valuable experience. The tests should address:

- Recoverability from backup media
- Synchronization of recovery teams
- Internal and external connectivity
- System performance with alternate equipment
- Restoration of normal operations
- Notifying relevant parties

Exercise formats include:

- *Classroom exercises*: This involves a walkthrough of the contingency plan procedures. None of the recovery operations are actually carried out, but it helps prepare teams for functional exercises.

- *Functional exercises*: Here, the disasters are simulated and the teams are expected to carry out the contingency plan as if it were, in fact, a real emergency.

Exercises should be planned in advance so that the team members are mentally ready and are available for the exercise.

Plan Maintenance

IT systems undergo numerous changes due to technology upgrades, changing business needs, and the policies of the organization. The contingency plan should be updated as these changes occur, in order for it to remain effective. The plan should be reviewed and modified regularly, at least once per year. Some elements may require more frequent changes, including:

- Operational and security requirements
- Redundancy of electronic data
- Technical procedures
- Hardware, software, and other equipment

- Contact information of the team members, vendors, and personnel at alternative sites and off-site
- Requirements of alternate and off-site facilities

Organizations should maintain a record of changes to the plan.

IT Contingency Plan Development

IT contingency plan development involves the following five phases:

1. Supporting information
2. Notification/activation phase
3. Recovery phase
4. Reconstitution phase
5. Plan appendices

Supporting Information

The supporting information consists of two components:

1. Introduction
2. Concept of operations

These components give key information to help in understanding, implementing, and maintaining the contingency plan. They also act as a guide and help the contingency plan coordinator in decision making.

The introduction component contains five sections:

1. *Purpose*: This defines why the IT contingency plan is being developed and its objectives.
2. *Applicability*: This subsection documents the business functions of the organization impacted by the contingency plan. Related plans that complement the IT contingency plan are identified and added to the appendix.
3. *Scope*: Specific issues that are addressed by the contingency plan are discussed here. This section also involves identifying the IT system for which the plan is being designed. The scope should also discuss any assumptions that were made in formulating the plan.
4. *References/requirements*: This subsection identifies laws and regulations that should be followed in preparing the contingency plan.
5. *Record of changes*: All changes made to the plan should be recorded and located at the beginning of the plan documentation.

The concept of operations component includes:

- *System description*: This gives a general description of the IT system for which the contingency plan is being formulated. The description should include system architecture, security devices installed in the system, and the location of the system. This information can be gathered from the system security plan.
- *Line of succession*: This section identifies the personnel member who will take over if someone is unable to perform his or her duties for the contingency plan.
- *Responsibilities*: This section includes the roles and responsibilities of the teams that are involved in implementing the IT contingency plan and the hierarchy of the teams. Responsibilities should be set to a team as a whole, not to individuals.

Notification/Activation Phase

This phase defines the primary actions that should be taken once an emergency is declared. It includes notifying the designated personnel (recovery staff), assessing the damage to the system, and implementing the contingency plan. After this stage, the designated personnel must be ready to implement the plan and recover the system functions.

- *Notification procedures*: System disruption can occur with or without warning. The recovery staff should be notified about the disruption as early as possible, so that they may be able to shut down the system and perform other preparatory actions. Procedures should be set as to how to notify the recovery staff during business and nonbusiness hours. The recovery personnel must be advised to regularly check their e-mails to avoid missing important security updates. The contingency plan should include the contact information of the recovery personnel and assessment teams.

- *Damage assessment*: To determine how the contingency plan will be implemented following an emergency, it is essential to assess the nature and extent of the damage to the system. The damage assessment team must be immediately notified about the disruption and then should assess the following as soon as possible:
  - Cause of the disruption/emergency and the areas affected
  - Chances of further disruptions and damages
  - Type of damage to the physical infrastructure and equipment
  - Inventory and functional status of IT equipment
  - Equipment to be replaced and the time required for returning to normal operations
- *Plan activation*: The IT contingency plan can be activated only when one or more activation criteria are met, as determined by the damage assessment team. The plan coordinator activates the plan after the damage assessment team gives its report. The criteria that should be identified in the contingency plan include:
  - Safety of personnel
  - Damage to the facility
  - Damage to the system
  - Importance of the system
  - Estimated time of the disruption

Recovery Phase

The activities in this phase involve repairing the damages and restoring the functions of the system to their normal operational conditions. If the damages cannot be repaired quickly, steps are taken to relocate the operations to an alternate site.

The system recovery sequence follows the priorities set in the BIA. Recovery procedures include:

1. Acquiring permission to visit the area of the disrupted system
2. Notifying internal and external business partners associated with the system
3. Acquiring supplies for recovery
4. Acquiring and installing hardware
5. Acquiring backup media and installing it
6. Restoring operating system and application software
7. Restoring system data
8. Testing system functionality and security controls
9. Connecting the system to the network
10. Operating alternate equipment

Reconstitution Phase

In this phase, business operations and systems are completely restored to their normal functional state. If normal operations cannot be restored to the original facility, the operations are transferred to a new facility. This phase also defines the teams that restore the system and the site.

The activities in this phase include:

- Ensuring basic infrastructure support and supplies
- Installing system hardware, software, and firmware
- Connecting the system to the network
- Testing the functionality of the restored system

- Backing up operational data on the contingency system and uploading to the restored system
- Shutting down the contingency system
- Terminating the contingency operations
- Securing sensitive materials at the contingency site
- Arranging for recovery personnel to return to the original facility

Plan Appendices

Additional relevant details that are not covered in the contingency plan documentation should be included in the appendices section. These details may include:

- Contact information of vendors and the contingency planning team
- Procedures and checklists for system recovery
- Detailed information about the equipment vital to support system operations
- Vendor SLAs and agreements with other organizations
- Details of the alternate site

Technical Contingency Planning Considerations

Contingency plans are necessary for several different IT platforms, and they may slightly differ for each platform, based on that platform's specific requirements.

Desktop Computers and Portable Systems

Computers and portable systems are the most common platforms used in organizations, so they are extremely important in contingency plans. Contingency considerations for computers and portable systems include:

- Storing backups off-site
- Encouraging individuals to back up data
- Providing guidance on saving data on personal computers
- Standardizing hardware, software, and peripherals
- Documenting system configurations and vendor information
- Using results from the BIA

Organizations need to consider the following when choosing backup media:

- Equipment interoperability
- Storage volume
- Storage life of the media

The following are a few types of backup media:

- Tape drives
- Removable storage devices
- Compact discs
- Network storage
- Replication or synchronization with portable devices
- Internet backup

One effective method of backing up data is *imaging*. Imaging involves creating a single file with the complete contents of a storage device. This creates a large file, but it makes it possible to restore the contents of the device with no changes whatsoever.

Servers

Any disruption in the server could bring a business to a standstill. The following contingency considerations address server vulnerabilities:

- Store backup media and software off-site.
- Standardize hardware, software, and peripherals.
- Document system configurations and vendors.
- Coordinate with security policies and system security controls.
- Use results from the BIA.

The BIA helps in selecting the right contingency solution for enhanced recovery capabilities. The security of critical data should be considered when selecting a contingency solution. Servers can have backup drives of their own, or a centralized backup system can be deployed by attaching a backup drive to one central server. Server data can be backed up in the following ways:

- *Full backup*: A full backup stores all data in a folder or a disk onto a single backup medium. This makes it easy to retrieve a particular file, but the backup process takes a long time.
- *Incremental backup*: Only the files that were created or modified after the last backup are captured here. It does not take long to make the backup, as less information is being backed up than the original full backup, but retrieving data to recover a system would require restoring the last full backup and then each sequential incremental backup from oldest to most recent in order to achieve a complete restoration.
- *Differential backup*: The files that were created or modified after the last full backup are stored. This takes less time than a full backup but more time than an incremental backup, as each time the differential backup is made, it will include all information that has been modified since the last full backup. It requires fewer media for system restoration because retrieving the data to recover the system involves only restoring the data from the last full backup and the latest differential backup.
- *Redundant Array of Independent Disks (RAID)*: A RAID is a type of virtual hard drive consisting of two or more hard disks. Because RAID uses multiple disks, reliability is increased.

Web Sites

These measures should be considered for Web site contingency planning:

- Document the Web site's hardware, software, and configuration.
- Document any programming changes.
- Coordinate contingency solutions with appropriate security policies and security controls.
- Coordinate contingency solutions with incident response procedures.
- Use results from the BIA.

When planning contingency solutions for a Web site, organizations should consider the sites' supporting infrastructures. This infrastructure includes the server hosting the Web sites and the local area network (LAN).

Load balancing is one solution, in which more than one server shares Web traffic. This provides redundancy, enabling at least one server to work when the other fails. Load balancing can be achieved by using DNS or reverse proxy.

- *DNS*: A URL request typed in a browser is directed to a DNS server. This maps the request to an IP address and then directs it to one of the servers.
- *Reverse proxy*: A proxy server is stationed between the client and the server. It receives requests from the clients, passes them to one of the servers, and then sends the response back to the client from the server. The reverse proxy server gathers all browser requests together, reducing the bandwidth.

Local Area Networks (LANs)

A LAN can be implemented using two architectures:

1. In a peer-to-peer network, users can transfer files from one computer to another.
2. In a client-server model, all computers in the network connect to a server and access data from that server.

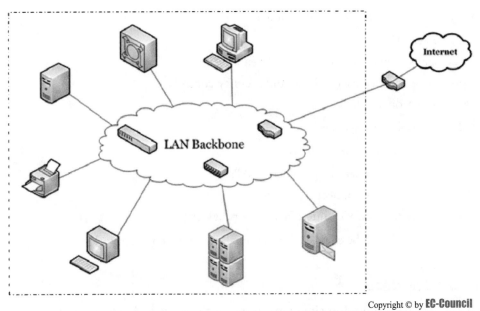

Figure 4-5   In most workplaces, computers are networked together.

Figure 4-5 shows a local area network.
Organizations should consider these measures for LAN contingency planning:

- Diagram the LAN.
- Document system configuration and vendor information.
- Coordinate with security policies and security controls.
- Use results from the BIA.

The BIA identifies key devices in the LAN, including:

- Cabling systems
- Network connecting devices (hubs, routers, and bridges)
- Remote access provided by servers on the LAN

Wireless networks may act as a contingency solution when wired LAN service is disrupted.

Wide Area Networks (WAN)

A WAN is a long-range communications network, which could use one or more of the following:

- Dial-up connections
- Integrated Services Digital Network (ISDN)
- T1
- T3
- Cable Internet
- DSL
- Fiber optic Internet
- Frame relay
- ATM
- Synchronous optical network (SONET)
- Wireless LAN bridge
- Virtual private network (VPN)

WAN contingency considerations include:

- Diagram the WAN.
- Document system configurations and vendors.
- Coordinate with security policies and security controls.
- Use results from the BIA.

WANs have these contingency solutions:

- Redundant communications links
- Redundant network service providers (NSPs)
- Redundant network connecting devices
- Redundancy from NSP or Internet service provider (ISP)

The NSP or ISP should be checked for the reliability of its core networks.

Distributed Systems

Distributed systems are used in situations in which the users and clients are dispersed over wide geographical areas. All these systems should be synchronized to avoid any processing errors. They have the following considerations:

- Standardize hardware, software, and peripherals.
- Document system configurations and vendors.
- Coordinate with security policies and security controls.
- Use results from the BIA.

Because the distributed systems are located over wide geographical locations, the BIA should address the risk of the system and its infrastructure. The contingency solutions for distributed systems are reflected in the solutions for LANs and WANs, because these systems are dependent on them. Any changes in the primary system should be reflected in the rest of the systems.

Mainframe Systems

Mainframes are large computers with the ability to perform critical and complex functions. These systems have centralized architecture in which the clients receive the output but are not involved in the processing.

The considerations for a mainframe are similar to the contingency considerations for other platforms discussed. A mainframe lacks the redundancy of a distributed system, making it very important to back up critical information. The following elements should be considered to determine the contingency requirements for a mainframe system:

- Store backup media off-site.
- Document system configurations and vendors.
- Coordinate with network security policy and system security controls.
- Utilize results from the BIA.

The contingency solutions should consider the fact that storage in a mainframe system exists at a single location, unlike distributed systems where the data is replicated at various locations. Organizations should use UPS and power monitoring systems to ensure that the system does not crash due to a power failure. They should also consider diesel- or gas-run generators to help ensure that power is always available.

Maintaining a warm or hot site is a good solution, although the size and expense of installing such a large system at an alternate site is not viable for most organizations. It may be possible to share a replacement mainframe system with other organizations.

Vendor support is a must for mainframe systems. Although vendors may not be able to fix the system within the outage time, they might help in replacing critical equipment. Service agreements with vendors should be updated regularly.

Preventive Controls

Preventive controls help mitigate risks. Some of these controls include:

- The organization should be designed to allow segregation of duties and roles.
- Standardize policies and procedures.
- Personnel should be trained to perform a particular job.
- Systems should follow standard design and architecture.

User Account Maintenance

Securing the user account information is a critical part of avoiding damage from intrusions. Login information in the wrong hands could lead to data theft or system crashes. User passwords can be secured using authentication methods such as Pluggable Authentication Module (PAM)–based authentication and database-based authentication. Installing filters and firewalls also helps protect the system from unauthorized access.

Processes for Timely Deletion of Accounts

Once accounts become inactive, system administrators should delete them in order to prevent attackers from using them. In the case of an employee leaving the organization, that user's account should be deleted after taking a backup of all the important data from that particular account profile. Users leaving the organization must assist the service/departmental managers in locating important files and e-mails required for further operations.

Virtualization Disaster Recovery

Virtualization makes use of a single physical server for running multiple virtual machines. That way, multiple users interact with the system as if they were each using their own individual system. Virtualization can be performed by a software layer called a virtual machine monitor (VMM). This increases efficiency, decreases costs, and increases the scalability and availability of enterprise storage environments.

Virtualization disaster recovery (VDR) technology allows organizations to quickly and effectively recover important business systems. VDR solutions reduce the downtime associated with traditional storage recovery solutions, allowing the organization to recover data immediately after the disaster recovery solution is installed, at a fraction of the cost.

Virtualization Benefits

Virtualization offers several benefits for organizations, including:

- Greater flexibility/agility in IT environments
- More balanced server workload
- Reduced physical size of the data center
- Reduced power consumption
- Reduced costs

Workload Portability

Workload portability means that workloads can be detached from their original hardware configuration, and entire software stacks can be moved to another physical or virtual host. This means that workloads can be circulated between similar virtual hosts in order to balance workloads.

Typical workload portability scenarios include:

- Physical-to-virtual host portability
- Virtual-to-physical host portability
- Physical-to-physical host portability
- In-and-out-of-imaging formats

Workload portability improves the flexibility, agility, and overall competency of data centers, allowing organizations to tackle challenges such as:

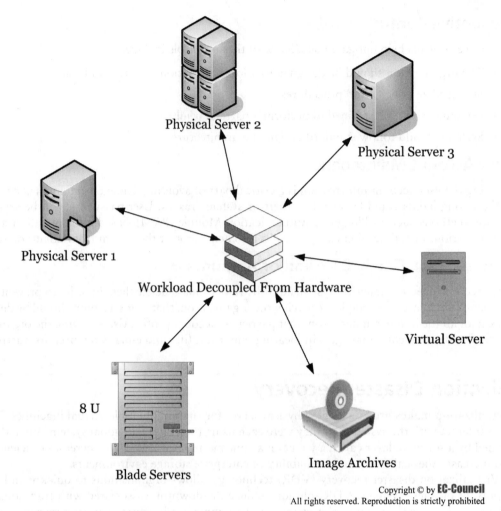

Figure 4-6 Virtualization allows for workload portability, where workloads
can be circulated among similar hosts.

- End-of-lease hardware migration
- Server consolidation
- Disaster recovery

Figure 4-6 demonstrates workload portability.

Workload Protection

Workload protection involves copying the server's workload to a secondary location in case of a primary server outage or disaster. Keeping a bootable archive of the workload on the virtual recovery platform makes it much easier to quickly recover.

Using a virtualization process, multiple workloads are duplicated to a single virtual recovery environment over a WAN. This process gives complete protection to the physical or virtual workloads, providing an ability to replicate the entire workload, rather than just application data, to the virtual machine environment. It ensures that anything that is required to restore operations is present in a bootable virtual machine on the recovery server, at a significantly lower cost than one-to-one solutions.

Figure 4-7 shows workload protection with consolidated recovery.

Rapid Recovery

When a primary server outage or disaster strikes, the virtualized recovery server is activated to run the workload immediately. The workload executes in the virtual recovery environment until the primary server is restored. That way, recovery time and point objectives are achieved without requiring a high-cost and complex clustering environment.

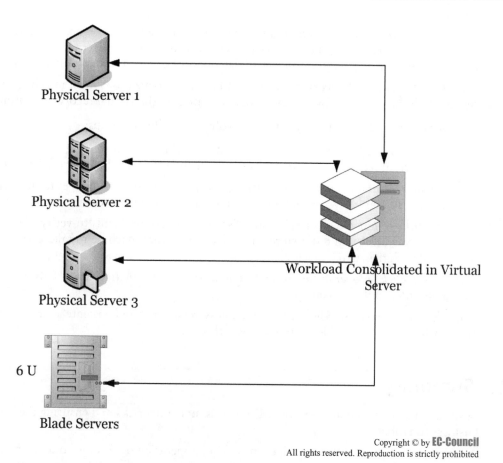

Figure 4-7 Protecting workloads in a virtual recovery environment has many of the benefits of one-to-one solutions at a significantly lower cost.

When planning a virtualized recovery environment, organizations should check for sufficient computer power and capacity to run the recovery workload for as long as it will take to restore the production server. If the physical host is insufficiently sized, the workloads may have to run in a degraded state, which may impact business operations.

At the recovery planning stage, a workload profiling and analysis solution is required. These solutions are used to monitor the workload and resource utilization trends for a certain period of time to estimate everything about resource utilization. These solutions guarantee that the recovery environment is perfectly balanced to take care of present and future workload requirements.

Ease of Testing

Organizations must thoroughly check their disaster recovery strategies, solutions, and methodologies. Conventional recovery solutions are complex in nature, so they cannot be tested regularly. Virtualization recovery solutions are easier to test, and these tests can be run without interrupting business operations.

Planning and Implementing an Virtualized Recovery Solution

The implementation of a successful virtualized recovery solution starts with creating a detailed plan. The steps in the planning phase are:

1. *Discover server inventory*: In this step, organizations discover and list all the assets in the IT environments, including the physical and virtual servers and data, applications, and operating systems. This information is included in the disaster recovery plan.

2. *Monitor server utilization*: Organizations monitor for workload information such as CPU, disk, memory, and network utilization rates in a particular period of time. This collected information provides invaluable workload profiling and capacity planning data.

3. *Build the disaster recovery plan*: Organizations develop the recovery plans to determine the exact virtual recovery site capacity. They must build sufficient headroom at the target virtualized recovery environment to ensure sufficient capacity to run consolidated workloads and resources in case of a disaster.

4. *Configure the virtual recovery environment*: Finally, organizations must match the physical production servers with the virtual recovery machines and configure the virtual recovery environment.

Implementing a virtualized recovery solution involves the following steps:

1. *Initial system backup*: Execute a complete system backup by transferring the entire server workloads to the target virtual recovery environment with the help of the workload portability solution.

2. *Ongoing incremental backups*: Automatically propagate all source changes to the target virtual recovery environment so that it always contains a current copy of the production environment.

3. *Run fire drills to test DR readiness*: Run disaster recovery fire drills to verify the application's integrity and recovery time. Run a test restore on the backup virtual machine to take an image of the virtual file associated with the virtual machine.

4. *Initiate one-click failover in case of system outage*: If the production server fails, initiate a system failover to rapidly start up the session.

5. *Rapidly restore systems*: When the production system is repaired, execute a virtual-to-physical workload transfer for restoring workloads to the original server.

Chapter Summary

- Business continuity management (BCM) involves managing risks and ensuring the availability of business functions.

- An emergency response plan describes the role and operation of all units and personnel during an emergency.

- An organization should have alternate worksites identified for business resumption and recovery.

- Organizations should implement evaluation and maintenance programs to keep the business continuity plan relevant.

- IT contingency planning represents a broad scope of activities designed to sustain and recover critical IT services following an emergency.

- Virtualization disaster recovery (VDR) technology allows organizations to quickly and effectively recover important business systems.

Review Questions

1. What are the elements of business continuity management?

_____

_____

_____

_____

2. What is a BCP?

_____

_____

_____

_____

3. What is an emergency response plan?

_____

_____

_____

_____

4. What is a crisis communication plan?

_____

_____

_____

_____

5. What are the five goals of a BCP?

_____

_____

_____

_____

6. What is a contingency plan?

_____

_____

_____

_____

7. How can a contingency plan be worked into the system development life cycle?

_____

_____

_____

_____

8. How do you conduct a BIA in the contingency planning process?

_____

_____

_____

_____

9. How is a contingency plan maintained?

_____

_____

_____

_____

10. What is virtualization?

_____

_____

_____

_____

11. What is workload protection?

_____

_____

_____

_____

12. What are the steps in planning and implementing a virtualized recovery solution?

_____

_____

_____

_____

_____

Hands-On Projects

HANDS-ON PROJECTS

1. Read about IT risk management.
   - Navigate to Chapter 4 of the Student Resource Center.
   - Open Industry_BCM_Managing_Information_Technology_Risk.pdf and read the content.

2. Read about risk assessment.
   - Navigate to Chapter 4 of the Student Resource Center.
   - Open Risk Assessment Instructions.pdf and read the content.

3. Read about technology risk.
   - Navigate to Chapter 4 of the Student Resource Center.
   - Open Unpan.pdf and read the content.

4. Read about enterprise risk management.
   - Navigate to Chapter 4 of the Student Resource Center.
   - Open COSO_ERM_ExecutiveSummary.pdf and read the content.

5. Read about contingency planning for IT systems.
   - Navigate to Chapter 4 of the Student Resource Center.
   - Open Contingency Planning Guide for Information Technology Systems.pdf and read the content.

6. Read about the contingency planning process.
   - Navigate to Chapter 4 of the Student Resource Center.
   - Open contingency_planning_process.pdf and read the content.

7. Read about continuity of operation.
   - Navigate to Chapter 4 of the Student Resource Center.
   - Open coop.pdf and read the content.

8. Read about the benefits of virtualization.
   - Navigate to Chapter 4 of the Student Resource Center.
   - Open Benefits of Virtualization for BCDR.pdf and read the content.

9. Read about using virtualization for disaster recovery.

   ▪ Navigate to Chapter 4 of the Student Resource Center.

   ▪ Open Virtualization for Disaster Recovery.pdf and read the content.

10. Read more about virtualization for disaster recovery.

   ▪ Navigate to Chapter 4 of the Student Resource Center.

   ▪ Open Virtualization Technologies and Their Impact on Disaster Recovery Planning.pdf and read the content.

Chapter 5

Managing, Assessing, and Evaluating Risks

Objectives

After completing this chapter, you should be able to:

- Conduct risk management
- Explain the importance of risk management
- Integrate risk management into SDLC
- Follow the risk management methodology
- Follow the risk assessment methodology
- Conduct system characterization
- Use security countermeasures
- Calculate residual risk
- List the responsibilities of an information systems security officer (ISSO)
- Evaluate information systems
- Conduct information system acquisition and disposition

Key Terms

Impact analysis   a type of analysis that determines the impact that a threat could have on a system

Residual risk   the risk that results from issues that were not covered by the assessment or that come up after the assessment

Risk assessment   a quantitative or qualitative process that deals with the identification of possible risks and their impacts, and provides measures to be taken to reduce the risks

Risk mitigation   a process that involves the implementation of risk control measures to minimize risk to an acceptable level

Risk variables   the elements or factors in an environment that cause a corresponding degree of change in the exposure to a risk

Security countermeasures   the actions or solutions used to prevent attacks

Security requirements checklist   a document that comprises essential and basic security standards that can be used to methodically evaluate and identify the vulnerabilities of information system assets in the management, operational, and technical security areas

Technical surveillance countermeasure (TSCM) techniques   techniques used to detect and neutralize the hostile penetration technologies used to gain unauthorized access to confidential and sensitive information

TEMPEST   a government project studying compromising electrical, mechanical, or acoustical energy emissions unintentionally emitted by electrical equipment/systems such as computers, monitors, or transmission lines, allowing the information therein to be captured

Threat   any event that could have a negative impact on the operations of the organization

Threat source   any incident or occurrence with the potential to cause harm to an information system

Vulnerability   any weakness in the operations or systems of an organization that could be exploited by a threat agent

Introduction to Managing, Assessing, and Evaluating Risks

Risk management is performed to identify threats and prevent them from severely affecting an organization. Risk management is an integral part of business continuity planning and all disaster recovery efforts. A *risk assessment* is a quantitative or qualitative process that deals with the identification of possible risks and their impacts, and provides measures to be taken to reduce those risks. When a risk assessment is complete, *risk mitigation* is performed to implement risk control measures to minimize the risk to an acceptable level. It involves all the risks identified in the risk assessment process. The efficiency of the risk management program and its implementation is then tested, and the results of this process are used to update the risk assessment and mitigation processes.

The DAA (designated approving authority) and the system-authorizing official are responsible for risk management and checking that risks remain within acceptable limits. If risks exceed the acceptable level, the authorities also provide additional security controls that need to be executed to remove the residual risks.

Importance of Risk Management

Risk management helps organizations avoid heavy losses. These losses can be financial or data-related losses. Risk management is important for the following reasons:

- It protects organizations' information assets.
- It protects business continuity and enables organizations to accomplish their business objectives.
- It minimizes the effect of risk on organizations' finances and earnings.
- It provides organizations with a sense of security.
- It helps organizations control IT systems-related mission risks.
- It enables organizations to maintain a balance between operational and financial costs.
- It helps organizations' management identify suitable controls for implementing required security measures.

Integration of Risk Management into the System Development Life Cycle (SDLC)

Integration of risk management into the system development life cycle (SDLC) enables an organization to minimize risks and helps management to select and implement appropriate risk control measures. Risk management should be integrated completely into SDLC to develop a more secure and robust system. The following phases comprise an IT system's SDLC:

1. Initiation
2. Development or acquisition
3. Implementation
4. Operation or maintenance
5. Disposal

SDLC Phases	Phase Characteristics	Support from Risk Management Activities
Phase 1—Initiation	Defines the requirements of an IT system and documents its scope	Recognized risks help in supporting the development of system requirements
Phase 2—Development or Acquisition	The IT system is designed and developed	Recognized risks help in supporting security analyses
Phase 3—Implementation	The security measures in a system are configured, activated, and tested for efficiency	The risk management process checks whether the system is implemented according to the modeled operations or checks against its requirements
Phase 4—Operation or Maintenance	The system is functioning and requires changes or modifications regularly based on the policies, processes, and procedures	Risk management activities aid in system reauthorization in case of changes made to the system
Phase 5—Disposal	This involves destroying, archiving, and moving information, hardware, or software	Performed on the system components to dispose of or change the hardware and software

Table 5-1   The risk assessment process is performed in each phase of SDLC

The risk management process is performed in each major phase of SDLC. Table 5-1 describes the characteristics of each phase.

Risk Management Methodology

It is important for organizations to maintain business continuity. Risk management is a part of the overall business continuity and disaster recovery processes. Successful risk management ensures that the risks facing an organization remain within acceptable levels and are mitigated before they cause harm. Organizations should also develop and maintain efficient risk management plans to overcome legal compliance issues.

Risk management plans are developed after a comprehensive risk assessment and require active management involvement. Management's involvement ensures that the effective risk controls can be identified and implemented successfully. Risk management involves the following steps:

1. *Risk identification*: This step involves the identification of all the risks facing an organization that may affect normal business operations.
2. *Risk assessment*: This step involves the determination of the potential impact of risks on business assets and operations.
3. *Risk prioritization*: Risk prioritization aids in the categorization of risk control methods. Risks are categorized according to the criticality of the systems and processes they may affect.
4. *Risk analysis*: Risk analysis is a systematic analysis of the causes of risks. It involves the analysis of threat sources and factors that give rise to risks.
5. *Development of strategies to manage the identified risks*: Different strategies are developed for the proper and effective management of the identified risks.
6. *Implementation of risk management plan*: After developing the strategies, the best suitable solution is established to counter the risks. Then the solution is implemented according to the plan.

Risk Assessment

Risk assessment may be defined as a set of guidelines and procedures used to identify and assess the risks that pose a threat to the business or project environment. It involves identifying and prioritizing security risks according to critical information assets and key business processes. It determines the probability and magnitude of the possible threats, vulnerabilities, and risks associated with an IT system. It also determines the level of risk and the resulting security requirements for each system.

Risk assessment for a new system is conducted at the beginning of the system development life cycle. Risk assessment for an existing system is conducted when major modifications are made to the system's environment.

Risk assessment also involves training the staff to understand the risks in business operations and make them aware of certain best practices that would prevent sensitive information from being exposed. The output of the risk assessment process enables the identification of security measures to minimize risk and aid in the risk mitigation process. The organization should plan, implement, and monitor a set of security measures for the identified risks.

Risk Variables

Risk variables are the elements or factors in an environment that cause a corresponding degree of change in the exposure to a risk. These variables determine the risks to an organization. The risk assessment process is a function of these elements. All the risk variables are interdependent and affect the probability of each other.

The risk identification phase of a risk assessment relies on the determination of risk variables. Accuracy in determination of risk variables influences the effectiveness of a risk assessment and risk mitigation controls. Risk variables are often determined by evaluations of certain assumptions or management's perception of risks in the operating environment, along with a statistical analysis of various business indicators. The determination is also influenced by management's previous disaster recovery efforts.

Threats

Information assets in an organization are vulnerable to threats. A *threat* is any event that could have a negative impact on the operations of the organization. Threats may be internal or external. Internal threats originate from within an organization, whereas external threats are created by outsiders who attempt to breach organizational security. For example, if an employee tries to breach the data access policies and tries to get control of information assets, it is an internal threat; if an outsider plants a Trojan in the organization's network and tries to steal information, it is an external threat.

The types of threats can be differentiated as follows:

- Intentional actions
- Unintentional actions
- Problems caused by system hardware or software
- Other events
  - Power failure
  - Telecommunication failure
  - Natural disaster

These threats can result in disclosure of assets, damage to assets, destruction of hardware or software, etc.

Risk Assessment Methodology

The following steps are involved in the risk assessment process:

1. System characterization
2. Threat identification
3. Vulnerability identification
4. Control analysis
5. Likelihood determination
6. Impact analysis
7. Risk determination
8. Recommendations to control the threats
9. Results documentation

Step 1: System Characterization

In this step, the limits of an IT system are determined in order to set the scope of the risk assessment, as shown in Figure 5-1. The IT system is characterized along with the circumstances under which it operates. To identify

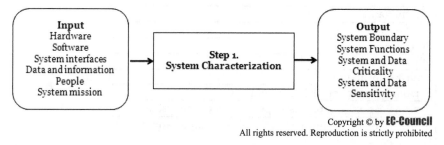

Figure 5-1   System characterization involves determining the scope of the risk assessment.

the risk to a system, a good knowledge of the system's processing environment is necessary. The organization needs to collect the following system-related information:

- Organization's hardware assets, including computer systems, networking devices, and other equipment
- Software assets
- System interfaces
- Data and information
- Users of the IT system
- Objective of the system
- System and data criticality
- System and data sensitivity

The following techniques can be used to gather information about an IT processing environment. The methods can be applied individually, or they can be combined to collect information.

- Preparing a checklist of questions that the technical and nontechnical management staff can use in on-site visits and interviews. This checklist should contain various management or operational controls planned or practiced by the IT system.
- Using automated tools to collect technical information such as vulnerability details.
- Collecting the following data on the planned IT system's security controls:
  - Policy documents
  - System documentation
  - System administration manual
  - System design documentation
  - Security-related documentation
  - Use of automated scanning tools

After gathering all the required information, the organization should design a system characterization template, such as the one in Figure 5-2.

Step 2: Threat Identification

In this step, different threats and threat sources are identified, as shown in Figure 5-3. A *threat source* is any incident or occurrence with the potential to cause harm to the information system. A threat source does not present a risk if there is no vulnerability that can be exercised for that particular threat source.

The following threat sources are common:

- *Human threats*: Human threats are more difficult to predict and identify due to their uncertain nature. The following human threats are common:
  - False data entry or deletion of data
  - Inadvertent acts

System Name:
Hardware
Software
System Interfaces
Data & Information
Persons who support the IT system
System mission (e.g. processes performed by the system)
System & data criticality (system's value or importance to the organization)
Functional requirements of the IT system
Users of the system
System Security policies (organizational policies, federal requirements, industry practices, laws)
System security architecture
Current network topology (e.g. network diagram)
Current information storage protection that safeguards system & data CIA
Flow of information relating to the IT system
Management controls used for the IT system (e.g. security planning, rules of behavior)
Operational controls (e.g. back-up, contingency, and resumption and recovery operations, personnel security...)
Physical security environment (e.g. facility security, data center policies)
Environmental security (temperature control, water, power)

Figure 5-2 A system characterization template is used to show the characteristics of a system.

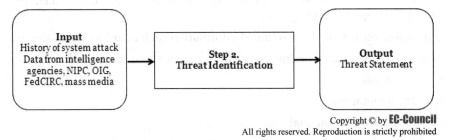

Figure 5-3 Threat sources must be identified in a risk assessment.

- Eavesdropping
- Impersonation
- Shoulder surfing
- User abuse or fraud
- Theft, sabotage, vandalism, or physical intrusions
- Espionage
- *Technical threats*: These threats arise due to system misconfigurations and errors in application development. Though there are procedural solutions for most technical threats, the complexity in current evolving technologies and weak interrelations between various stakeholders in the field make them difficult to avoid. The following technical threats are common:
  - Breaking passwords for unauthorized access to system resources
  - Sniffing and scanning of network traffic

- Data/system contamination
- Malicious code infection
- Spam and mail frauds
- Phishing that may result in loss of confidential private information
- DDoS attacks
- Application coding errors
- Unauthorized modification of a database
- Session hijacking
- System and application errors or failures

The threat identification process is performed in two steps:

1. *Threat-source identification*: The main objective of this step is to recognize the probable threat sources and develop a list of identified threat sources that are applicable to the information system being evaluated. While identifying threat sources, it is vital to consider all probable threat sources that may cause harm to the information system and its operations.

2. *Determination of motivation and threat actions*: The motivations for and resources used to perform an attack make humans potentially hazardous threat sources. A review of existing threat identification reports helps security personnel identify human threat sources that have a potential to harm an information system. The following reports are valuable sources of information on threat sources:

   - System break-in report
   - Security violation reports
   - Security incident reports

After identifying a potential threat source, security personnel must develop a report or estimation of motivation and resources to carry out a successful attack. The threat report, containing probable threat sources, should be tailored to the individual organization and its processing environment.

Step 3: Vulnerability Identification

A *vulnerability* is any weakness in the operations or systems of an organization that could be exploited by a threat agent. The main objective of this step is to prepare a list of information system vulnerabilities that could be exploited by the probable threat sources, as shown in Figure 5-4. Different types of vulnerabilities exist in information systems, and methods required to decide whether the vulnerabilities are present generally depend on the nature of the information system.

If the information system has not yet been developed, the identification of potential vulnerabilities should focus on security policies, intended security procedures, and system requirement definitions of the organization. If the information system is in the process of being implemented, the search for potential vulnerabilities should be expanded to include the intended security features described in the security design plan and the outcome of the system certification process and evaluation. If the information system is operational, the search for potential vulnerabilities should focus on analysis of security features and security controls.

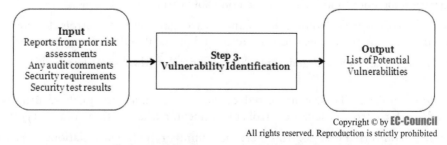

Figure 5-4 Vulnerability identification is performed through the use of security tests and prior reports.

The vulnerability identification process includes the following methods:

- *Vulnerability sources*: Potential vulnerabilities associated with an information system's processing environment can be recognized with the help of information-gathering techniques. A review of other organizational resources also helps in preparing useful questionnaires to recognize vulnerabilities that may be applicable to particular information systems. The Internet is also a good source for information gathering. Many vendors post known system vulnerabilities and their remedial measures to eliminate vulnerabilities. The following documented vulnerability sources should be considered in a vulnerability analysis:
  - Previous risk assessment reports on the information system.
  - Information system audit reports, security reports, and system test and evaluation reports.
  - Known vulnerability lists gathered from the Web.
  - Vendor advisories.
  - System software security analyses.
- *System security testing*: Many system security-testing methods are used to identify information system vulnerabilities depending on the criticality of the information system and available resources. This includes the following system security-testing methods:
  - *Automated vulnerability scanning tool*: This type of tool is used to scan system networks or a group of hosts for known vulnerable services.
  - *Security test and evaluation (ST&E)*: This method is used to identify system vulnerabilities during the risk assessment process. This method includes the development and implementation of a security test plan. The main objective of this method is to test the effectiveness of the information system security controls.
  - *Penetration testing*: This method is used to complement the review of system security controls and guarantee that different facets of the information system are secured. The main objective of this method is to test the information system from the perspective of a threat source and to spot potential failures in the information system security plans.
- *Development of security requirements checklist*: This step is performed by risk assessment personnel to verify whether the security requirements stipulated for the information system and gathered during system characterization are being met by present or intended security controls.

A *security requirements checklist* document comprises essential and basic security standards that can be used to methodically evaluate and identify the vulnerabilities of information system assets in management, operational, and technical security areas, as shown in Figure 5-5.

Step 4: Control Analysis

The organization analyzes the controls that are planned to be implemented or are already implemented in order to reduce the probability of a threat, as shown in Figure 5-6. The following aspects are included in a control analysis:

- *Control methods*: The following two methods must be incorporated to achieve security control:
  1. *Technical controls*: Technical controls are safeguards that are integrated into system hardware, software, or firmware, such as access control mechanisms, identification and authentication mechanisms, encryption methods, and intrusion detection software.
  2. *Nontechnical controls*: Nontechnical controls are management controls that include operational procedures, security policies and personnel, and physical and environmental security.
- *Control categories*: Technical and nontechnical control methods are classified into the following two categories:
  1. *Preventive controls*: These controls reduce the attempts made to violate security policies and thus include such controls as access control enforcement, authentication, and encryption.
  2. *Detective controls*: These controls alert the administrator when violations or attempts at violations of security policies occur. They include controls such as checksums, audit trails, and intrusion detection methods.

Introduction		
	Date carried out:	
	Testing Team details:	
	Network Details:	
	Scope of test:	
Executive Summary		
	OS Security issues discovered with appropriate criticality level specified:	
	Application Security issues discovered with appropriate criticality level specified:	
	Physical Security issues discovered with appropriate criticality level specified:	
	Personnel Security issues discovered with appropriate criticality level specified:	
	General Security issues discovered with appropriate criticality level specified:	
Technical Summary		
	OS Security issues discovered:	
	Web server security:	
	Database server security:	
	General Application Security:	
	Business Continuity Policy:	
Annexes	1:	
	2:	
	3:	

Figure 5-5   A security requirements checklist document comprises essential and basic security standards.

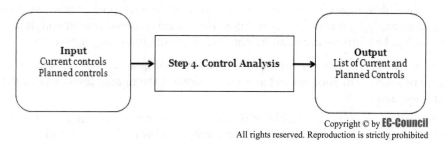

Figure 5-6   Control analysis evaluates current and planned controls.

It is essential to maintain and update the security requirements checklist, as the use of this checklist would be a benefit in analyzing controls efficiently. The security requirements checklist can be used to validate security compliance and noncompliance.

Step 5: Likelihood Determination

This step determines the likelihood of the occurrence of a threat, as shown in Figure 5-7. The following factors help in deriving the overall likelihood rating:

- Motivation and capability of the threat source
- Nature of the vulnerability
- Efficiency and existence of current controls

The likelihood level of a threat source can be described as high, medium, or low. These are described in Figure 5-8.

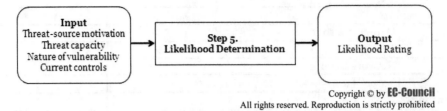

Figure 5-7   A number of factors determines the likelihood of a successful threat.

Likelihood Level	Likelihood Definition
High	The threat-source is highly motivated and sufficiently capable, and controls to prevent the vulnerability from being exercised are ineffective.
Medium	The threat-source is motivated and capable, but controls are in place that may impede successful exercise of the vulnerability.
Low	The threat-source lacks motivation or capability, or controls are in place to prevent, or at least significantly impede, the vulnerability from being exercised.

Figure 5-8   Threats must be assessed according to their likelihood.

Step 6: Impact Analysis

An *impact analysis* determines the impact that a threat could have on a system, as shown in Figure 5-9. To perform an impact analysis, it is necessary to know the system mission, system and data criticality, and system and data sensitivity. This information can be obtained from the following reports:

- *Mission impact analysis report*: Based on a qualitative or quantitative assessment of the sensitivity and criticality of assets, a mission impact analysis prioritizes the impact levels associated with the compromise of those assets.

- *Asset criticality assessment*: An asset criticality assessment identifies and prioritizes the sensitive and critical information assets that support the critical missions of the organization.

If these reports do not exist, the system and data sensitivity can be evaluated depending upon the confidentiality, integrity, and availability of the information. The three qualitative categories—high, medium, and low—are described in Figure 5-10.

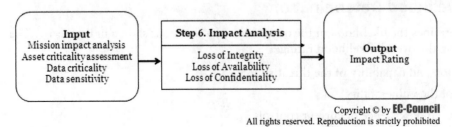

Figure 5-9   An impact analysis determines the effect that a threat could have on an organization.

Magnitude of Impact	Impact Definition
High	Exercise of the vulnerability (1) may result in the highly costly loss of major tangible assets or resources; (2) may significantly violate, harm, or impede an organization's mission, reputation, or interest; or (3) may result in human death or serious injury.
Medium	Exercise of the vulnerability (1) may result in the costly loss of tangible assets or resources; (2) may violate, harm, or impede an organization's mission, reputation, or interest; or (3) may result in human injury.
Low	Exercise of the vulnerability (1) may result in the loss of some tangible assets or resources or (2) may noticeably affect an organization's mission, reputation, or interest.

Figure 5-10   Impact ratings help organizations assess the value of addressing threats.

During an impact analysis, qualitative and quantitative assessments are also taken into account. A qualitative impact analysis prioritizes the risks involved and thus identifies the immediate improvement areas. A quantitative impact analysis provides the impact's magnitude measurement, which in turn is used for a cost-benefit analysis of the recommended controls.

Step 7: Risk Determination

Risk determination is a crucial task in a risk assessment effort, as shown in Figure 5-11. It is a complex process and depends upon various tangible and intangible factors. Though it is generally difficult to determine the exact level of risk to different organizational processes and assets, a careful consideration of various risk determinants gives an overall perception of risks faced by the organization. Risk determination involves a consideration of the following factors:

- *The probability of occurrence of an anticipated incident*: An incident is the result of a threat source exploiting system vulnerabilities.

- *The tangible and intangible impact of an incident on organizational resources*: Tangible impacts of an incident are easier to measure and can be represented by statistical analysis, whereas intangible impacts such as loss of reputation and customer trust are difficult to assess and can be determined only as a perception.

- *The control measures used to minimize impact*: Selection and implementation of control measures is based on risk determination and various management issues such as cost-benefit analysis and availability of resources.

Various standards bodies such as NIST have developed risk scales and risk matrices based on a categorization of risk levels as low, medium, and high, which help in determining the security posture of an organization.

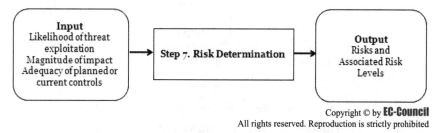

Figure 5-11   Risk determination takes all of the previous calculations and finds risks with associated risk levels.

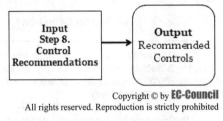

Figure 5-12   Recommended controls
are the results of the entire risk
assessment process.

Step 8: Recommendations to Control the Threats

Control recommendation and implementation is the main purpose of the whole risk assessment exercise, as shown in Figure 5-12. Risk assessment teams recommend the controls based on the likelihood, impact, and criticality of risk for a business operation.

Risk assessment teams need to consider these factors when recommending risk control measures:

- The control should meet the basic principle of a cost-benefit ratio.
- Controls should be implementable within the organization's ethics and security policy.
- The recommended solutions should be compatible with the organization's existing system.
- Controls must be within legislative and regulatory boundaries.
- The reliability of controls should be verified by using previous case studies and preimplementation tests.
- The controls should not go against the safety requirements of personnel and resources.

The implementation of controls depends on many business and management issues. Senior management in the organization has to determine the effectiveness of controls based on technical feedback and available case studies.

Step 9: Results Documentation

Each step of a risk assessment and the results should be properly documented, as shown in Figure 5-13. Documentation is critical to a risk assessment. An official, detailed, and clear risk assessment report helps senior management make decisions on policies, procedures, and system, operational, and management changes.

The documentation should be well structured and include supporting information. It should provide miscellaneous information that could help senior management implement mitigation strategies and allocate resources to mitigate risks in order to reduce potential losses. Figure 5-14 is a general risk assessment report.

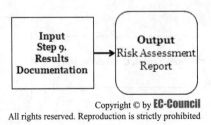

Figure 5-13   The final product of
the risk assessment process is a risk
assessment report.

Risk No.	Vulnerability	Threat	Risk	Risk Summary	Risk Likelihood Rating	Risk Impact Rating	Overall Risk Rating	Analysis of Relevant Controls and Other Factors	Recommendations

Figure 5-14   A risk assessment report is the final result of a risk assessment.

Attack Methods

Attacks against information systems have a number of potential targets. These attacks are differentiated in the following ways

- Attacks aimed at disclosing information; the following attacks are common examples:
  - Manipulation of a user's client
  - Eavesdropping on the network
  - Stealing a user's session
  - Manipulating the program files on the application server
  - Stealing backup copies with a known password
  - Exploiting vulnerabilities in the server operating system
- Attacks against information integrity; the following attacks are common examples:
  - Stealing an existing user ID
  - Circumventing the system's security controls
  - Manipulating data when they are transferred over the network
- Attacks aimed at causing unavailability; the following attacks are common examples:
  - Physical destruction
  - Crashing network interface software or the operating system
  - Manipulation of the network's components
  - Flooding
  - Attacking an operating system
  - Attacking an application file server

Attack Phases

By assessing the different phases of an attack, security personnel can understand the security measures necessary for each phase, as shown in Figure 5-15. The following three phases constitute an attack:

1. *Probing stage*: This is the stage in which the attacker finds loopholes in the security system. If the attack is detected at this stage, it will be easy to mitigate the risk before damage is done to the system.

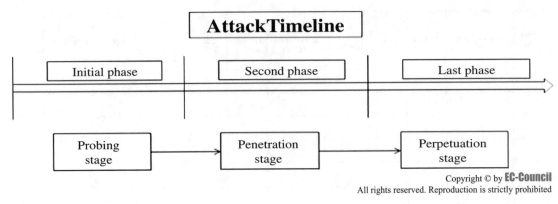

Figure 5-15   Attacks occur in three phases.

2. *Penetration stage*: In this stage, an attacker attempts to surpass the security controls so as to harm the information security system. This phase can cause harm to a system, but it is not targeted specifically at information, so the damage is usually repairable. It is similar to a thief damaging a fence or an alarm system. Attacks such as unauthorized access and denial of service (DoS) are examples of this type of attack.

3. *Perpetuation stage*: In this stage, the attacker successfully penetrates into the network or system to perform malicious activities. These attacks can result in disclosure of information, manipulation of data, and destruction of information.

Countermeasures

Security Countermeasures

Security countermeasures are the actions or solutions used to prevent attacks. The following types of controls are implemented to prevent attacks:

- Technical security controls
- Operational security controls
- Management security controls

Technical Security Controls

Technical security controls involve the use of technological measures to control risks. The following are some examples of technical controls:

- Supporting technical controls; this includes the following controls:
  - Identification
  - Cryptographic key management
  - System protections
- Preventive technical controls; this includes the following controls:
  - Authentication and authorization
  - Access control enforcement
  - Protected communications and transaction privacy
- Detection and recovery technical controls; this includes the following controls:
  - Auditing and restoration of the secure state
  - Intrusion detection and containment
  - Virus detection and eradication

Operational Security Controls

These controls are implemented by the organization considering the present set of requirements and good organizational practices. Operational security controls include the following examples:

- Preventive operational controls:
  - Control the media access to data
  - Restrict the data distribution to external sources
  - Safeguard the computing facility
  - Provide backup capability
  - Secure IT assets from damage due to fire
  - Provide an emergency power source
- Detection operational controls:
  - Maintain physical security
  - Ensure environmental security

Management Security Controls

These controls, in combination with technical and operational controls, are implemented to handle, control, and minimize the risk of loss and to secure the mission of an organization. These include the following controls:

- Preventive management security controls; the following controls are common examples:
  - Allocate security responsibility so that sufficient security is maintained
  - Develop and maintain system security plans
  - Implement personnel security controls
  - Organize security awareness programs and technical training
- Detection management security controls; the following controls are common examples:
  - Execute personnel security controls
  - Perform reviews of security controls
  - Perform periodic system audits
  - Conduct ongoing risk management
- Recovery management security controls; the following controls are common examples:
  - Provide continuity of support
  - Establish an incident response capability

Technical Surveillance Countermeasures

Technical surveillance countermeasure (TSCM) techniques are used to detect and neutralize the hostile penetration technologies used to gain unauthorized access to confidential and sensitive information.

TSCM programs recognize and allow the user to correct utilizable technical and physical security vulnerabilities. TSCM techniques involve the following procedures:

- *Detection*: Detecting devices that contain threats
- *Nullification*: Using passive and active measures to neutralize the threat devices
- *Isolation*: Restricting the use of secure areas and ensuring the proper construction for those areas
- *Education*: Providing education to people regarding threats, installation of new equipment, and renovation

Weighing the Costs and Benefits of Risk Management

The cost of a potential attack can be calculated according to the data loss and the business affected by the data loss. The execution of the attack handling and response plans also incurs costs for resources and materials.

The cost of an attack is calculated depending on estimates of the following necessities:

- Loss of business because the information resources are not available
- Compromising productivity from non-IT staff
- Labor and materials cost of the IT staff related to detection and repair of the breached resources
- Labor cost of obtaining forensic evidence and prosecuting the attacker
- Public relations consulting costs

Risk Countermeasure Analysis

A risk countermeasure analysis is conducted to weigh the effectiveness and economic benefits of countermeasures. Countermeasure analysis is conducted through the following steps:

1. *Prioritize actions*: After the risk assessment is finished, the first step is to give priority to the task with the highest risk.
2. *Evaluate the recommended control options*: The suggested controls are analyzed to judge their effectiveness.
3. *Conduct the cost-benefit analysis*: The worthiness of the countermeasures is taken into consideration before they are implemented.
4. *Select the cost-effective control*: The most cost-effective solution is chosen from the various solutions suggested.
5. *Assign responsibility*: The appropriate person must be given the responsibility to implement the controls.
6. *Develop a safeguard implementation plan*: The countermeasures should be implemented as per the plan, and all the safety precautions should be taken while doing this.
7. *Implement selected control*: Finally, the countermeasures should actually be implemented.

Cost-Benefit Analysis

A cost-benefit analysis is performed on the solutions suggested for countering the risk. The cost of the risk mitigation controls is compared with the probable economic impacts of the threat. Organizations look for other options if the cost of the data loss due to the risk is less than the cost of the proposed controls.

Cost-benefit analysis also helps organizations decide the most effective solution to implement. If there is more than one option to counter the risk, then the cost-benefit analysis will help the organization choose the most economically viable solution. Figure 5-16 illustrates the cost-benefit analysis process.

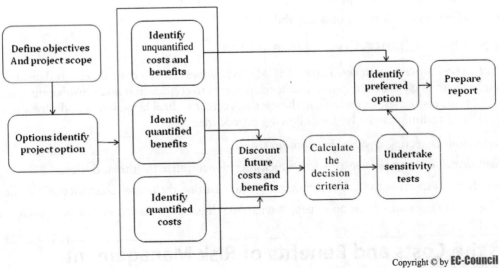

Figure 5-16 The cost-benefit analysis process allows organizations to gauge the economic viability of countering risks.

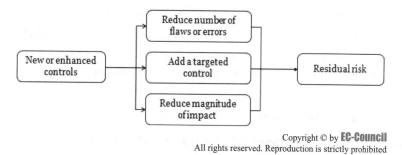

Figure 5-17   Residual risk takes unforeseen issues into account.

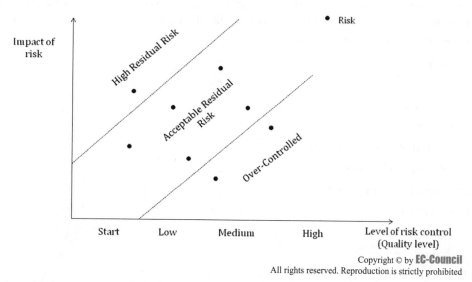

Figure 5-18   Residual risk can be graphed to determine its severity.

Residual Risk

After the implementation of countermeasures to counter the risk factors, there may still be issues that were not covered or that come up after the assessment. This possibility is called *residual risk* (Figure 5-17). It is impossible to be sure that all risks have been taken into account. Thus, the residual risk is always there, even after the implementation of the best suitable countermeasures.

Residual risk should always be taken into account by organizations performing a risk assessment. Sometimes, there are issues that cannot be mitigated by the implementation of any possible solution; those kinds of issues are also categorized as residual risk. The graph in Figure 5-18 can be used to determine the severity of residual risk.

Risk Assessment Responsibilities

Information Assurance

Information assurance refers to policies, procedures, and solutions that help minimize the risks in an information system. There are five common security principles that system developers and risk acceptors should consider when deciding on an appropriate level of information assurance:

1. *Confidentiality*: Confidential information should not be disclosed to unauthorized individuals, processes, or devices.

2. *Integrity*: Protecting the information against unauthorized modification or destruction.

3. *Availability*: Providing reliable information access to authorized users.

4. *Authentication*: Verifying the authorization of individuals to receive specific categories of information.

5. *Nonrepudiation*: The sender of the information should be given a delivery proof, and the recipient of the information should be given the identity of the information sender, so neither can deny having processed the data.

Maintenance Responsibilities

System Activities for Chronological, Analytical Reconstruction and Maintenance of System Components

Information systems acquire, process, and store information. These systems are accessed by users and organizations for normal operations and decision making. Maintenance of information assurance depends on access controls implemented in systems. Organizations should keep chronological records of all system processes and accesses to ensure security and responsibility for any incident involving the information system. System activity records should include the following activities:

- File access
- Buffer activity
- System call statistics
- Disk activity
- Page-out and memory operations
- Kernel memory allocation
- Interprocess communication
- Page-in activity
- Queue activity
- Unused memory
- CPU utilization
- System table status
- Swap activity
- Terminal activity

Security Product Integration

With the evolution of technology, integrating different security products such as firewall, antivirus, and anti-spam systems becomes increasingly complex. Providing the functionality of these products is an essential aspect of establishing a consistent security profile. Finally, the association of these technologies is also essential for the delivery of technology solutions to support compliance programs that are more critical to organizations in today's business environment.

Security product integration provides the following benefits:

- Provides increased efficiency by creating a unified system
- Provides complementary technologies designed to help the organization's IT security
- Reduces network outages caused by worms and viruses
- Contains association of the features and functions across different product types
- Offers functionalities such as installation, implementation, tuning, and training

Maintenance of User Accounts

The process of user account maintenance begins with the creation of a new user account. For example, when a new employee joins the company, his or her new account should be created and assigned to the correct organizational unit (OU) in the Active Directory structure. The organization should assign the correct group policies to the OU. When an employee changes positions at the company, that employee should also be moved within the OU structure. When an employee quits, the account should be disabled and moved out of the ordinary OU structure. Short-term or temporary employees should be given accounts with a particular expiration date.

Processes for Timely Deletion of Accounts The timely deletion of user and group accounts is important for information assurance. Attackers can exploit unused accounts to gain unauthorized access to system resources and compromise system security. Account deletion policies should consider these factors:

- *Expiration period*: An expiration time is set on an employee's account to provide a grace period before the employee's account is actually inaccessible to the user.

- *Suspension period*: After the user's expiration period has elapsed, the user's account is suspended for a set number of days, during which the user cannot access the account.

- *Account deletion*: After the end of the suspension period, all the data associated with the account are deleted.

- *Backup cycle time*: After the account is deleted, the data associated with the account will still be stored on the backup media for a set period of time.

Change Control

Change control is a method used to ensure that the changes to a system are made in a controlled and coordinated manner. It minimizes the possibility of making unnecessary modifications to the system. A change control method should be implemented for the following reasons:

- Minimal disruption to services

- Reduction in back-out activities

- Cost-effective utilization of resources

Change control is commonly used in different products and systems. For IT systems, it is the main feature of the broader discipline of change management. Change controls for computer and network environments include the following examples:

- Patches to software products

- Installation of new operating systems

- Upgrades to network routing tables

- Changes to the electrical power systems

Maintenance Procedures Concerning Life Cycle Operations and Analysis Issues

The maintenance of an application system starts when the system is put into operation, as shown in Figure 5-19. In the maintenance phase of the system life cycle, ongoing system maintenance should be performed to ensure the performance and functionality of the system match the business requirements of the users.

System maintenance includes the following steps:

1. *Maintenance planning*: The maintenance plan should be prepared well before the system is put into operation. The following information should be included in the maintenance plan:

    - Role assignments

    - Maintenance activities

    - Maintenance resources and facilities

2. *System nursing*: This period should start before the development team delivers the system to the maintenance team. Monitoring and tuning is conducted during this period to ensure a smooth transition of the system.

3. *System monitoring and tuning*: This step involves continued monitoring and tuning of the application system operations and should be performed to ensure smooth operation and to increase efficiency and effectiveness.

4. *System maintenance cycle stage*: System maintenance goes through these stages:

    - Initiation

    - Impact analysis

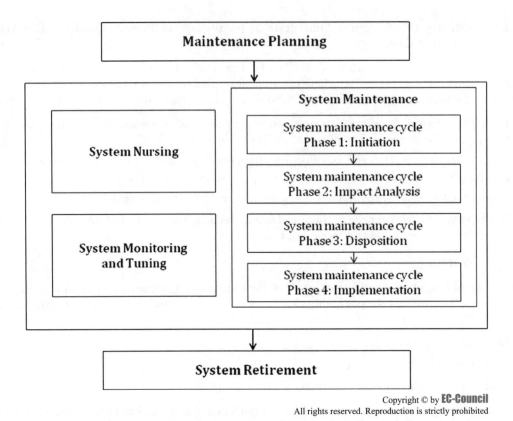

Figure 5-19   System maintenance is an essential aspect of risk management.

- Disposition
- Implementation

5. *System retirement*: This is the process of removing an existing system from active use by replacing its operations with a new system. This process should be designed with detailed procedures.

Responsibilities of Security Personnel

Responsibilities of Information Systems Security Officer (ISSO)

Information systems security officers (ISSOs) have the following responsibilities:

- Ensure that information systems are operated in accordance with security policies
- Implement the security policies and safeguards on all personnel having access to information systems
- Report the security status of information systems to the information systems security manager (ISSM)
- Maintain the system security plan
- Ensure that TEMPEST measures have not been altered; *TEMPEST* is a government project studying compromising electrical, mechanical, or acoustical energy emissions unintentionally emitted by electrical equipment/systems such as computers, monitors, or transmission lines, allowing the information therein to be captured
- Ensure that all computers display access warning banners
- Provide training and awareness activities to users
- Work with the physical security personnel to provide physical security for information system assets
- Provide protective or corrective measures when a security problem is identified
- Support the accreditation of the information systems

- Ensure that security audits are reviewed periodically and that audit records are archived for future reference
- Report incidents to an ISSM by creating a security incident reporting mechanism
- Develop proactive and corrective measures to prevent security problems

Responsibilities of System Administrator

The system administrator is a member of the IT department who maintains the computer system and network. The administrator's responsibilities may vary from one organization to another.

Generally, administrators are responsible for installing systems, supporting and maintaining servers, and planning the IT infrastructure to support the organization's business objectives. The administrator is also responsible for responding to service outages and other system-related problems.

The system administrator should make decisions in the following areas:

- *Audit mechanism*: Ascertain the validity and reliability of information.
- *Software options*: Decide which software is to be installed and allowed on a system.
- *Access permissions*: The access to important information should be given only to authorized personnel.
- *Maintenance of user authentication data*: Maintain data for user authentication purposes.
- *Detecting and preventing unauthorized system access*: Use tools and software to restrict unauthorized access to the system.

Responsibilities of Information System Owner

The information system owner is a member of senior management who defines objectives and priorities, oversees and approves the development of all deliverables documents, manages resource allocations, and decides on the acquisition of new services for an information system.

The responsibilities of the system owner and data owner may be different, depending on the size of the system. The system owner is accountable for all modifications and improvements made to a system, including making decisions for the overall replacement of a system. The system owner plays the role of steering committee chairperson and allocates portions of the budget and high-level resources for system maintenance. The system owner also manages the accreditation process that determines when a system change is ready for implementation. The system owner must also be aware of new technologies, risks, threats, regulations, and market trends.

Responsibilities of System Developers

The system developer is the expert who has the technical knowledge necessary for providing solutions related to an information system's services and requirements. The system developer controls the process of system development. System developers obtain information about the customer's requirements and develop the system according to those requirements.

System developers have the following responsibilities:

- Defining the process for selecting and purchasing new information technology
- Verifying the functionality of an application
- Providing risk methodologies to evaluate measures taken to protect the system
- Analyzing maintenance practices, procedures, and measures to ensure an acceptable level of risk

Responsibilities of Agency Vendors as Members of the Risk Management Team

Members of the risk management team are responsible for the following tasks:

- Identifying the organization's exposures to accidental loss
- Implementing the required financial protection measures with the help of the risk transfer, risk avoidance, and risk retention programs
- Developing and updating a system to communicate the components of the risk management program throughout the organization
- Designing master insurance and self-insurance programs
- Maintaining sufficient insurance coverage at a reasonable cost

- Determining cost-effective ways to build a protection system for loss prevention
- Implementing loss prevention or loss retention programs
- Providing guidelines to handle all property and liability claims involving the organization
- Managing claims for both insured and uninsured losses
- Complying with local insurance laws
- Establishing deductible levels
- Distributing insurance premiums
- Issuing certificates as necessary
- Developing risk management policies and procedures

Automated Testing

Automated tests contain consistent and repeatable test methods. They provide a high degree of efficiency by allowing testers to rapidly test predefined controls. In addition, the automated tools help to test the system's security. Creating automated tests requires a thorough understanding of a system's architecture in order to make sure the tests cover as much of the system as possible.

There are two major issues regarding the use of automated tools:

1. They are limited to testing the parameters for which they were designed.

2. It may be difficult to map the use of an automated tool to all necessary requirements.

Information System Auditing

Information system auditing involves the evaluation of a system's processes and security to verify the validity and reliability of information. It involves recording events such as modifications, access, deletions, and additions of data in an information system.

Auditing procedures must include the following tasks:

- Creating an annual audit program
- Selection of the auditor and team leader
- Planning specific types of audits
- Conducting audits
- Recording observations
- Determining corrective actions
- Implementing corrective actions
- Confirming the effectiveness of the corrective actions

Verification of Tools and Techniques

Verification of Techniques

Verification of information assurance tools and techniques is a complex process and requires a thorough analysis of various functional and structural components. Verification techniques can be broadly categorized in the following ways:

- *Dynamic testing*: Dynamic testing refers to the verification of tools and techniques in their operational state. It involves the execution of the system components. In this testing, the system is made to run on different test input cases, and the results are analyzed to determine the efficiency of tools and techniques. Dynamic testing is categorized into the following three types:
  - *Functional testing*: This refers to testing the functional efficiency of the system.
  - *Structural testing*: This testing makes use of knowledge of the internal structures of an information system to assess the performance of the system and its various components.

- *Random testing*: Random testing involves selecting test cases from all possible test cases. It uses randomly determined inputs to detect the faults that cannot be easily detected by other testing techniques.
- *Static testing*: Static testing does not involve the implementation of a system or component. Some static testing techniques are performed manually, while others are automated. Static testing is categorized into the following two types:
  - *Consistency techniques*: This testing checks for the consistency of various system variables and program properties.
  - *Measurement techniques*: Measurement testing is a quantitative testing that aims to determine the probability of vulnerabilities in a system, considering various determinants such as understandability and the structure of the system.
- *Validation techniques*:
  - *Formal methods*: Formal methods involve the use of mathematical and logical techniques to determine the characteristics of the hardware and software components of a system.
  - *Fault injection*: This method involves the intentional creation of faults to test how the system operates under different fault conditions.
  - *Dependability analysis*: Dependability analysis is a method that involves identifying hazards and providing methods to reduce the risk of hazards.
  - *Hazard analysis*: Hazard analysis is a method that involves identifying hazards, their root causes, and potential countermeasures.
  - *Risk analysis*: Risk analysis is a process identifying the possible consequences of each hazard and the possibility of it occurring.

Acquisitions

System Acquisition

System acquisition is a process that starts from the time the decision is made to select a new system until the time a contract has been negotiated and signed. The process of selecting or acquiring a system can take anywhere from a few days to a couple of years depending on the size, structure, and needs of an organization.

The system acquisition process includes the following steps:

1. Define the project's objectives.
2. Determine the system's goals.
3. Determine the system's requirements.
4. Find a potential supplier or vendor.
5. Develop and distribute the Request for Information (RFI) and Request for Proposal (RFP).
6. Identify other options for acquiring the system.
7. Evaluate the vendor's proposal.
8. Conduct a cost-benefit analysis.
9. Prepare a summary report.
10. Conduct a contract negotiation.

Selecting and Purchasing New IT Solutions

The following points should be kept in mind when selecting an IT solution:

- *Understand and prioritize business objectives*: Understanding business objectives allows management to identify what a business really needs. It is essential to review all available solutions in an organization before selecting a new system.
- *Vendor demonstration*: When purchasing a new solution, management should make sure the vendor demonstrates how the solution will meet the business and operational needs. In the demonstration, vendors will explain all the features of their solution. This is a good time to ask questions about the solution.

- *Compare prices accurately*: To compare prices accurately, management should ask vendors if their figures contain real-time agent adherence, Web access for agents and supervisors, maintenance and support, and training. Comparing prices will give a clear idea about the price of the solution compared to other solutions.
- *Seek solutions that can be remotely installed*: Management should find a vendor who provides solutions that can be installed remotely. On-site installation will increase the ownership cost and also require more time compared to a remote installation.
- *Make ROI calculations*: Many vendors provide an ROI (return on investment). Some vendors make statistical adjustments. Creating an ROI tailored to the organization will aid the decision-making process.

Software Acquisitions

The software acquisition process includes the following steps:

1. *Requesting software*: This step involves identifying the software needs and obtaining approval from the IT department to purchase that software.
2. *Purchasing licenses for software*: In this step, the complete purchase order request is sent to the IT department for verification and approval. If any changes are required in the request order, the IT department contacts the requesting department.
3. *Receiving software*: After receiving the software, the IT department follows the company's check-in procedure to ensure that the new software is added to the software inventory.
4. *Distributing software*: The IT department provides the software to the requesting department. The IT department also contacts the requesting department to schedule the installation of the software.
5. *Ensuring software documentation is available to end users*: Copies of the end-user license agreement should be made available to the end users in the receiving department.

System Disposition/Reutilization

The system disposition plan is a major consideration in the disposition of an information system. The purpose of this plan is to provide an approach for ending the operating life of the system. It ensures that all data are properly archived or transferred to another system.

System disposition/reutilization includes the following procedures:

- *Notifications*: The plan for identifying the users of a system before it is shut down and notifying those users
- *Data disposition*: The plan for archiving, deleting, or transferring the data files from one system to another system, before the system is shut down
- *System documentation disposition*: The plan for archiving, deleting, or transferring documentation from one system to another system, before the system is shut down
- *Equipment disposition*: The plan for archiving, removing, or transferring hardware and other devices from one system to another system, before the system is shut down

Tools

Xacta IA Manager

Xacta IA Manager (Figure 5-20) combines security compliance and risk assessment functionality with business process automation to establish a centralized governance, risk, and compliance management platform that facilitates compliance assessment, continuous risk assessment, sustained compliance management, and security process automation.

Xacta IA Manager includes the following functions:

- Enforces processes for compliance with FISMA, FDCC/SCAP, DIACAP, DCID, GLBA, HIPAA, ISO 17799, SOX, and more
- Collects extensive IT asset inventory data

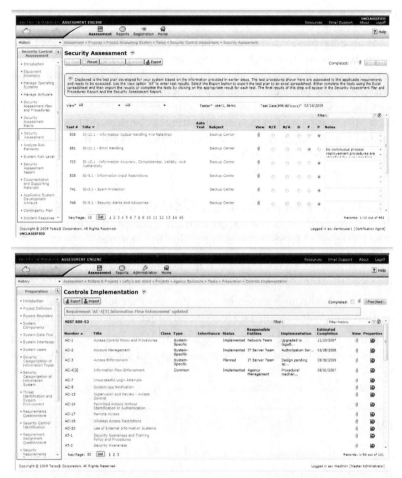

Source: http://images.telos.com/files/external/XIAM-SP8d-Brochure.pdf. Accessed 9/2009.

Figure 5-20   Xacta IA Manager handles many aspects of risk management.

- Detects, identifies, and remediates threats to system security
- Continuously assesses security posture
- Automates security policies and enforces procedures
- Generates the reports and documentation needed for regulatory compliance

SecureInfo RMS

SecureInfo RMS supports all phases of the DoD Information Assurance Certification and Accreditation Process (DIACAP) and National Institute of Standards and Technology (NIST) certification and accreditation process, and guides users through the steps necessary to create consistent documentation. It includes a content library that links and maps all federal, Department of Defense (DoD), service branch (Air Force, Army, Navy, Marines), and intelligence community security requirements to applicable information assurance (IA) controls. It includes the following features:

- Complete set of standards documents and templates
- Flexible workflow, including e-mail alerting, document management, privilege-based access/control, and expired certification and accreditation package alerts
- Extensible reporting framework supports Federal Information Security Management Act (FISMA) reporting, plans of action and milestones (POA&Ms), DIACAP reporting, and user-defined configurable reports
- Common enterprise directory support enables a centralized database for system users (supports Lightweight Directory Access Protocol [LDAP] and Microsoft Active Directory)

Trusted Agent FISMA (TAF)

Trusted Agent FISMA is an enterprise compliance and oversight tool that manages the collection and reporting of a component's information associated with key information security practices and controls. It comes with a digital dashboard that aggregates the data collected in Trusted Agent FISMA and is used as a visual tool using a traffic light display to gauge the progress of the department-wide information security program.

The digital dashboard serves as a management tool to ensure the components take a risk-based, cost-effective approach to secure their information and information systems, identify and resolve current information security weaknesses and risks, and protect against future vulnerabilities and threats. It allows management to monitor the components' remediation efforts to identify progress and problems.

eMASS

The Enterprise Mission Assurance Support System, or eMASS, is a government-owned, commercial off-the-shelf (COTS) software-based certification and accreditation solution. It is purposefully designed to be flexible for future upgrades and changes. eMASS includes the following features:

- eMASS Web certification and accreditation is a government-developed package that facilitates and automates the security certification and accreditation process.

- The product leads the user through a step-by-step process that identifies risks and assesses network and system configuration compliance with DITSCAP and other applicable regulations.

- eMASS's functionality includes the ability to explain and distribute security directives, handbooks, and detailed technical security configuration guidelines and security best practices to system administrators.

Chapter Summary

- The maintenance of an application system starts when the system is put into operation.
- Risk analysis is a process identifying the possible consequences of each hazard and the possibility of [it] occurring.
- Residual risk is the risk or danger that remains after the implementation of new or enhanced controls.
- Risk assessment is the process of identifying and assessing the resources that pose a threat to the business or project environment.
- Risk management is the process of identifying risk, addressing risk, and taking steps to eliminate or reduce risk to an acceptable level.
- Risk management should be implemented in all phases of SDLC.
- IT system administrators should have a thorough knowledge of the system processing environment.

Review Questions

1. Discuss the roles and responsibilities of the system administrator in the risk evaluation process.

2. Explain the different steps of the system acquisition process.

3. What are the responsibilities of system developers?

_____

_____

_____

_____

4. Explain the risk analysis process.

_____

_____

_____

_____

5. Discuss the importance of cost-benefit analysis for the implementation of risk control measures.

_____

_____

_____

_____

6. What are residual risks? Suggest appropriate controls to contain residual risks within an acceptable limit.

_____

_____

_____

_____

7. Discuss the various steps of the risk assessment methodology.

_____

_____

_____

_____

8. Describe the process of threat identification.

_____

_____

_____

_____

9. Explain how risk management can be integrated with an IT system's SDLC.

_____

_____

_____

_____

10. Explain the characteristics of the development and acquisition phase from a risk management perspective.

_____

_____

_____

_____

Hands-On Projects

1. Navigate to Chapter 5 of the Student Resource Center. Open IMAToolsTechniques.pdf and read the following topics:

   ■ Executive Summary

   ■ Risk Identification Techniques

   ■ Analysis of Risk by Drivers

2. Navigate to Chapter 5 of the Student Resource Center. Open ai00033.pdf and read the following topics:

   ■ Introduction

   ■ Risk Management Cycle

3. Navigate to Chapter 5 of the Student Resource Center. Open FRMWRK_ERA.pdf and read the following topics:

   ■ Introduction

   ■ PROBLEM FORMULATION

4. Navigate to Chapter 5 of the Student Resource Center. Open 4014.pdf and read the following topics:

   ■ Scope Applicability

   ■ Infosec Performance Standard for the ISSO (Entry, Intermediate & Advanced Levels)

Chapter 6

Risk Control Policies and Countermeasures

Objectives

After completing this chapter, you should be able to:

- Determine countermeasures
- Develop policies for risk analysis
- Conduct a cost-benefit analysis
- Categorize information
- Conduct configuration management
- Identify system security policies
- Implement change control policies
- Develop access control policies
- Manage electronic records
- Develop policies for capturing audit logs

Key Terms

Countermeasure   any action, device, procedure, or technique used to reduce vulnerabilities or risks

Introduction to Risk Control Policies and Countermeasures

Because there are inherent risks in running any business or organization, they must be dealt with in a number of different ways. Some risks can be totally eliminated if doing so will not harm the organization; however, other risks are necessary factors in running particular types of organizations. For example, running a publicly accessible Web site increases the risk of hacking attacks, but Web sites are necessary for most organizations.

After risks to an organization have been identified, organizations must respond to them through the use of countermeasures. *Countermeasures* are any actions, devices, procedures, or techniques used to reduce vulnerabilities or risks. Specific devices, such as firewalls, can eliminate certain risks, but there are other risks that must be dealt with through the use of policies. For example, mistakes by staff and personnel often pose a threat to information that can equal or surpass the threat of malicious hackers. This problem cannot be solved by a device, so a policy must be enacted to deal with it. Risk control policies take into account the degree of risk that an organization is willing to accept in a number of different areas and mitigate risks accordingly.

Countermeasures

Determining Security Countermeasures

Because there are different vulnerabilities possible, it is necessary to determine the specific countermeasures for each type of threat. Countermeasure determination is an important factor in the success of any risk management and business continuity effort.

Countermeasures should be selected based on the following criteria:

- Threat statement and assets to be protected
- Incident and events type
- The relevant resources that are available
- Effectiveness to handle the threats

Determine Countermeasures Based on Threat Capabilities and Motivations

Organizations can determine the proper countermeasures using the following steps:

1. Identify potential countermeasures to reduce the threats.
2. Identify the level of risk reduction with the use of countermeasures.
3. Determine the cost required for the chosen countermeasures.
4. Conduct the cost-benefit analysis and the trade-off analysis of countermeasures.
5. Analyze the options to be prioritized and recommend those options to the decision-maker.

Risk Control Policy Development Factors

Development of IA Principles and Practices

Development of information assurance principles and practices takes the factors discussed in the following sections into account.

Organizational Security Policy

Organizational security policies are the basis of any information assurance effort. Organizations should develop and implement appropriate security policies in order to achieve IA. The security policies should be developed after the risk assessment process and should be based on commonly accepted policy standards defined by various organizations such as NIST (National Institute of Standards and Technology) and the ISO (International Organization for Standardization).

Implementation of organizational security policies in accordance with organizational business objectives ensures long-term information security for the organization. These security policies must be well documented and made available to all concerned stakeholders. Management should develop a comprehensive program to make employees aware of these security policies.

Defined and Documented Security Infrastructure

The security infrastructure includes all the control measures implemented in an organization to protect information systems, such as intrusion detection systems, firewalls, and antivirus systems. The security infrastructure varies according to the operating environment and risk perception of an organization.

Organizations should clearly define and document the entire available security infrastructure in order to provide an immediate response to the security requirements of the system. Documents related to security infrastructure should be readily available to all the users and user groups that are responsible for information assurance.

Education

Training and awareness are major components of an information assurance program. Policy and control implementation will be useless if employees and other stakeholders are not aware of these policies. Information assurance principles encourage organizations to develop comprehensive training and awareness programs. These training programs should cover anyone who has access to the information system. Employees of the organization should be aware of security issues related to their field of work and duties.

Asset Management

Information asset management in an organization refers to the acquisition, maintenance, and security of all the assets that store or process information. Organizations should develop and implement asset management policies to ensure the accountability of information systems. Asset management provides a baseline for information assurance and helps the organization develop appropriate security controls for the system.

Business Continuity

Business continuity and information assurance are interdependent concepts in an information system. Any compromise related to information assurance may lead to business discontinuity and vice versa. Organizations should develop and implement comprehensive business continuity plans that help protect information in case of a disaster or security incident. These plans should include technical and procedural controls to back up and restore data in case of a disaster.

Regulatory Compliance

Regulatory compliance ensures that an information system meets a certain base security level. Compliance issues are often interlinked with information assurance in an organization. Organizations should develop and implement required policies, controls, and infrastructures to achieve compliance with established standards and laws. This ensures information security and also saves organizations from legal liabilities arising due to any compromise in information assurance.

Laws and Procedures in Information Assurance (IA) Policy Implementation

The following domestic and international laws address IA policy implementation:

- *Official Secrets Act*: The Official Secrets Act is used for the protection of official information related to national security. This act requires employees to avoid unauthorized disclosure of information. It requires employees who are working with confidential information to sign a statement that they agree to follow the restrictions of the Official Secrets Act.

- *Data Protection Act*: The Data Protection Act is mainly used for the protection of sensitive and confidential data. This act requires that personal data be protected safely and accessed only by authorized users. This act is part of a piece of legislation that manages the protection of personal data.

- *Computer Misuse Act*: The Computer Misuse Act is a law that makes activities such as hacking computer systems, helping a person access the information of another person, and the unauthorized modification of computer materials illegal.

- *Freedom of Information Act*: The Freedom of Information Act provides the right to access information held by public authorities unless there are good reasons to keep it confidential. This act defines the agency's records that can be disclosed, provides a list of mandatory disclosure procedures, and provides nine exceptions to disclosure.

Security Test and Evaluation

Security test and evaluation (ST&E) is performed to review the security controls of information systems. Testing helps to ensure a secured operating environment by fulfilling the security requirements.

The objective of ST&E is to uncover flaws present in the design, implementation, and operations performed by information systems. The ST&E team has the following responsibilities:

- Developing the test plan
- Executing the plan
- Documenting the test results

Security Test and Evaluation Methodology

The main objective of ST&E is to verify whether the system configuration and operational environment covers the basic security requirements of the information system, which is a prerequisite for the certification and accreditation process. The security test and evaluation methodology uses the following steps:

1. *Establish test objectives*: This helps to ensure the protection of the information systems by deciding how to test whether the appropriate security controls and the best practices and procedures for risk mitigation have been implemented.

2. *Develop the initial ST&E plan*: In this phase, the team creates a draft of the ST&E plan, which should include all the basic test objectives, procedures, and execution processes that are to be initiated while testing; the separate test procedures for each and every component of the information system; and the complete test procedures for management, operational, and technical security controls. In this phase, the involvement of the system owner can identify the components of the system and thus help the team in finalizing the plan.

3. *Develop ST&E procedures*: In this step, the test objectives are validated using test procedures that were developed initially. The team then verifies whether the system has met the stated test objectives. The team develops the initial security test and evaluation procedures depending upon the validated objectives, which include all the steps in detail so as to verify the effectiveness of all security controls. Once the effectiveness of all security controls is verified, the team has to perform a dry-run execution in order to check if all the objectives, procedures, and scripts are compatible with the system being tested.

4. *Conduct ST&E and document results*: Documentation should be clear and concise and should cover all the aspects of the ST&E procedure.

Roles and Responsibilities of the ST&E Team

The ST&E team has the following responsibilities:

- *Executing test procedures*: The ST&E team executes the test using the test procedures that are provided in the plan. It is essential for other technical personnel, such as system administrators, to be present during testing so they can witness and aid in the execution of the test procedures.

- *Interpreting the results*: The ST&E team must record the results such as whether the objectives being tested were met, not met, or not tested.

- *Conducting out-brief*: Once the results of the testing are documented, an informal out-brief is conducted between the ST&E team and the system owner in order to discuss and fix the critical findings (failure comments).

- *Developing the ST&E report*: The ST&E team develops an ST&E report, which includes the results documentation of each and every component of the information system tested, comments related to test objectives and procedures, and the findings of all the objectives. Each finding should include the following information:

  - *Test objective*: A test objective verified by the ST&E team
  - *Test objective number*: Identifier for the test objective
  - *Finding description*: A detailed description of how and why the test objective was not met while testing
  - *Control tested*: Document whether the management, operational, or technical controls were tested
  - *Recommendation*: Recommended steps to correct the findings

Automated Security Tools

Automated security tools enable security personnel to automate various incident management processes in an information system. These security tools may be used for traffic filtering and pattern analysis, log monitoring and management, security alerts, and operating system security. Automated tools acquire information from various system and traffic indicators, analyze the information, and alert administrators about any suspicious behavior in the system and network. The features and functionalities of automated security tools depend on the factors discussed in the following sections.

Event Logs

Event logs are important sources of system information on Windows systems. Automated security tools can analyze event logs for any suspicious system event. They can query large log databases for a historical analysis of patterns in system events and detect specified anomalies.

Processes

Automated tools monitor system processes for any suspicious processes and alert the system owners. Automated tools may detect the processes associated with malware in the system. System administrators should be aware of essential system processes and be able to recognize suspicious processes, because automated tools may also give false positives and terminate essential services.

Automated security tools can also alert in case a critical process is not available or turned off unexpectedly. They can be programmed to restart these processes and prevent essential services from being turned off.

Automated tools should be carefully configured to avoid false positives and negatives. Before reacting to any security alerts from these tools, administrators should manually verify the results. Though human intervention is required, automated tools can simplify the complex monitoring and analysis process.

System Counters

System counters are system performance indicators. Automated tools can use these indicators to alert system owners about suspicious system activity. System counters include cache memory usage, CPU utilization and usage history, paging file usage, and others. Any sudden changes in these counters indicate suspicious activity. For example, automated tools can alert administrators if virtual memory usage suddenly or unexpectedly increases or if the activity of the Winlogon process suddenly increases.

Services

Services offered by systems and their availability provide an indication of a system's health and security. Any loss in availability of these services may be an indication of system compromise. Automated tools can monitor the availability of these services and alert system administrators if there is any variation in expected service characteristics. These automated tools can also be configured to alert for the presence of any unnecessary or suspicious services. Automated tools can ensure the availability of critical system services.

Files

Files are the main repositories of information in any system. The creation, deletion, and manipulation of important files should be recorded and reported to system owners so that they can verify the file operations. Creating fake large files and deleting and manipulating important system and user files are the main characteristics of malware programs. Automated tools can alert system owners about any suspicious file operations.

There are a large number of commercial off-the-self security tools available that offer easy and affordable security capabilities to organizations, but the procurement of these automated security tools should follow a stringent process; otherwise, there are chances that the organization may end up with certain tools that are either not able to meet security requirements or may even create vulnerabilities in the system.

Cost-Benefit Analysis

A cost-benefit analysis (CBA) determines how well, or how poorly, a planned action will turn out. It shows whether the costs related to a planned action are worth the benefit the planned action will provide. Various CBA opportunities include staff addition, purchasing assets/equipment, developing a new workflow or modifying the workflow, and remodeling facilities.

CBA justification is organized into the following categories:

- *Hard dollar savings*: These are quantitative and easily calculated savings that represent real savings. They deal with the reduction and elimination of expenses through staff or supplies. Hard dollar savings provide the strongest case of justification.

- *Soft dollar savings*: These savings are qualitative and less directly calculated. They represent savings that cannot be recovered. They include saving management time or freeing up record space.

- *Cost avoidance*: Cost avoidance addresses the future cost reduction of the organization. Some of the items that are considered cost avoidance are temporary staff, additional file equipment/assets, and overtime.

Developing a Risk Assessment Methodology

The following are the steps in developing a risk assessment methodology:

1. *Build the risk assessment team*: Creating a risk assessment team is an important task for an organization because this team is responsible for reporting assessment results to management.

2. *Set the scope of the project*: A risk assessment team should identify the following parameters:
   - The objective of the assessment project
   - Department that needs to be assessed
   - Responsibilities of the team members
   - Persons to be interviewed
   - Standards to be used by the team
   - Documentation that has to be reviewed
   - Operations to be observed

3. *Identify assets covered by the assessment*: It is important to identify the assets that are involved in the assessment project. An assessment project may cover assets such as software, hardware, data, facilities, and current controls that protect those assets.

4. *Classify potential losses*: The team must classify the potential losses that could result from damages to an asset. Potential losses to assets may result from the following:
   - Physical damage to an asset
   - Denial of service
   - Modifications to an asset
   - Unauthorized access
   - Disclosure of information

5. *Identify threats and vulnerabilities*: In this step, the team identifies threats that exploit vulnerabilities to attack an asset. The following are some of the types of threats to an asset:
   - Natural threats
   - Accidental threats
   - Human accidental threats
   - Human malicious threats

6. *Identify existing controls*: Controls are protection measures that minimize the possibility of threats. The team should identify the controls that are presently implemented and determine their effect in the context of the current analysis.

7. *Analyze the data*: Data will be analyzed by collecting the required information to determine the risks. The following techniques are used to analyze data:
   - Preparing a list of assets
   - Corresponding threats to an asset
   - Determining the type of loss to an asset
   - Determining the vulnerabilities of an asset

8. *Determine cost-effective safeguards*: The following factors are necessary to determine a cost-effective safeguard:
   - Cost required to implement the safeguard
   - Total annual cost required to operate the safeguard
   - Duration or validity of safeguard

9. *Generate the report*: The team generates a risk assessment report that contains the following:

- List of assets covered by the assessment project
- Threats and vulnerabilities to an asset
- Determination of risk
- Safeguards to minimize the effect of threats
- Cost-benefit analysis to evaluate the cost of the assessment project

Security Requirements

Security requirements are defined to ensure a reasonable level of security for computer systems and networks. They refer to the level of security necessary to ensure that computers and networks are not compromised in any manner. Security requirements are defined for the following reasons:

- Controlling user access
- Detecting intrusions by unauthorized users
- Preventing unauthorized malicious programs
- Preventing intentional data corruption
- Keeping confidential data and communication private
- Enabling security personal to audit the status and usage of security mechanisms

Security requirements for information assurance adhere to the following principles:

- *Integrity and consistency*: Integrity and consistency refer to the assurance that information can be accessed and modified only by authorized users. The main function of this security requirement is to protect the information from being modified by unauthorized users and to ensure a logical consistency of information.

- *Identification, authentication, and auditing*: Identification and authentication are the basic security requirements for information assurance. They refer to the process of verifying a user before granting access to information. The main purpose of performing the process of identification and authentication is to provide security to the information so that unauthorized users do not have access to it. Auditing is also a security requirement for information assurance because it helps to monitor all events related to security.

- *Authorization*: Authorization is the process of controlling access to resources such as services and files. It determines if a user should be granted access to a particular resource or information.

Physical Security Requirements

Physical security describes the measures taken to protect personnel, critical assets, and systems against deliberate attacks and accidents. Physical security is intended to prevent attackers from accessing the resources of an organization.

Physical security is necessary for every organization to secure its assets. Physical security measures are usually taken according to needs and circumstances. To guard property and prevent unauthorized entry, security guards and/or intruder detection systems should be used at access points.

The need for and location of security barriers depends on the cost of what is being protected. For systems and other information facilities, it is important to define a highly secure area (a sealed place in the building), such as a locked room, office, or utility cabinet.

The following physical security measures should be implemented by all organizations:

- Lock up the server room, so that no one can physically damage the server.
- Set up surveillance cameras to monitor and record when someone is in a high-security area.
- Place network devices in locked rooms.
- Use rack-mount servers.
- Protect portable devices such as laptop and handheld computers.
- Back up all data so that they can be recovered later in the event of a disaster.
- Disable unnecessary drives and ports so that employees cannot copy company information.
- Secure printers.

Information Categorization

The information of an organization is categorized according to its sensitivity to loss or disclosure. This categorization is used to define necessary access control requirements. Whoever is responsible for the information should assess its sensitivity level based on its value to the organization and the impact its loss would have. After the categorization, an overall management review must be performed. An overall data assessment method should be used to make any adjustments. All personnel who are responsible for information categorization must agree to use the same definitions.

Information Categorization Levels

The following categorization levels are commonly used:

- *Sensitive*: This type of information requires special protection measures to ensure its integrity by protecting it from unauthorized modification or deletion. This type of information requires higher assurance of accuracy and completeness. Financial transactions and regulatory actions are the best examples of this type of information.

- *Confidential*: This type of information is the most sensitive and can only be used within the organization. It is free from disclosure under the provisions of the Freedom of Information Act or other applicable federal laws and regulations. Its unauthorized disclosure may seriously impact the organization.

- *Private*: This is personal information that can only be used by an employee. Disclosure of this information can seriously impact the employee. Examples of private information include the following:
  - Contact details
  - Work product information
  - Credit card details

- *Public*: This is information that does not belong to any of the above-mentioned categories. Disclosure of this information does not have any serious impact on the organization.

Risk Acceptance

Risk acceptance is the process of accepting the possibility and consequences of a particular risk. It is the final stage in the risk management process. Business risk presents an opportunity to gain profit and the potential to take losses. Organizations should manage their risks to maintain balance between the opportunities for gain and the potential for loss.

The amount of risk that an organization can accept is also known as its *risk appetite* or *risk tolerance*. Risk appetite or risk tolerance is different for every organization, depending on the culture, the industry, the line of business, and the potential gain.

Risk acceptance depends on the following factors:

- Financial capacity of organization to absorb the consequences of risk
- Level of conservatism of the decision maker
- Amount of risk inherent in the business activity normally carried out by the organization
- Diversity of the business
- Extent to which risk can be transferred or reduced

Risk Acceptance Process

The risk acceptance process is a top-level approach for integrating the concept of risk acceptance into a system safety program. It provides the framework for satisfying the requirements of the Discretionary Function Exclusion under the U.S. Federal Tort Claim Act. The Discretionary Function Exclusion protects both the government and contractors, if they follow an intelligent discretionary decision process.

The risk acceptance process involves the following steps:

1. *Develop a risk acceptance statement for remaining exposures*: This statement includes detailed information on residual risks, probability of occurrence of a security incident due to such risks, possible impacts of such risks, and methodologies used to assess such risks. Senior management, who can decide on the

risk acceptance level for the organization, must endorse this statement. Risk acceptance statements are required to achieve compliance with established standards and overcome legal issues that may arise due to residual risks.

2. *Approve the risk acceptance statement*: After the development of the risk acceptance statement, it is sent to the risk management team for assessment. This statement is also forwarded to other stakeholders that may be affected by the risk acceptance.

3. *Document results*: The outcomes of the risk acceptance process should be thoroughly documented and made available to all stakeholders. This document acts as a guide for the chief information officer to maintain risk control measures implemented in the organization.

Accuracy and Reliability of an Information System's Data

Information systems depend on data to fulfill their purpose. The accuracy and reliability of the data are critical for the system's normal operation. Organizations should implement preventive controls to detect and prevent undesirable data from entering the information system. Inappropriate or malicious data may give rise to several system vulnerabilities or may even lead to a system crash.

The preventive controls for maintaining the accuracy and reliability of an information system's data include the following:

- Maintenance of access privileges to appropriate personnel
- Verification of sensitive transactions
- Authentication before allowing users to enter and manipulate data

Configuration Management

Configuration management is a field of management that focuses on establishing and maintaining the integrity of an information system throughout its life. It is responsible for making changes to hardware, software, firmware, and test documentation throughout the life cycle of an information system. It ensures that project documentation correctly describes and controls the functional and physical characteristics of the end product being developed.

Configuration management policies cover the following activities:

- Configuration management planning
- Configuration identification
- Configuration change management process implementation
- Configuration status accounting documentation
- Configuration verification and audit process
- Configuration interface management

Configuration management helps the organization manage information and track changes that take place during the life cycle of the information. Noting the changes helps in finding the origin of problems and solving them as quickly as possible.

System Configuration and Management Board (SCMB)

The system configuration and management board (SCMB), also known as the configuration control board (CCB), is a group that plays a vital role in an organization's information systems. This board is managed by the chief information officer (CIO) and is made up of voting representatives from every department of the organization.

The main goal of the SCMB is to make decisions that increase network efficiency and utility. Security is an important part of this decision-making process, so members of this board must provide for security concerns during every phase.

There are two main responsibilities of the SCMB:

1. Controlling the baseline
2. Evaluating and approving the planned changes

System Certifiers and Accreditors

- *System certifiers*: Activities of system certifiers are as follows:
  - Performing complete multidiscipline assessment of technical and nontechnical security features
  - Supporting accreditation process
  - Identifying assurance levels to meet all applicable security policies
- *System accreditors*: System accreditors are responsible for the following tasks:
  - Approving the system for operation
  - Ensuring that the system is adequately tested prior to accreditation
  - Developing certification, security, and security evaluation plans
  - Implementing the certification process
  - Evaluating the risk assessment and developing a residual risk statement

Risk Management Methodologies to Develop Life-Cycle Management Policies and Procedures

Risk management methodologies to develop policies and procedures for information system life-cycle management must include the following steps:

1. Assess the life-cycle management policies and procedures.
2. Define roles and responsibilities.
3. Perform a system characterization.
4. Analyze vulnerabilities and controls.
5. Identify the threat sources.
6. Calculate the probability of each threat's occurrence.
7. Perform an impact analysis.
8. Determine the level of risk.
9. Develop a risk mitigation policy.
10. Estimate the level of residual risk.
11. Prepare the risk assessment report for business decisions.

Role of Security Awareness as Part of a Risk Management Plan

A security awareness program allows organizations to improve their security posture by providing required training to their employees to protect information assets. To protect the organization's information assets, employees must understand the organization's security policies and their responsibility in protecting the assets.

The security of an organization must be an ongoing process and should include continuous training, communication, and support. A one-time security action is not sufficient to identify the ever-growing threats to the organization.

Security awareness programs enable organizations to accomplish the following goals:

- Comply with laws and regulations
- Reduce unpredictable costs
- Improve security posture
- Protect information assets
- Reduce information security risk

Education, Training, and Awareness

Education, training, and awareness are important from the perspective of the organization because a trained employee increases productivity and also saves time. Educated staff will always help protect organizational data from leakage. Many times, data breaches are caused by the mistakes of employees who make uninformed mistakes. Educating employees reduces the chances of these types of mistakes.

Security Laws and Applicability to Risk Management Plan

- *Federal Information Security Management Act of 2002 (FISMA)*: The Federal Information Security Management Act provides a legal framework for protecting federally owned and operated computer systems. It covers non–national security systems. It assigns data protection responsibility in the federal government to various agencies. This act requires the head of an agency to conduct annual reviews of information security programs in order to reduce risk.

- *Gramm-Leach-Bliley Act (GLBA)*: The Gramm-Leach-Bliley Act requires financial institutions to protect the security and confidentiality of a customer's financial information. This act contains three sections:

  1. *Financial privacy rule*: This controls the disclosure of financial information.

  2. *Safeguards rule*: This rule states that financial institutions must use security measures to protect financial information.

  3. *Pretexting provisions*: This prohibits pretexting activities such as obtaining private information using false pretenses.

- *Health Insurance Portability and Accountability Act of 1996 (HIPAA)*: This law ensures the integrity and confidentiality of individually discovered information. It requires health care units to implement new security policies for disclosure of health information. It protects against reasonably anticipated threats and unauthorized disclosure. The health care units covered by HIPAA include:

  - Health care plans

  - Health care clearinghouses

  - Health care providers

- *Sarbanes-Oxley Act*: This law provides protection to investors against corporate accounting fraud. It sets guidelines to improve the accuracy and reliability of corporate disclosures. This act includes the following provisions:

  - CEOs and CFOs are responsible for the financial reports of their organizations.

  - CEOs and directors may accept loans from their organizations.

  - Insider trades are immediately reported.

  - Insider trades are prohibited during fund blackouts.

- *Counterfeit Access Device and Computer Fraud and Abuse Act of 1984 (CFAA)*: This law governs an array of computer-related crimes. The main purpose of this act is to focus directly on computer abuses. It helps federal prosecutors prosecute criminal computer activities.

- *Electronic Communications Privacy Act (ECPA)*: This act makes provisions for the access, use, disclosure, interception, and privacy protections of electronic communications. This act prohibits illegal access and certain disclosures of communication contents.

Policy Development

The process of developing policy commonly involves research, analysis, discussion, and synthesis of the information to produce proposals. Policy development contains the following steps:

1. *Define the issue or problem*: Policy development begins with defining the issues or problems for which the policy is being developed.

2. *Collect the required information on the issue*: This step of policy development deals with collecting the information required for developing a successful policy. The following information is collected in this step:

   - Sample policy language

   - Experience from other policies

- Local inputs
- Education research
- State association seminars
- State laws and regulations

3. *Secure recommendations from the supervisor*: After collecting the information, the board listens to recommendations for developing the policy.

4. *Discuss the issue with the management board*: In this step, the superintendent, who is responsible for managing the policy development, discusses the issues that were defined in previous steps.

5. *Outline the policy*: After discussing the issues with management, the superintendent obtains solutions from management to develop a policy. The superintendent develops and submits a sample policy to verify that this policy will cover all the issues of the organization.

6. *Adopt the policy*: In this step, management verifies a sample policy and approves the policy to be implemented in the organization. Before approving the policy, management goes through the various steps to verify the policy.

7. *Distribute the policy document to the organization's employees*: Once management has approved the policy, the policy document is distributed to all the employees of the organization. Every employee must follow this policy before performing any activity or operation on a computer.

8. *Oversee the policy's implementation*: This step deals with managing the policy's implementation after distributing it to all the employees.

9. *Review and evaluate the policy*: In this step, the policy is evaluated and reviewed to identify any necessary modifications.

Information Security Policy

Information security policies define a set of standard procedures and methodologies to protect information and information systems from various attacks. The policy statements clearly define the objectives of information security efforts in conjunction with an organization's business objectives and outline the control measures to safeguard the information.

Information security policies are developed after a thorough analysis of perceived business risks and criticality of information systems in achieving business objectives. In general, information security policies provide guidelines for the following tasks:

- Preparing an information security plan and implementing security control measures
- Performing an information security risk assessment and estimating the acceptable level of risk
- Periodically testing the security control measures to find out the efficiency of the information system
- Performing an audit of the information infrastructure

System security administrators should identify the existing policies implemented in the organization before creating new policies and updating the existing policies. Implemented policies can be identified by testing organizational procedures for standard policy guidelines.

Standard Information System Security Policies

The following information system security policies are standard:

- *Protect passwords*: Information systems rely on passwords for authentication and authorization of system users. Any compromise of passwords may enable unauthorized people to access sensitive and confidential information. Password security is a key for the information security in an information system. Passwords can be protected by taking the following protection measures:
  - Do not share passwords with others.
  - Do not use dictionary words, keyboard sequences, words spelled backward, or foreign words.
  - Use as many characters as allowed.
  - Use punctuation marks or symbols.

- Use a mix of uppercase and lowercase characters.
- Do not write passwords where someone else can see them.
- Change passwords every 90 days.

- *Protect confidential information*: Users should never place confidential data such as Social Security and credit card numbers in an unlocked area on the computer. They should not post Social Security numbers or user IDs in a public location or on the Internet.

- *Update systems with patches and security fixes, and update antivirus software*: Administrators should ensure that all systems contain the latest patches, security fixes, and antivirus software. Unprotected computer systems are vulnerable to outside attacks and data loss, and leave the organization's network vulnerable to damage and failure.

- *Use secure applications*: Users should not use unsecured applications. Unsecured applications collect and transmit personal data and leave organizations open to network attacks.

- *Back up data*: Administrators should protect important information and data on systems by backing up computer data.

- *Use a password-protected screensaver*: All users should utilize password-protected screensavers to lock the computers when they are not in use. This helps protect information systems from insider threats and helps ensure information privacy.

- *Use discretion when dealing with e-mail*: E-mail attacks are common. The following steps should be taken to secure e-mail accounts:

  - Evaluate the source of the received mail before opening and responding.
  - Disable the preview feature of the e-mail client.
  - Treat each received attachment as a possible virus attack.
  - Avoid submitting e-mail addresses on Web sites.
  - Implement spam filters.
  - Quarantine suspicious e-mail.
  - Conduct vulnerability tests on e-mail systems.

Change Control Policies

Change control is the process used to request, review, plan, approve, and implement changes to a system. It helps an organization maintain the changes taking place. Information changes and system changes can be documented using change control policies. These policies are decided on by management and are implemented to assess changes within an organization.

The following steps should be followed for the change control process:

1. Change request submitted
2. Change evaluated
3. Validation assessed
4. Implementation planned
5. Approval to implement given
6. Implementation and qualification
7. Approval to close change
8. Special treatment of "emergency changes"
9. Special treatment of "routine changes"

Change control policies provide the following guidelines:

- The possible impact of any change should be evaluated prior to accepting a change request.
- Changes in an information system should be carried out in a way that will not affect the existing system in a harmful way.

- A change log/directory should be maintained.
- Changes should be premeditated and access to make changes should be given only to qualified personnel.
- All changes should be controlled through the change management process.
- Reviews should be done prior to implementation of any change.
- Changes should be planned only for those systems that are capable of carrying out the work.

System Acquisition Policies and Procedures

System acquisition policies should adhere to the following guidelines:

- Examine the sufficiency of the planned system as a solution for the data processing problems under consideration.
- Assess the impact of the acquisition on the organization's personnel.
- Assess the impact of the acquisition on the organization's information systems.
- A cost-effective substitute should be considered.
- Recognize the possible growth of expenses and ensure that the financial needs associated with the acquisition are understood.
- Satisfy the organization's reporting and authorization requirements.

Acquisition and Upgrade of Software Components

The software acquisition policy should contain the following steps:

1. *Requesting software*: The requesting personnel should work with the IT department to identify the software needs. He or she should then obtain approval from the IT department manager to purchase the software.
2. *Purchasing licenses for software*: The requesting personnel then sends the completed purchase order request to the IT department for verification and approval. The IT department then sends the approved purchase order request to the purchasing department, where it is processed.
3. *Receiving software*: After receiving the software, the IT department follows the organization's check-in procedure to ensure that the software is added to the software inventory.
4. *Distributing software*: The IT department provides the software to the requesting department.
5. *Ensure that software documentation is available to the end users*: A copy of the end-user license agreement and manuals related to the software must be provided to the receiving department.

Risk Analysis Policies

Risk analysis policy should include the following steps:

1. Identify the frequency of a particular type of disaster.
2. Determine the effect of the disaster.
3. Analyze the speed of occurrence of the disaster.
4. Approximate the duration of the disaster.
5. Determine the impact of the disaster based on whether or not vital records are destroyed.
6. Identify the effects of the disaster such as:
   - Employee availability
   - Employee injuries
   - Loss of operating resources
   - Loss of organizational assets
   - Damages to facilities

7. Identify the required redundancy levels in the organization to accommodate critical systems and functions, including:

- Hardware
- Information
- Communications
- Personnel
- Services

8. Estimate the potential dollar loss, including the following losses:

- Loss of business opportunities
- Loss of financial management capabilities
- Loss of organizational assets
- Negative media coverage
- Loss of stockholder confidence
- Loss of goodwill
- Loss of income
- Loss of competitive edge
- Legal actions

9. Determine the cost of contingency planning.

General Risk Control Policies

General risk control policies should abide by these guidelines:

- Create clear objectives, and identify and estimate the major risks involved in achieving those objectives.
- Incorporate risk responses into a system of internal controls to protect the company's assets.
- Check the effectiveness of the risk and internal control management system.
- Follow the company's group guidelines and standards.
- Provide accountability to manage risks within approved boundaries.

Access Control Policies

An access control policy defines access to information systems for different categories of users. Access control standards are applied by the organization to control access to its information assets. These standards ensure suitable access controls for an organization's operation and security needs.

A security policy for access control depends upon the following points:

- *Managing access control standards*: Management must establish access control standards for information systems and must provide restrictions to prevent unauthorized access to increase the operational efficiency of the organization.

- *Managing user access*: The owner of a system must authorize access to the system. The following information security issues should be considered when implementing the security policy:

  - Unavailability of managed access controls may result in unauthorized access to information systems.

  - Logon screens and banners must be removed because they help unauthorized users gain access.

  - Assigning inappropriate privileges to inexperienced staff may result in processing problems and accidental errors.

- *Protecting unattended equipment*: Equipment must be protected appropriately, especially when left unattended. Unauthorized access to unattended equipment may result in harmful and fraudulent activities.

- *Managing network access control*: Access to network resources must be maintained strictly to prevent unauthorized access. Computing and information systems and peripherals must be accessed only after explicit authorization.

- *Securing access to operating system software*: Organizations must restrict access to operating system commands to only those persons who are authorized to perform system administration activities. All systems, from small PCs to large servers, must be hardened to remove needless development tools and utilities prior to delivery to end users.

- *Monitoring user system access and utilization*: Access to user systems must be logged and observed to recognize potential misuse of the systems. Sometimes, users may perform unofficial activities that are against the company's policy, which may cause damage or information loss. System access must be monitored regularly to prevent unauthorized access and to confirm that access control standards are effective.

- *Controlling access to files and documents*: Access to shared files must be carefully controlled to ensure that only authorized individuals have access to them. Uncontrolled access may result in unauthorized copying and modifying of information.

- *Controlling remote user access*: Remote-access control processes must provide proper safeguards through strong detection, verification, and encryption techniques. Remote users may need to communicate directly with their organization's systems to send and receive data. These types of users are physically remote and also connect through public networks, which may increase the threat of unauthorized access.

Personnel Security Policies

Personnel security policies provide the following guidelines:

- The roles and responsibilities as mentioned in the information security policy should be documented in the job descriptions as applicable.

- Verification of permanent employees should be performed at the time of job application through the following processes:
  - Character references
  - Confirmation of qualifications
  - Identity checks through documents such as passports
  - Proof of submission of passport application

- Managers should be aware of the activities of their employees.

- All employees should sign confidentiality and nondisclosure agreements at the start of employment.

- Employment terms and conditions should be precisely stated in the confidentiality agreement.

- Appropriate actions should be taken to separate duties in order to reduce the chance of unauthorized modification of information.

- Resources of information processing should not be used for other purposes.

Communications Security Policies

Communications security policies provide the following guidelines:

- Data paths related to online processing must be error free and secure.
- Telecommunication devices such as routers and hubs must be protected.
- Valuable information must be encrypted before being sent over a communications network.
- Virtual private networks (VPN) must use encryption according to the organization's cryptography policy.
- Internal/external desktop modems in the organization must be handled only by authorized personnel.
- Contractor sites must comply with an organization's security policies to obtain access to the organization's network.
- Communication cables that carry data must be protected from interception or damage.
- The data owner must ensure that communication protection measures are established for each data system.

Security Policies for Types of Permitted and Prohibited Actions on a System

The following actions on a system are prohibited:

- Sharing, transferring, and distributing information or data in violation of any applicable laws
- Performing an action that violates system or network security
- Performing an illegal action that may result in a criminal or civil liability
- Using a computer to irritate, harm, abuse, or harass others
- Sharing passwords with other people
- Installing or running unauthorized software on the computer
- Downloading and storing pornographic material on the computer

Declassification and Destruction Policies

Media Declassification Information that the organization no longer uses should be destroyed. Declassification of media is done by the following methods:

- *Declassifying tapes*:
  - A tape containing confidential and important information should be degaussed before being released for destruction.
  - All markings and labels indicating the previous use of the tape should be removed.
  - The tape should be destroyed by incineration or disintegration.
- *Declassifying disks*:
  - Disks containing information that is no longer useful should be disposed of after removing the labels.
  - Disks can be destroyed using metal destruction, incineration, or a chemical destroyer.
- *Declassifying memory*:
  - Magnetic core memory should be declassified and destroyed by pulverizing, smelting, and incinerating methods.

Policies for Destruction of Sensitive Information Information stored at a location other than the office may be at risk, as theft and hacking of the information is possible. Physical media that are used for data storage should be kept at a secured location.

It is advisable to destroy sensitive information storage devices as soon as the information is no longer needed. The information storage media destruction should be done in a thorough manner, as it is important to destroy the information completely.

Some media and data destruction methods are as follows:

- *Nonvolatile magnetic media, such as hard disk drives*: Pattern wiping, incineration, and physical destruction
- *Write-once optical media, such as CD-ROMs and DVD-Rs*: Abrasion, incineration, and physical destruction
- *Write-many optical media, such as CD-RWs and DVD-RWs*: Abrasion, incineration, and physical destruction
- *Solid-state media*: Pattern wiping and physical destruction
- *Paper-based media*: Shredding and incineration

Emergency Destruction Planning and Procedures (EDPP) Emergency destruction planning must address the following issues:

- Reporting fire incidents and initial firefighting by assigned personnel
- Assigning on-scene responsibility for protecting the organization's resources
- Securing or removing classified material and evacuating the area

- Protecting resources when admission of outside firefighters is necessary
- Reporting possible exposures to the organization's resources from unauthorized personnel during the emergency
- Posting emergency inventory of classified resources and reporting losses

Emergency destruction procedures must address the following issues:

- Adequate number of destruction devices
- Availability of electrical power
- Secure storage facilities
- Sufficient protected destruction areas
- Personnel assignments

Organizations must ensure the following to develop a successful destruction plan:

- All duties under the plan must be clearly described.
- All authorized persons must be aware of the plan.
- All assigned personnel under the plan must know their responsibilities.
- Training exercises must be conducted periodically.

Policies for Capturing Audit Trails

Audit trails maintain a record of information system activity. With the help of appropriate tools and procedures, they also detect security violations, performance problems, and errors in applications.

An audit trail contains a list of computer events about an operating system, an application, or activities of a user. Computer systems may contain many audit trails, each of which is related to a particular user activity. Auditing is the process of analyzing management, operational, and technical controls.

An audit trail is used to help system administrators make sure that the information system has not been adversely affected by hackers, insiders, or technical problems. Audit trails also help to achieve the following security-related objectives:

- Individual accountability
- Reconstruction of events
- Intrusion detection
- Problem analysis

The following policies should be implemented for capturing audit logs:

- Logs must be protected from unauthorized users and integrity problems.
- To protect the integrity of logs, there should be proper segregation of duties among those who administer system/network accounts.
- Consideration should be given to the location of logs and moving logs to a central spot.

Policies Regarding Audit Data Usage, Management, and Maintenance

- Proper controls and audit logs should be designed into the application of information systems.
- Control and audit logs should include the justification of input data, internal processing, and output data.
- Log records must be categorized into the following types:
  - Accounting records
  - Database records
  - Audit logs

Audit Record Policies

Auditable Events Audits help to maintain the security and integrity of critical information and processes. Information security audits check the level of information security in an organization. The audit process identifies risks in the operating environment. The auditor identifies the events that are needed to control and operate efficiently and effectively in order to minimize risk.

Auditable events are categorized into three categories:

1. Technical
2. Physical
3. Administrative

The following practices should be included when auditing events:

- Create a policy statement, develop an audit plan, and educate employees before implementing the audit policy.
- Clearly define the auditable events.
- Determine the tools, databases, and procedures to collect, organize, and analyze the audit data before starting the auditing process.
- Test the audit configuration settings before implementing them.
- Collect account logon and management event logs.
- Collect policy change events.
- Audit application and service success or failure events.
- Audit directory service access.
- Audit access and privilege assignments.

Personal Access Policies A policy for auditing personal access to computer systems provides the following guidelines:

- Systems are required to log users' system logins and logoffs with dates and times.
- Systems must be able to read, create, update, delete, and print user access for systems containing confidential data.
- All audit records must be identified by record keys or numbers.
- Systems must log unsuccessful login attempts and access violations.
- Functions of security administrators must be logged.
- Functions of system administrators must be logged.
- Unauthorized access, modifications, and deletions of audit records must be restricted.
- Audit records must be available for 90 days and must be backed up for a minimum of two years.

Risk Associated with Agency-Specific Policies and Procedures

Organizations should avoid agency-specific policies and procedures due to these risks:

- Agency-specific configuration management policies and procedures leave organizations unable to adopt new technologies.
- Agency-specific policies and procedures may render an organization noncompliant to some of the established standards.
- Configuration change management becomes difficult if a loophole is discovered in the products and services of the agency.
- Switching to different solutions from another vendor requires a significant financial and human resource investment.

Chapter Summary

- Understanding the system's processing environment is necessary while identifying the risks in a system.

- A cost-benefit analysis determines whether the cost to implement an action is worth the benefit the action will have.

- The system configuration management board (SCMB), also known as the configuration control board (CCB), is a group that plays a vital role in an organization's information systems.

- The process of developing policy commonly involves research, analysis, discussion, and synthesis of information to produce proposals.

- System certifiers perform comprehensive multidiscipline assessments of technical and nontechnical security features.

- System accreditors ensure that a system is adequately tested prior to accreditation.

- Risk management is the process of identifying risk, addressing risk, and taking steps to eliminate or reduce risk to an acceptable level.

Review Questions

1. Explain the change control procedure.

   _____

   _____

   _____

   _____

2. Explain configuration management. How do access controls and other administrative measures help in configuration management?

   _____

   _____

   _____

   _____

3. How are media declassified?

   _____

   _____

   _____

   _____

4. What are different media and data destruction methods?

   _____

   _____

   _____

   _____

5. What are the considerations in developing ST&E plans and procedures?

_____

_____

_____

_____

6. Discuss the laws that influence IA policy implementation.

_____

_____

_____

_____

7. Describe the policies and procedures for capturing audit logs.

_____

_____

_____

_____

8. Discuss the role of emergency destruction planning and procedures in information assurance.

_____

_____

_____

_____

9. What are the physical security requirements that organizations should implement in order to achieve IA?

_____

_____

_____

_____

Hands-On Projects

1. Navigate to Chapter 6 of the Student Resource Center. Open MBT_Automated_Security_Testing.pdf and read the following topics:

   ▪ Introduction

   ▪ Modeling Variables and Data Types

2. Navigate to Chapter 6 of the Student Resource Center. Open NAVSO P5239-07 ISSO Guide.pdf and read the following topics:

   ▪ INFORMATION SYSTEMS SECURITY OFFICER ROLE

   ▪ INFORMATION SYSTEMS SECURITY OFFICER RESPONSIBILITIES

3. Navigate to Chapter 6 of the Student Resource Center. Open RMPoliciesandProcedures.pdf and read the following topics:

   ■ Objectives

   ■ Authority and Responsibilities

4. Navigate to Chapter 6 of the Student Resource Center. Open costbenefit.pdf and read the following topics:

   ■ Identification of the Assets and Values

   ■ Management and Control

Chapter 7

Data Storage Technologies

Objectives

After completing this chapter, you should be able to:

- Use network attached storage (NAS)
- Use direct attached storage (DAS)
- Understand the difference between NAS and DAS
- Use storage area networks (SAN)
- Understand the difference between SAN and NAS
- Secure storage area networks with iSCSI
- Implement SAN security

Key Terms

Data phase the phase in which data are transmitted between the SCSI initiator and the SCSI target

Introduction to Data Storage Technologies

Home users are usually able to store as much data as they need on their desktop's hard drives, but many organizations require much more space. In addition, they need to be able to share data with others in the organization quickly and reliably. This chapter familiarizes you with three different data storage technologies: network attached storage (NAS), direct attached storage (DAS), and storage area networks (SANs).

Network Attached Storage (NAS)

Network attached storage (NAS) is a dedicated, hard disk–based storage technology. It is attached directly to a computer network, providing data access to network clients using a client-server design.

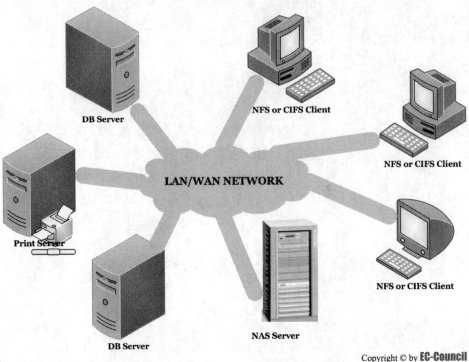

Figure 7-1   All of these clients can access the NAS server.

The hardware device, called a NAS box or NAS head, functions as the interface between NAS and network clients. It runs on an embedded operating system.

Clients usually access NAS through an Ethernet connection. NAS appears as a single node on the network with the IP address of the head device. NAS can store any type of file and includes built-in features such as secure authentication and disk space quotas.

Figure 7-1 shows the topology of a network including NAS.

NAS Architecture

A basic NAS may contain only one head, or it may share internal storage space across multiple heads to increase bandwidth. The storage capacity of NAS systems is determined by drive support, the number of drives present, and the capacity of the drives. NAS systems commonly use low-cost, high-density SATA drives, as well as some other drives including ATA, SCSI, and SAS drives. Higher-end NAS models use Fibre Channel drives.

Workgroup-type NAS systems contain at least a terabyte (1 TB) of capacity, spread across two or more hard disks. Enterprise-class NAS systems can use many disks to provide substantially more storage. Several NAS systems include RAID support to protect data, implementing common RAID levels such as RAID 0, RAID 1, RAID 5, RAID 6/DP and RAID 10. NAS systems also contain onboard RAM to cache data from all the disks. Small NAS devices contain a 128-MB to 256-MB cache, while enterprise-class NAS systems contain can contain 8 GB or more.

Some NAS products provide multiple Ethernet connections for network interface aggregation, redundancy, or failover. NAS boxes operate independently and can be aggregated into clusters. Similar to clustered computing, NAS clusters are used as a single device in the LAN. Each clustered element can share the data load, and each box in the cluster can provide failover if another box fails, which improves storage performance.

Figure 7-2 shows an example NAS architecture.

NAS Protocols

NAS uses the following protocols to communicate with clients in the LAN:

- *Networking protocols*:
    - *IPX (Internetwork Packet Exchange)*: This protocol connects clients and servers using Novell's NetWare. It functions at the network layer of the communication protocols, so it does not require a direct connection to exchange packets.

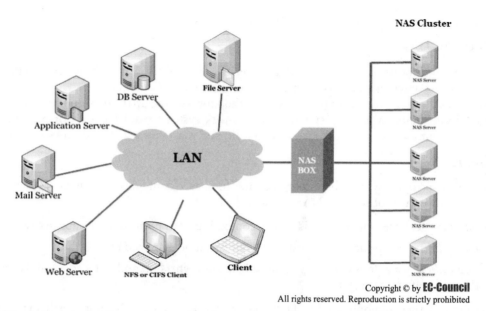

Figure 7-2   Note that a cluster of NAS servers can be behind a single NAS box.

- *NetBEUI*: This is an advanced version of NetBIOS. It is mainly used to communicate between computers within a local area network running Windows NT, LAN Manager, and Windows for Workgroups products.
- *File exchange protocols*:
  - *Network File System (NFS)*: This protocol was developed by Sun Microsystems and uses the Remote Procedure Call (RPC) method to communicate.
  - *Server Message Block (SMB)*: This protocol is used by the client application to read and write files on the server. It is used on the Internet on top of the TCP/IP protocol or other protocols such as Internet Packet Exchange (IPX) and NetBEUI.
- *Internet application protocols*:
  - *File Transfer Protocol (FTP)*: This is a standard Internet protocol that enables file exchange between computers on the network using the TCP/IP protocol.
  - *Hypertext Transfer Protocol (HTTP)*: This is an application protocol that runs on top of the TCP/IP protocol on the Internet.

The Need for NAS

NAS is useful for the following reasons:

- *Security*: A properly implemented NAS system offers a level of data security. Most NAS implementations are based on the Linux OS, making them less vulnerable to viruses and other malware when compared to Windows-based systems.
- *Power consumption*: NAS systems are energy efficient. In the case of a power failure, NAS can shut down the hard disk drives and remain idle. The power utilization of NAS, depending on how many hard disk drives are included, is about 5 W to 20 W.
- *Network access*: Network storage restricts unwanted or unauthorized network communications to the Internet. It is possible to set up a home page using NAS, providing a Web server with DDNS (Dynamic DNS). In addition to regular Web content, it can be used to access cameras as a remote surveillance server.
- *Larger storage capacity*: NAS was originally designed to offer larger storage capacity than existing storage media. However, with increasing growth in the storage market, NAS capacity looks smaller than it used to.
- *NAS hardware platform*: The present NAS model consists of SATA-II slots, USB 2.0 high-speed host ports, and Gigabit Ethernet. NAS looks similar to a regular PC, without display and input devices. NAS typically uses a RISC-based embedded application computer or x86 PC.

NAS Types

NAS Disk-As-Disk

A NAS disk-as-disk target is a disk array that stores the disk behind a NAS head, creating a single shared volume. This type of system is easier to maintain than traditional disk arrays.

A disk-as-disk target provides an inexpensive method for backing up the disk and provides additional benefits when used with traditional backup systems. Disk-as-disk systems require a SAN or NAS unit. SAN units are more powerful but are also more difficult to maintain and share; they will be discussed later in this chapter.

Scalable NAS

Scalable NAS is a storage system that accommodates file-based content that is always growing and must always be available. Advantages of scalable NAS include:

- *Scalability*: Scalable systems provide more computing power and storage capacity when necessary.
- *Manageability*: Newly added content and devices can be managed efficiently.
- *Affordability*: Scalable systems have reduced cost of ownership and reduced administrative expenses due to their ease of management.

NAS solutions are commonly used by IT managers because they can be more easily managed than DAS and SAN systems. The NAS market is divided into two separate segments: low priced and low performance. Non-scalable NAS are well suited for homes and offices. More expensive devices that provide high performance and scalability require special management skills. Scalable NAS is perfectly suited for sites that require a high degree of data growth.

Scalable NAS is commonly used by providers and distributors of high-definition material. This can include any form of rich media such as video pre- and postproduction, prepress, 3-D modeling, satellite imagery, and many aspects of high-performance computing.

Scalable NAS is useful for companies involved in the following:

- Delivering streaming video to users
- Providing Web 2.0 file servers
- Digital archiving
- Storing any other massive amounts of data

Open-Source NAS Implementations

FreeNAS

FreeNAS has the following features:

- Occupies less than 32 MB memory once installed on the hard disk
- Can be run directly from a storage device
- Supports protocols such as CIFS (via Samba), FTP, NFS, SSH, rsync, AFP, UPnP, iTunes/DAAP Server and BitTorrent
- Provides FreeBSD IPFW packet-filter and traffic-accounting facility
- Provides extensions for SlimServer via SlimNAS and XBMSP via ccXstream
- Contains iSCSI targets to create virtual disks
- Supports all network cards (wired and wireless) supported by FreeBSD
- Supports all hardware RAID cards supported by FreeBSD
- Has a Web-based configuration interface, shown in Figure 7-3

Installing FreeNAS To install FreeNAS, follow these steps:

1. Download the latest FreeNAS ISO image and burn it onto a CD.
2. Boot the system from that CD.
3. Select option 7 to install FreeNAS on the hard disk.

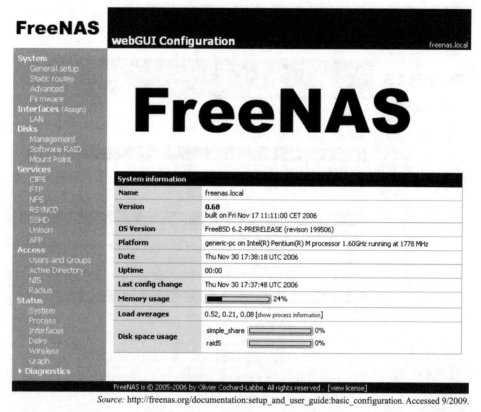

Source: http://freenas.org/documentation:setup_and_user_guide:basic_configuration. Accessed 9/2009.

Figure 7-3   This is the FreeNAS Web configuration interface.

4. Select option **2** to create two UFS partitions on the hard disk. One partition will be for FreeNAS, and the other will be for storage space.

5. The installer will show the names of the detected CD-ROM drives. Enter the name of the CD-ROM drive with the FreeNAS disc.

6. The installer will show the names of the detected hard drives. Enter the name of the hard drive to which FreeNAS should be installed.

7. Once installation is complete, press Enter to continue.

8. Select option **2** to return to the main menu, and then select option **5** and press Y to reboot the system.

9. Once the system reboots, it is necessary to configure the network. First, select option **1** to assign the network interface.

10. FreeNAS provides the list of interfaces. Type the name of the interface to use, or enter **A** to autodetect.

11. To add another LAN interface, enter its name, or just press Enter to move on.

12. Press Y to reboot FreeNAS.

13. Once FreeNAS reboots, select option **2** to set the LAN IP address that FreeNAS will use.

14. FreeNAS will ask if it should use DHCP. Press N.

15. Enter a static IP address for the system.

16. Enter the subnet mask.

17. FreeNAS will confirm that the IP has been set and will give instructions for entering the Web GUI. Press Enter.

18. Select option **6** to test the network connection.

19. Enter a known internal IP address. FreeNAS will attempt to ping it. If the ping is successful, FreeNAS is installed correctly. Press Enter.

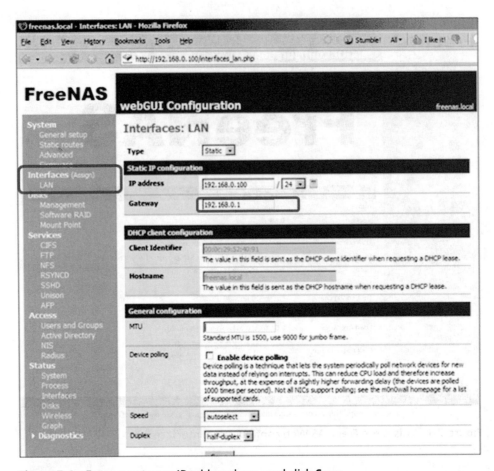

Figure 7-4 Enter a gateway IP address here, and click **Save**.

Configuring FreeNAS To configure FreeNAS after it has been installed, follow these steps:

1. Log into the FreeNAS Web interface by entering its IP address, assigned during setup, into a Web browser on any system on the network.

2. Enter the login information. The default username is **admin**, and the default password is **freenas**.

3. The welcome page will be displayed.

4. In the left navigation pane, click **LAN** under **Interfaces**.

5. Enter a gateway IP address, as shown in Figure 7-4, and click **Save**.

6. On the FreeNAS machine, return to the FreeNAS terminal.

7. Select option 5 to reboot the system, and press Y to confirm.

8. Return to the Web interface.

9. On the left navigation pane, click **General setup** under **System**.

10. Fill in the two DNS servers and change the administrator password, as shown in Figure 7-5, and click **Save**.

Configuring a Hard Drive for Use with FreeNAS To configure a hard drive for use with NAS, follow these steps:

1. Enter the FreeNAS Web interface.

2. In the left navigation pane, click **Management** under **Disks**.

3. Click on the + sign.

4. Select the disk from the drop-down list.

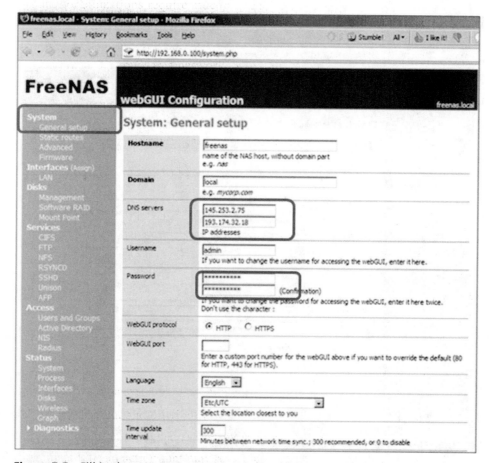

Figure 7-5 Fill in the two DNS servers and change the administrator password, and then click **Save**.

5. Select **UFS** under **Preformatted FS**, as shown in Figure 7-6, and click the **Add** button.

6. On the next page, click the **Apply changes** button.

7. Next, the partition must be mounted before it can be used. In the left navigation pane, click **Mount Point** under **Disks**.

8. Click on the + sign.

9. Select the information that matches the disk that was just added, and create a share name and description for this disk. Then click the **Add** button.

Enabling Services on the FreeNAS Server To enable a service, click on that service under **Services** in the left navigation pane. Click the check box on the top right of the page that loads, and then click **Save**. It may be beneficial to enable the following services:

- CIFS
- FTP
- SSHD

Openfiler

Openfiler, from Xinit Systems, converts an industry-standard x86/64 system into a full-fledged NAS/SAN appliance or IP storage gateway. It is based on Linux and has the following features:

- Supports protocols including NFS, SMB/CIFS, HTTP, FTP, and iSCSI
- Supports network directories including NIS, LDAP, Active Directory, Windows NT4 domain controller, and Hesiod

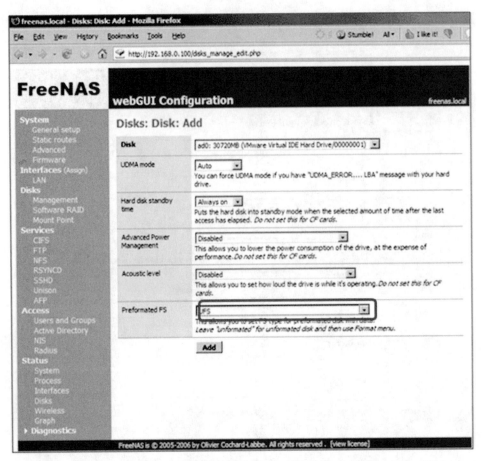

Figure 7-6 Select **UFS** under **Preformatted FS**, and click the **Add** button.

- Supports the Kerberos authentication protocol
- Supports volume-based partitioning such as ext3, JFS, and XFS
- Supports both hardware and software RAID with monitoring and alert facilities, volume snapshot, and recovery
- Supports active/passive high-availability clustering, MPIO, and block-level replication
- Scales to over 60 TB

NASLite

NASLite turns a basic computer into a dedicated SMB/CIFS, NFS, AFP, FTP, HTTP, and rsync file server. It boots from a variety of IDE, SATA SCSI, USB, Firewire, or hardware RAID devices. Content can be accessed simultaneously using any of the supported protocols. Its features include:

- Fully automated monitoring and intelligent resource management
- Daily mirror backups between local or remote drives to ensure data safety
- Easy to operate and to administer
- Remote administration through telnet
- Boots directly into RAM
- Large partition and file support
- S.M.A.R.T. support
- Wide range of PCI hardware support

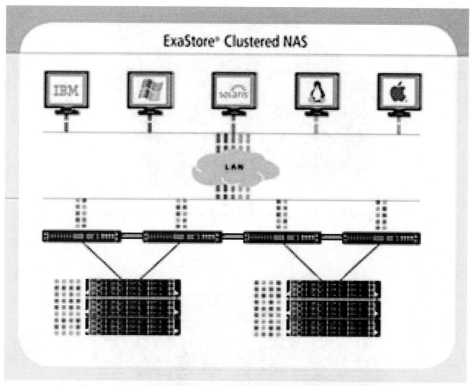

Source: http://www.exanet.com/. Accessed 9/2009.

Figure 7-7   ExaStore Clustered NAS is both high performance and scalable.

ExaStore Clustered NAS System

ExaStore Clustered NAS is a high-performance, scalable solution, allowing administrators to expand capacity and performance as needed without affecting applications or users. It is an enterprise-class storage system offering the following features:

- Data protection
- Data vaulting
- Digital media
- Broadcasting
- Postproduction
- Disaster recovery
- Global content delivery
- High-performance computing
- Hosted storage services
- Web services

A diagram of ExaStore Clustered NAS is shown in Figure 7-7.

NAS Appliances

ioSafe R4 NAS

ioSafe R4 NAS is designed for businesses, enterprises, remote/branch offices, and government agencies. It is both fireproof and waterproof, and it is powered by ReadyNAS. R4 NAS is shown in Figure 7-8.

Figure 7-8   R4 NAS is both fireproof and waterproof.

Figure 7-9   The ioSafe 3.5 Pilot hard drive is an internal
fireproof and waterproof hard drive.

ioSafe 3.5 Pilot Hard Drive

The ioSafe 3.5 Pilot hard drive is an internal fireproof and waterproof hard drive for digital data storage. The Pilot series of disk drives are compatible with home media servers, desktops, storage arrays, and external storage devices. They work with Windows, Linux, and Mac systems over the SATA I interface. These fire-safe disks have a 5,400-rpm rotational speed, 8-MB buffer size, 5.5-ms average latency, 12.0-ms read seek time, and 2.0-ms average track-to-track seek time. One of these disks is shown in Figure 7-9.

ioSafe 3.5 Squadron Hard Drive

The ioSafe 3.5 Squadron Hard Drive is another internal fireproof and waterproof hard drive for digital asset storage. The Squadron series of internal disk drives are compatible with desktops, storage arrays, home media servers, and external hard drive enclosures, and work with Windows, Linux, and Mac systems over the SATA II interface. The Squadron hard drive is shown in Figure 7-10.

ioSafe Solo Hard Drive

The ioSafe Solo is an external hard drive that uses a standard USB connection and usually requires no setup. The Solo is available in 500-GB, 1-TB, and 1.5-TB models. The Solo is able to withstand fires and is rated up to 1,550°F per the ASTM E119 industry standard. The Solo can also be submersed in freshwater or salt water for three days at a depth of up to 10 feet. The Solo is shown in Figure 7-11.

Figure 7-10   The ioSafe 3.5 Squadron hard drive supports SATA II.

Figure 7-11   The ioSafe Solo is a simple but sturdy USB hard drive.

Figure 7-12   Disk2Disk can be either fixed capacity or scalable.

Disk2Disk

TCG America's Disk2Disk NAS solutions can be either fixed capacity or scalable. The Disk2Disk system is shown in Figure 7-12.

LaCie 5big Network

The 5big Network is a five-bay RAID solution for small and medium workgroups or offices with capacities of up to 7.5 TB. It supports seven RAID modes, including RAID 5 and RAID 6, and is housed in a sleek and durable aluminum tower with five lockable, removable drive trays.

Its stackable design helps to save space, and its browser-based access and management system allows administrators to quickly set up the 5big Network and allow multiple users to share, store, and access data without using the bandwidth of a central server. This solution additionally features Active Directory support for easy integration into Windows-based networks and a wake-on-LAN function. Compared to traditional four-disk RAID towers, it uses 25% less energy and makes 37% less noise.

The LaCie 5big Network is shown in Figure 7-13.

Figure 7-13   The LaCie 5big Network is an aluminum tower with five drive trays.

Figure 7-14   The RELDATA 9240i uses virtualization to perform multiple replication functions.

RELDATA 9240i Unified NAS Storage System

RELDATA's 9240i Unified Storage System delivers integrated iSCSI SAN, NAS, and WAN replication functions on a single virtualized platform. It is shown in Figure 7-14, and its features include the following:

- Reliable, high duty-cycle SAS storage
  - High-performance and high-capacity drives
- Storage system investment protection
  - Redeploy and add legacy third-party disks with RELDATA heterogeneous virtualization
  - No vendor storage lock-in
- Software licensing per 9240i instead of onerous licensing based on capacity
- High-performance networking
  - Six Gigabit Ethernet ports (expandable up to 16 ports)
  - Up to eight 10-Gigabit Ethernet ports for even higher performance
- Integrated local and WAN data replication
- Optional integrated iSCSI
- Clustered storage systems
  - Linearly scalable capacity from gigabytes to petabytes
  - Linearly scalable performance in IOPS and throughput

Synology RS407

The Synology RS407 is a four-bay NAS shown in Figure 7-15 with the following features:

- Hot-swappable hard disks
- RAID 0/1/5/5 + spare/6 support
- Uses 21 W to 68 W of power
- Windows Active Directory support
- IP camera video recording
- Encrypted network backup
- Encrypted FTP with hack prevention
- Multiple Web site hosting with PHP + MySQL

Figure 7-15 The Synology RS407 is a four-bay NAS.

NAS Vendors

The following companies manufacture NAS products:

- Addonics
- BlueArc
- Freecom
- Hitachi
- Broadberry

Direct Attached Storage (DAS)

A direct attached storage (DAS) system is directly attached to a single host computer or server. When it is attached to a server, network workstations must access that server to connect to the storage device. DAS can use one of many types of drives, including ATA, SATA, SCSI, SAS, and Fibre Channel. The main alternative for direct attached storage is storage area network (SAN), discussed later in this chapter.

DAS is an inexpensive storage system for small- and medium-sized businesses. Small organizations use DAS for file transfer and e-mail, while larger organizations are more likely to use DAS in mixed storage environments such as those that also use NAS and SAN. Organizations that begin with DAS but later switch to networked solutions can use DAS to store less critical data.

Table 7-1 and Figure 7-16 show the differences between NAS and DAS.

Storage Area Network (SAN)

A storage area network (SAN) is a high-speed subnetwork used to transfer large amounts of data. Typically, a SAN is connected to several data storage devices containing disks for data storage. SAN supports data storage, data recovery, and data duplication for enterprise networks via high-end servers, multiple disk arrays, and Fibre Channel interconnection technology. It provides an interface between storage devices that enables systems to access data backups as if they were available locally.

SAN architecture, shown in Figure 7-17, consists of links from the storage system to the user, servers, and network equipment.

DAS	NAS
Directly attached to a computer or server	Attached to the network and provides centralized data access to multiple clients
Used for localized file sharing in environments with a single server or a few servers	Used by organizations to achieve fast data access in a simple, cost-effective manner
Provides block-level I/O	Provides file-level I/O via CIFS and NFS
Provides disk-level high availability with the help of RAID solutions	Provides disk-level high availability with the help of RAID solutions

Table 7-1 These are the differences between NAS and DAS

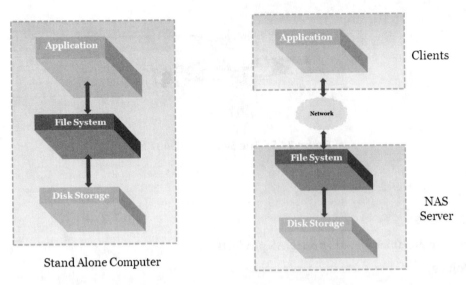

Figure 7-16 The fundamental difference between NAS and DAS is that NAS includes the network.

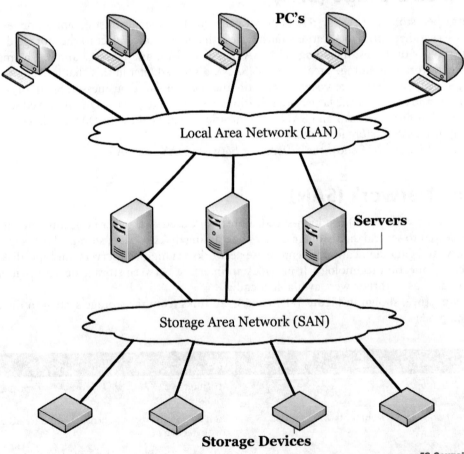

Figure 7-17 A storage area network (SAN) links storage devices to other parts of the network.

SAN Protocols

The protocols used in storage area networks include:

- *Fibre Channel Over Ethernet (FCoE)*: This protocol is used for mapping Fibre Channel frames over full-duplex IEEE 802.3 networks. It makes it possible to move Fibre Channel traffic across existing Ethernet infrastructures and extend the capacity of a SAN. This is mainly useful in data centers.

- *Small Computer System Interface (SCSI)*: SCSI is a bus that connects devices like printers, hard disks, and scanners to a computer. It provides higher data communication rates compared to standard ports, allowing more than one device to be connected to a single port. There are many variations of this interface, including SCSI-1, SCSI-2, SCSI-3, and SAS.

- *Serial Attached SCSI (SAS)*: This standard is a substitution for the parallel SCSI physical storage interface, providing faster data transmission and easier configuration. The SAS controller can be connected to several ports using a SATA cable for communication between devices. This cable is a thin point-to-point connection using a simple cable mechanism that does not require the interconnecting of devices. Using SAS can enhance the performance of every drive in an array by 1.5 Gbps.

- *Network Data Management Protocol (NDMP)*: This protocol is used to manage network databases throughout an organization. It controls data backup, restoration, and transfer between the main storage devices and the secondary storage devices via network-based mechanisms. The architecture of NDMP is based on the client-server model.

- *Internet Storage Name Service and iSNS Protocol (iSNS and iSNSP)*: Fibre Channel devices and iSCSI are discovered automatically and configured using this standard. iSNS allows for the configurate of each storage device with its respective initiators and targets using a management model.

- *Internet Small Computer System Interface (iSCSI)*: iSCSI is based on the TCP/IP protocol used to establish connections between IP-based storage devices, hosts, and clients. It aids in quick data transfers between the elements of a data storage network.

- *Internet Fibre Channel Protocol (iFCP)*: This standard provides Fibre Channel fabric services to Fibre Channel devices over a TCP/IP network.

- *Fibre Channel over IP (FCIP)*: This protocol is used to interconnect clusters of Fibre Channel SANs over IP-based networks and thus form a single SAN in one Fibre Channel fabric. The connectivity between SAN clusters through LANs or WANs depends on IP-based networks.

Working of SAN

While SAN is used for storage, it is significantly different from a server or any other storage device. SAN is highly scalable and can provide added security by only offering files to users on the same network. SAN is also capable of transferring data rapidly between two separate servers—for instance, transfers between an FTP server directory and a user's file server. It also connects networks that are separated by large distances. Since the devices on a SAN are connected together, backing up data requires only one backup server, reducing backup requirements.

Differences Between SAN and NAS

SAN and NAS have the following key differences:

- SAN is a devoted network that is connected via multiple gigabit Fibre Channel switches and host bus adapters, while NAS is directly connected to a network via TCP/IP using Ethernet CAT 5 cables.

- Because NAS runs on a TCP/IP network, it is subject to latency and broadcast storms. It is in contention with other users and network devices for bandwidth. SAN does not have this issue.

- SAN is highly secure thanks to its zoning and logical unit numbers, while NAS is not very secure, typically using access control lists for security.

- While NAS does support RAID levels, two different levels cannot be mixed in the same device.

iSCSI

Internet Small Computer System Interface (iSCSI) is an IP-based storage networking standard for linking data storage facilities. iSCSI is used to handle data storage over large expanses. Because it is IP-based, data can be transmitted over the Internet, LANs, or WANs.

The protocol architecture is based on the client-server model when the devices are present in close proximity and connected using SCSI buses. The main function of iSCSI is encapsulation and reliable delivery of data. This protocol provides a method for encapsulating SCSI commands over an IP network and operates on top of TCP/IP.

Working of iSCSI

iSCSI is the transmission of SCSI (Small Computer System Interface) commands over an IP network. It contains two types of devices: initiators and targets. A SCSI initiator is a server that starts the communication by sending the command to be executed, while a SCSI target is a storage device that responds to the initiator and carries out the commands.

Figure 7-18 shows the layers of iSCSI.

The target responds to and executes the commands that it receives from the initiator. These commands are exchanged using command descriptor blocks (CDBs), shown in Figure 7-19.

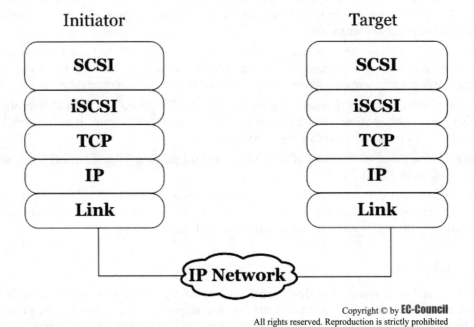

Figure 7-18 This shows the layers of iSCSI.

Bit	7	6	5	4	3	2	1	0
Byte								
0	Operation Code							
1		Command Specific Parameters						
n-1								
n	Control							

Figure 7-19 This is the structure of a SCSI command descriptor block (CDB).

SCSI commands are performed using data phases. In each *data phase*, data are transmitted between the initiator and the target. The SCSI command is terminated by the target once the operation is completed. Authentication between initiators and the user occurs using names provided by the vendors. iSCSI initiators establish a session to send a SCSI command to the target. In this session, the initiator forms numerous multiple TCP connections using a TCP port. The target connects via a TCP port to listen for incoming requests. The initiator then uses the login method to validate the initiator and target, and establishes the session as an iSCSI session.

The initiator transfers the data using SCSI commands via an iSCSI message. SCSI assigns the numbers to the commands, which are transferred from the initiator to the target, carried by the iSCSI protocol data unit (PDU) as Command Sequence Numbers (CmdSN). These numbers are unique for every session. It also assigns these numbers to the responses carried by the iSCSI PDU as the Status Sequence Numbers (StatSN). The initiator contains an Expected Status Sequence Number (ExpStatSN) to determine the status of a transfer request. If the StatSN and ExpStatSN are different, the connection may be indicated as a failed connection. The Domain Name Service (DNS) is used to resolve the iSCSI URL to an IP address. Basically, this just means that the initiator of the communication sends numbered pieces of data to the target, and the target responds with these numbers so that each system knows when to start and terminate the data communication.

Figure 7-20 shows the basic header statement (BHS) for a SCSI initiator command, while Figure 7-21 shows the BHS for a SCSI target response.

Securing Storage Area Networks with iSCSI

iSCSI provides a number of security features, including the following:

- An iSCSI SAN supports Gigabit Ethernet and a point-to-point architecture for the switched network, making packet sniffing difficult. It limits access to only particular users or administrators.

- A virtual private network (VPN) helps in protecting data transfers over a public network. This is done by encrypting the data transmitted between an iSCSI initiator and the client using the IPSec protocol.

- When packets are protected by IPSec and a firewall at the IP level, iSCSI uses authentication methods so that only authorized users can access the storage.

- iSCSI protects the data by physically regulating access to iSCSI SAN devices and separating SANs from other networks.

Fibre Channel SAN

Fibre Channel SAN is a multigigabit technology used for data storage running over a fiber-optic cable. The main purpose of Fibre Channel is to increase cable length and simplify connections rather than increasing the speed.

Byte	0	1	2	3
	Opcode	Opcode-specific fields Reserved		
4 8	Logical Unit Number (LUNs)			
12	Initiator Task Tag			
16	Expected Data Transfer Length			
20	CmdSN			
24	ExpStatSN or EndDataSN			
28 + 4	SCSI Command Descriptor Block (CDB)			

Figure 7-20   This is the basic header statement for a SCSI initiator command.

Byte	0	1	2	3
0	Opcode	Opcode—specific fields Reserved (0)		
4	Reserved (0)			
8				
12	Initiator Task Tag			
16	Basic Residual Count			
20	StatSN			
24	ExpCmdSN			
28	MaxCmdSN			
32	EndDataSN or Reserved (0)			
36	R2TEndDataSN or Reserved (0)			
40	Bidi-Read Residual Count			
44	Digests if any			
48	Response Data or Sense Data (optional)			

Figure 7-21   This is the basic header statement for a SCSI target response.

Fibre Channel SAN is a network technology in which servers are directly connected to storage devices using the SCSI bus protocol. Fibre Channel SAN offers a performance-enhanced network in which multiple servers communicate with multiple storage devices. It allows for any-to-any connectivity of the server to storage using components such as routers, hubs, gateways, and servers. It also allows for multiple servers to access multiple storage systems using redundant paths, resulting in high data availability and speed.

The following topologies are supported by Fibre Channel:

- Point to point
- Arbitrated loop
- Switched fabric

Fibre Channel SAN provides these benefits:

- Reduces the IT management costs associated with storage
- Allows for quick access to a storage device
- Allows organizations to create, store, share, and coordinate data
- Allows addition of a new device or removal of a failed device without interruption

Comparison of Fibre Channel SAN and iSCSI SAN

Both technologies have advantages and disadvantages. The iSCSI protocol is based on TCP/IP, which ensures data reliability using TCP acknowledgement and cyclic redundancy check (CRC). CRC must be enabled in the iSCSI SAN to ensure the integrity of the data.

Data on a Fibre Channel SAN are considered reliable because it runs over trusted connections such as Class 3, which provides error recovery at the upper-layer protocols. A Class 3 acknowledged connection also helps prevent long-term outages in the SAN.

Features	Fibre Channel SAN	iSCSI SAN
Industry specifications	Specified by Fibre Channel FC-0	Specified by IEEE, IETF, and Storage Networking Industry Association (SNIA)
Data rates	100 Mbps to 800 Mbps	10 Mbps to 10 Gbps
Communication media	Optical fiber, coaxial cable, and twisted pair	Optical fiber, coaxial cable, and twisted pair
Maximum distances for point-to-point links	50 m to 10 km	100 m to 120 km
Hunt groups	Group of associated N_Ports at a single node	Not available
Multicast	Transmits to all N_Ports on a fabric	Transmits to all N_Ports on a switched network
	Transmits to a subset of the N_Ports on a fabric	Transmits to a subset of the N_Ports on a fabric
Topology	Fabric or switched, point to point, and arbitrated loop	Switched, point to point, star, ring

Table 7-2   These are some of the differences between Fibre Channel SAN and iSCSI SAN

Fibre Channel SAN provides higher security than iSCSI because it provides isolation in the data center in order to prevent unauthorized access to the data. An improperly configured iSCSI SAN can be compromised by joining together unauthorized devices on the network. These risks can be prevented by an IT manager's implementing standard network security practices.

Table 7-2 shows some of the differences between Fibre Channel SAN and iSCSI SAN.

Benefits of SAN

SAN provides the following benefits:

- Storage consolidation reduces cost
- Storage or server can be easily added without interruption
- Data are backed up and restored quickly
- High-performance interface, over 100 Mbps
- Supports server clusters of eight or more servers acting as a single reliable system
- Disaster tolerance
- Reduced cost of ownership

SAN Security

A storage area network should protect data from internal and external threats and attacks, and must allow only authorized users to access the data. Consolidating servers on the network increases the risk of a single security breach having a widespread impact on the organization. The connectivity between the SAN and IP network may increase the risk of IP network threats including man-in-the-middle and denial-of-service attacks. A SAN must encrypt sensitive data during data transfer.

Data can be secured from unauthorized access by securing logical unit numbers (LUNs). A LUN is a secondary level of device recognition. There are pros and cons for both hardware-based LUN security and software-based LUN security. The security of a SAN is completely dependent upon the user's authorization or authentication.

SAN security includes these concepts:

- *Host adapter–based security*: Security measures for the Fibre Channel host bus adapter can be implemented at the driver level.

- *Switch zoning*: In a switch-based Fibre Channel SAN, switch zoning refers to the masking of all the nodes connected to the switch.

- *Storage-controller mapping*: Some storage subsystems accomplish their LUN masking in their storage by mapping all host adapters against LUNs in the storage system.

- *Software measures*: SAN security can be implemented using software tools to control access to data and maintain its reliability.

Though expensive, tools used to manage access to volumes also help prevent data corruption. These tools provide different access privileges to each user for accessing the different data volumes. Only one user can access a particular volume at a time.

Threats to a SAN

The storage area network may be vulnerable to risk because it stores and transfers critical data. There are different levels of threats faced by the SAN:

- *Level one*: These types of threats are unintentional and common in workplaces. They may result in downtime and loss of revenue. These threats can be prevented by administrators.

- *Level two*: These types of threats are simple malicious attacks using existing equipment and easily obtained information. Preventive measures used for level-one threats are also used for these types of threats.

- *Level three*: These types of threats are large-scale attacks, coming from skilled attackers using uncommon equipment. Level-three attacks are difficult to prevent.

Pros and Cons of Using a SAN

- *Reasons to use a SAN*:
  - Better disk utilization
  - Fast and extensive disaster recovery
  - Better availability for applications
  - Faster backup of large amounts of data
- *Limitations of a SAN*:
  - Installing an effective SAN is expensive
  - Increased administration cost
  - Impractical for use with a single application
  - Requires a fast WAN connection, which may be costly

SAN Considerations for SQL Server Environment

SAN provides these features for SQL servers:

- Increased database size
- Clustered environment
- Performance advantages
- Storage efficiencies
- Faster disaster recovery

Various considerations when using SAN with an SQL server are as follows:

- *Caching*: SAN provides a significant cache, but the availability decreases when multiple servers share this cache.

- *LUNs*: A SAN administrator divides the SAN storage into LUNs and considers these units as a partition or drive.

- *RAID*: Before purchasing, organizations should test the SAN using a representative load to ensure that RAID 5 performs well for tempdb, log files, and intensive filegroups.

SAN Network Management Systems

Apple's Xsan

Xsan is an enterprise-class SAN file system introduced by Apple. It is a 64-bit cluster file system specifically designed for small and large computing environments that demand the highest level of data availability.

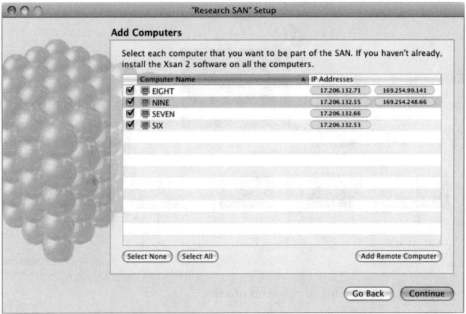

Source: http://www.apple.com/xsan/. Accessed 9/2009.

Figure 7-22   Xsan is an enterprise-class SAN system from Apple.

It enables multiple Mac desktop and Xserve systems to share RAID storage volumes over a high-speed Fibre Channel network. Each client can read and write directly to the centralized file system.

Xsan is shown in Figure 7-22, and its features include the following:

- Easily manage user access to data on SAN volumes
- Share terabytes of data simultaneously over a high-speed Fibre Channel network
- Use optimized workflow configuration settings for maximum performance
- Access volumes from multiple servers concurrently and copy data between them directly over high-speed Fibre Channel
- With Spotlight, Cover Flow, and Quick Look, scan through thousands of files on the SAN volume to find content
- Eliminate potential single points of failure with mission-critical redundancy

Xsan Components Xsan consists of the following components, shown in Figure 7-23:

- *SAN volume*: Xsan consolidates data into a single storage volume accessible to all systems on the storage area network (SAN). Adding capacity is as easy as attaching more RAID storage systems to the Fibre Channel network.
- *Fibre Channel network*: The SAN volume connects to the Xsan metadata controller and all Xsan clients through a high-speed Fibre Channel switch. Apple has qualified many popular third-party switches for use with Xsan.
- *Xsan metadata controller*: The metadata controller acts as the "traffic cop" for the SAN. When an Xsan client attempts to read or write to a file, it gets permission from the metadata controller, and then accesses the data directly on the SAN over high-speed Fibre Channel. Any Xserve or Mac Pro running Mac OS X Server can be an Xsan metadata controller.
- *Xsan clients*: Mac desktop or Xserve systems running Xsan have direct block-level access to files stored on the SAN volume and full read/write capability. As performance needs grow, Xsan allows the addition of servers and computers to the SAN. With Xsan, one SAN can handle hundreds of clients.
- *Ethernet network*: File system metadata is handled over a private Ethernet network shared by all systems connected directly to the SAN. This frees up Fibre Channel bandwidth for high-performance storage throughput.

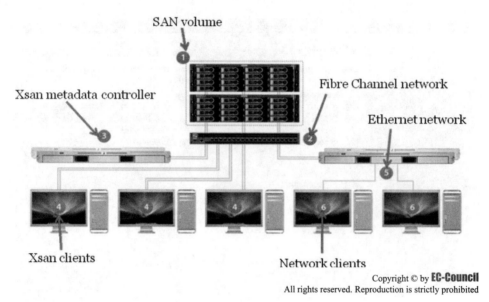

Figure 7-23 These are the components of Xsan.

- *Network clients*: An Xserve with Mac OS X Server and Xsan can share data from the SAN volume with an unlimited number of networked computers over the Ethernet network using file-sharing protocols, such as AFP, SMB/CIFS, and NFS.

Brocade Fabric Manager

Brocade Fabric Manager manages multiple Brocade switches and fabrics in real time. In particular, it provides essential functions for efficiently configuring, monitoring, dynamically provisioning, and managing Brocade data center fabrics on a daily basis.

As a single-point management platform, Brocade Fabric Manager facilitates the global integration of management tasks across multiple fabrics, thereby lowering overall storage costs. It is shown in Figure 7-24, and its features include the following:

- Monitors and administers large numbers of Brocade Fabric OS switches, directors, and the Brocade DCX Backbone—including multiple Brocade data center fabrics
- Performs end-to-end management tasks across multiple devices and fabrics in a single operation
- Optimizes fabric utilization and capacity planning through real-time and historical analysis and performance monitoring
- Visualizes and tracks changes to fabric configuration and state information through multiple views at multiple levels of detail
- Allows users to launch Brocade Fabric Manager from other enterprise management applications or to launch other applications from Brocade Fabric Manager
- Enhances asset management and analysis through detailed device tracking, including exporting to a spreadsheet
- Displays the fabric layout through a topology map that specifies Interchassis Link (ICL), Interswitch Link (ISL), switch, and device details
- Identifies, isolates, and manages data center events across large numbers of switches and fabrics

Cisco Fabric Manager

Cisco Fabric Manager is a Web-based application that simplifies the management of Cisco switches in SANs through an integrated approach to switch and fabric administration. The program offers storage administrators fabricwide management capabilities, including discovery, multiple-switch configuration, and continuous network monitoring and troubleshooting. This approach greatly reduces switch setup times, increases overall fabric reliability, and provides robust diagnostics for resolving network problems and configuration inconsistencies.

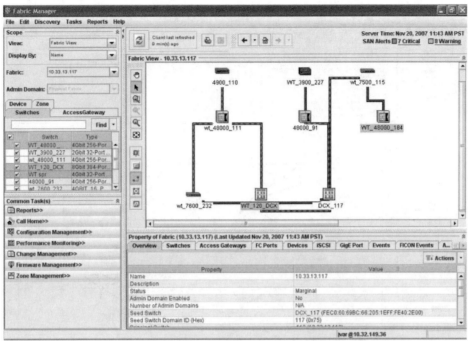

Source: http://www.brocade.com. Accessed 9/2009.

Figure 7-24 Brocade Fabric Manager manages multiple Brocade switches and fabrics in real time.

With the Cisco Fabric Manager GUI, storage administrators can compare switch configurations side by side, perform configuration policy checks across switches, set alarm thresholds to report to third-party fault-management applications, view individual device and aggregate statistics in real time, and analyze historical performance statistics. All these capabilities are available through a secure interface that facilitates remote management from almost any location.

Cisco Fabric Manager is shown in Figure 7-25, and its features include the following:

- *Switch-embedded Java application*: This application integrates switch and fabric management in a single performance-optimized tool that ships with every Cisco MDS 9000 Family and Nexus 5000 Family switch.

- *Fabric visualization*: Cisco Fabric Manager performs centralized automated discovery and displays storage network topology, connectivity, and zone and virtual SAN (VSAN) highlighting, allowing for the identification of network health and configuration concerns at a glance.

- *Multiple views*: Cisco Fabric Manager simplifies the configuration and monitoring of multiple switches and facilitates configuration replication with fabric, device, summary, and operation views.

- *Comprehensive configuration across multiple switches*: Cisco Fabric Manager provides integrated fabric-, switch-, and port-level configuration. It also simplifies zone, VSAN, Fibre Channel over IP (FCIP), Internet Small Computer System Interface (iSCSI), IBM Fiber Connection (FICON), and intelligent services configuration.

- *Flexible monitoring and alerts*: Cisco Fabric Manager presents real-time and historical performance-monitoring statistics in tabular and graphical formats. Performance-monitoring thresholds and configuration of threshold-based alerts, including Call Home, facilitate rapid response to exception conditions.

- *Historical performance monitoring*: Cisco Fabric Manager provides tabular and graphical reports showing daily, weekly, monthly, and yearly traffic for Interswitch Links (ISLs), host and storage connections, and traffic between specific Fibre Channel sources and destinations. Top 10 and daily summary reports present fabricwide statistics that greatly simplify network hotspot analysis.

- *Powerful configuration analysis*: Cisco Fabric Manager performs zone-merge analysis and configuration checking, simplifying resolution of problems, facilitating successful fabric merges, and resolving configuration inconsistencies automatically.

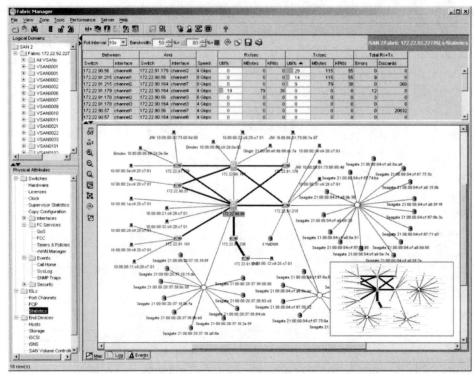

Source: http://www.cisco.com. Accessed 9/2009.

Figure 7-25 Cisco Fabric Manager is a Web-based program to manage Cisco systems in SANs.

- *Network diagnostics*: Cisco Fabric Manager probes network and switch health with Fibre Channel ping and traceroute, allowing administrators to rapidly pinpoint network connectivity and performance problems.

- *Comprehensive network security*: Cisco Fabric Manager protects against unauthorized management access with Simple Network Management Protocol version 3 (SNMPv3), Secure Shell (SSH) protocol, and role-based access control (RBAC).

SANmelody

SANmelody converts standard Intel/AMD servers, blades, or virtual machines (VMs) into fully capable storage servers that virtualize disks and serve them over existing networks to application servers. The program accelerates performance through built-in caching that minimizes delays from slower mechanical drives. The software equitably distributes the available disk space to multiple applications spread across several machines by carving out smaller logical disks from larger physical disks. Ethernet iSCSI host connections and Fibre Channel high-bandwidth ports are supported. Like other powerful Windows-based software, SANmelody runs on a variety of hardware platforms and disk drives on Windows, Linux, UNIX, NetWare, and Mac OS systems.

SANmaestro

SANmaestro is an analysis and decision support tool that monitors, reports, charts, gathers, and analyzes system performance and resource utilization information from multiple networked systems. It generates useful reports and charts, customized to fit the organization's reporting and analysis needs.

SANmaestro software is used to:

- Collect system performance and utilization metrics

- Analyze historical data accumulated over long periods (up to two years)

- Chart, tabulate, and analyze selected metrics with spreadsheets

- Perform hypothetical analyses

- Develop customized reports and charts with SANmaestro's development toolkit

- Export historical data to third-party tools and network management frameworks for further analysis, processing, or audit reporting

HP OpenView Storage Area Manager

HP OpenView Storage Area Manager (SAM) software allows the user to selectively monitor, manage, optimize, and plan storage and storage service availability, performance, usage, cost, and growth. OpenView SAM also enables management and planning for capacity related to Oracle and Microsoft Exchange applications.

The HP OpenView Storage Area Manager software suite consists of five functional modules:

1. *Storage Node Manager*: For device management
2. *Storage Builder*: For capacity management
3. *Storage Optimizer*: For performance management
4. *Storage Allocator*: For storage allocation and virtualized access control
5. *Storage Accountant*: For usage metering and billing

Each component functions either individually or together to enable integrated storage resource, application capacity, and infrastructure management. It integrates with third-party reporting tools and enterprise management tools, and supports Storage Management Initiative Specification (SMI-S)–based devices.

IBM SAN Volume Controller

IBM SAN Volume Controller (SVC) is a block-storage virtualization appliance. It implements an indirection, or virtualization, layer in a Fibre Channel SAN. It is shown in Figure 7-26 and is designed to:

- Combine storage capacity from multiple disk systems into a reservoir of capacity
- Help increase storage utilization by providing host applications with more flexible access
- Help improve productivity of storage administrators
- Support improved application availability by insulating host applications
- Enable a tiered storage environment in which the cost of storage can be better matched to the value of data
- Support advanced copy services from higher- to lower-cost devices

IBM TotalStorage SAN Volume Controller

The IBM TotalStorage SAN Volume Controller enables changes to physical storage with little or no disruption. It simplifies the storage infrastructure by combining the capacity from multiple disk storage systems into a single storage pool, which can be managed from a central point. Its features include the following:

- Manages large storage environments through expanded scalability
- Enables changes to physical storage systems with minimal or no impact to the applications running on the hosts
- Reduces downtime for planned and unplanned outages, maintenance, and backups
- Increases storage capacity utilization, uptime, administrator productivity, and efficiency
- Provides a single set of advanced copy services across multiple heterogeneous storage systems

Figure 7-26 IBM SAN Volume Controller implements a virtualization layer in a Fibre Channel SAN.

EMC VisualSAN

VisualSAN provides administrators with a single view of all devices across their storage networks and delivers advanced network, performance, and configuration management capabilities. The VisualSAN management suite includes three modules:

1. *VisualSAN Network Manager*: This is the base VisualSAN application for monitoring independent SAN devices. It serves as a common interface for other modules.
2. *VisualSAN Configuration Manager*: This module allows administrators to capture the state of a SAN configuration at a point in time for comparison, historical reference, change management, asset management, and replication of a specific SAN topology.
3. *VisualSAN Performance Manager*: The performance manager provides live and historical analysis of link statistics across a SAN.

EMC VisualSRM

VisualSRM is open management software that offers file-level reporting and centralized storage resource management across all of an organization's major storage and server platforms. It supports a wide range of applications, including Microsoft Exchange, Oracle, Sybase, and SQL Server databases. It also integrates with other storage management applications from backup and framework vendors such as IBM, Veritas, HP, CA, and BMC.

VisualSRM helps administrators to:

- Track system and individual storage consumption and enforce capacity utilization thresholds, ensuring capacity is available when and where needed
- Set policies for moving, deleting, compressing, and archiving files based on the age of the information, the time since the file was last accessed, and predefined capacity thresholds
- Categorize data and define category-based storage management policies that match the most appropriate and cost-effective storage media to the information stored on it

EMC Invista

EMC Invista is a network-based storage virtualization solution. It reduces the downtime associated with the movement of data across storage tiers in support of information lifecycle management (ILM) strategies. It can be used to copy, move, and migrate data across multiple tiers of heterogeneous storage arrays.

MetaSAN

MetaSAN is a high-speed file sharing SAN management software that is designed for cross-platform workgroup collaboration. It allows users of Windows, Linux, and Mac OS X to share files with one another. MetaSAN is shown in Figure 7-27.

Veritas CommandCentral Storage

Veritas CommandCentral Storage is a storage resource management solution providing centralized visibility and control across physical and virtual heterogeneous storage environments. It is shown in Figure 7-28, and its features include the following:

- Identifies current state of the storage infrastructure
- Implements prudent storage capacity management practices
- Transforms storage operations based on predefined policies
- Aligns storage operations with business objectives

DataPlow SAN File System

SAN File System (SFS) is DataPlow's flagship product that runs on devices ranging from consumer electronics to supercomputers. Its features include the following:

- Provides application compatibility
- Heterogeneous file sharing
- Highly available

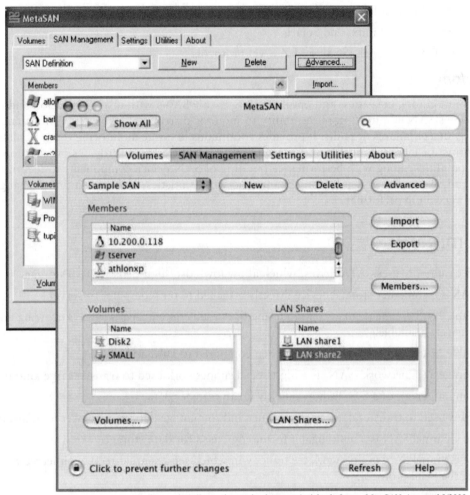

Source: http://www.tiger-technology.com/article.php?story=MetaSAN. Accessed 9/2009.

Figure 7-27   MetaSAN allows users of different operating systems to share files with one another.

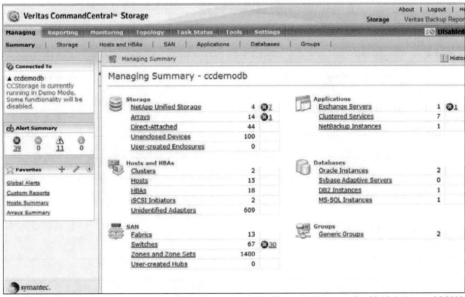

Source: http://www.symantec.com/business/products/screenshots.jsp?pcid=pcat_business_cont&pvid=19_1. Accessed 9/2009.

Figure 7-28   Veritas CommandCentral Storage provides centralized visibility and control across physical and virtual heterogeneous storage environments.

- Fine-grained tuning for optimal performance
- Supports Window, Linux, and Solaris
- Supports Fibre Channel, iSCSI, and Z-SAN protocols

NetWisdom

NetWisdom monitors, measures, and optimizes large-scale SANs with instrumentation and management software. It allows SAN administrators the ability to monitor distributed SANs for performance slowdowns and immediately detect failures or faults. It provides continuous line-rate monitoring that calculates statistics based on monitoring all Fibre Channel frames traveling through the SAN. It provides event recording and line-rate capture capabilities, along with performance trending of SAN device components to identify hardware degradation. It can also gather in-depth Fibre Channel network statistics, such as pending exchanges, to tune queue depths for maximum performance.

Chapter Summary

- NAS commonly uses SATA drives, which allow low-cost, high-density NAS storage.
- A DAS is a computer storage device directly attached to one computer or server.
- Scalable NAS is capable of accommodating file-based content that is always growing and must be pervasively available.
- Scalable NAS can be easily managed when compared to DAS and SAN.
- A storage area network (SAN) is a high-speed subnetwork used to transfer large amounts of data.
- The main benefit of a SAN is how quickly it can transfer data.
- iSCSI is used to transfer data on an intranet and to manage data storage over long distances.
- Fibre Channel SAN is a multigigabit technology used for data storage.
- Fibre Channel SAN is a network technology in which servers are directly connected to storage devices using the SCSI protocol.

Review Questions

1. Explain the NAS architecture.

_____

_____

_____

_____

2. What are the advantages of NAS?

_____

_____

_____

_____

3. What is scalable NAS?

_____

_____

_____

_____

4. What are the differences between NAS and DAS?

_____

_____

_____

_____

5. How is FreeNAS installed?

_____

_____

_____

_____

6. What is SAN?

_____

_____

_____

_____

7. What are the protocols used with SAN?

_____

_____

_____

_____

8. What are the components of Xsan?

_____

_____

_____

_____

9. What are the differences between SAN and NAS?

_____

_____

_____

_____

10. What is Fibre Channel SAN?

_____

_____

_____

_____

Hands-On Projects

1. Read about the differences between DAS, NAS, and SAN.

   ▪ Navigate to Chapter 7 of the Student Resource Center.

   ▪ Open DAS, NAS or SAN Choosing the Right Storage.pdf and read the content.

2. Read about IMB's NAS services.

   ▪ Navigate to Chapter 7 of the Student Resource Center.

   ▪ Open IBM Implementation Services for Network Attached Storage systems.pdf and read the content.

3. Read about massively scalable NAS.

   ▪ Navigate to Chapter 7 of the Student Resource Center.

   ▪ Open Massively Scalable NAS.pdf and read the content.

4. Read about using NAS for disaster recovery.

   ▪ Navigate to Chapter 7 of the Student Resource Center.

   ▪ Open Securing Data in Backup and Disaster Recovery.pdf and read the content.

5. Read about the evolution of SAN.

   ▪ Navigate to Chapter 7 of the Student Resource Center.

   ▪ Open SAN Evolution.pdf and read the content.

6. Read about SAN security.

   ▪ Navigate to Chapter 7 of the Student Resource Center.

   ▪ Open Security for SAN.pdf and read the content.

7. Read about using SAN for disaster recovery.

   ▪ Navigate to Chapter 7 of the Student Resource Center.

   ▪ Open iSCSI-based Storage Area Networks for Disaster Recovery.pdf and read the content.

8. Read more about SAN security.

   ▪ Navigate to Chapter 7 of the Student Resource Center.

   ▪ Open The Growing Need for Security in Storage Area Networks.pdf and read the content.

Chapter 8

Disaster Recovery Services and Tools

Objectives

After completing this chapter, you should be able to:

- Understand the importance of backing up data
- Understand computer backup practices
- Implement several backup techniques
- Use data backup and recovery tools
- Implement off-site backup
- Use enterprise backup tools

Key Terms

Job   a backup, restore, or utility operation

Introduction to Disaster Recovery Services and Tools

An organization's data can be even more critical and valuable than its physical assets. If anything happens to those data, be it by accident, attack, or any other disaster, the effects can be devastating. A good backup policy can reduce or even eliminate the damage caused by data loss, but far too many organizations rely on manual backups, which can be unreliable. This chapter teaches you how to implement effective and efficient data backup procedures.

Why Back Up Data?

The main purpose of data backup is to keep secondary copies of data in case the original data are lost. Data can be lost due to any number of reasons, including:

- Hardware failure
- Theft

- Data corruption
- Malicious attack
- Power outage
- Fire
- Flooding
- Virus or worm
- Human error

Backups can be used to access older versions of files, in case changes to files cause undesired effects. Backups can also reduce the amount of IT resources required to maintain an application, if the organization decides to archive older records and only work with current ones.

Preventing Data Loss

Organizations should take the following steps to protect data against loss:

1. *Back up often and wisely*: The most effective thing to do is back up data on a daily basis, but this can be costly and time-consuming. For the average business, the percentage of data that changes daily is between 2% and 5%, so it can save significant time by only backing up those changes.

2. *Prioritize data for disaster recovery*: An organization should prioritize each system and its related data, including e-mail, telephones, databases, file servers, and Web servers. Typically, systems are prioritized into three categories: redundant (required immediately), highly available (minutes to hours), and backed up (four hours to days).

3. *Archive important data for the long term*: Depending on federal and state regulations, data must be retained for between seven and 17 years. Older data should be stored in a separate physical storage location. Some businesses will choose a full-service company that picks up, stores, and delivers the data when it is needed.

4. *Store data cost-effectively*: Most small-to-midsize businesses do not have available IT resources to set up and manage a storage solution. These businesses may wish to purchase an integrated solution. The up-front cost may be a bit more, but in the long run, the time, money, and effort spent on a custom solution will be far greater.

Developing an Effective Data Backup Strategy

While developing a good backup strategy, the organization must first determine what data backup platform (hardware) is best for protecting the data. Tape backup systems are least expensive and are commonly used to back up large amounts of data. This technology only requires user intervention to physically change tapes; there are some technologies to automatically rotate tapes, allowing little chance of human error.

Organizations must next determine how much data must be protected and then choose a backup device suited for that amount. DDS (Digital Data Storage) tape backup systems are normally used in small organizations with less than 10 GB of data to protect. These systems are also best suited for small/home offices because they are economical and considered reliable. On the other hand, DLT (Digital Linear Tape) systems are best suited for larger businesses because they contain great data storage capacity. These systems contain automatic rotation systems to spread data across multiple high-capacity tapes.

The next step is to determine the best backup methodology. Many backup systems provide these options:

- *Full*: Stores a copy of all data to a tape backup, regardless of whether the data have been modified since the last backup was performed. This changes the archive property bit of the file from 1 to 0, indicating that the file has been backed up.

- *Differential*: Backs up every file on the drive that has been added or changed since the last full backup. This does not change the archive property bit of the file from 1 to 0, indicating that the file has changed since the last full backup. Thus, the file will be backed up each time a differential backup is performed. Compared to an incremental backup, it takes more time to run each differential backup and requires more space for each one, but a full restore operation requires only the last full backup and the last differential backup.

- *Incremental*: Backs up files that have been modified since the last backup operation. This changes the archive property bit of the file from 1 to 0, indicating that the file has now been backed up and will not be backed up on the next incremental backup. Compared to a differential backup, it takes less time to run each incremental backup and requires less space for each backup operation, but would require more time to restore the system, as the last full backup and each sequential incremental backup must be used.

The final step is to develop a rotation scheme and decide where to store the backup media. Many organizations store the physical backup media within about three feet of the server. This means that, should a disaster strike the server, it is likely to affect the backups as well. The best course of action is to place the physical media off-site, but still close enough to access it when needed.

Many organizations forget to secure backup data, which makes backups a common target for attackers. Off-site storage must be sufficiently secure. Organizations must always encrypt backup tapes.

A successful backup strategy should meet the following criteria:

- Off-site backup
- Scheduled backup
- Daily notifications
- Sufficient space
- Data availability at all times
- Adequate security
- Guarantee from provider
- Tested regularly

Backup Techniques

Disk Mirroring

Disk mirroring involves creating an exact bit-by-bit copy of all data on a physical disk drive. The mirrored disks are stored off-site and kept synchronized. This way, if the primary disk fails, important data can be accessed from the other disk. Disk mirroring can be done in two ways:

1. *Synchronous mirroring*: The disk is updated on every write request, which can affect application performance.

2. *Asynchronous mirroring*: Multiple changes to the primary disks are reflected in the secondary mirrored disk at predetermined intervals, which does not require an uninterrupted high-bandwidth connection.

Disk mirroring has a few drawbacks. If a file is deleted from the primary disk, it is also deleted from the secondary disk. Also, any effects from viruses or data theft will be synchronized. Establishing a disk mirroring infrastructure may require additional resources and continuous maintenance.

Snapshots

A storage snapshot contains a set of reference markers that point to data stored on a disk drive, on a tape, or in a storage area network (SAN). It streamlines access to stored data and hastens the data recovery process. There are two main types of snapshots:

1. *Copy-on-write snapshot*: Creates a snapshot of changes or modifications to stored data each time new data are entered or existing data are updated

2. *Split-mirror snapshot*: Physically clones a storage entity at a regular interval, allowing offline access and making it simple to recover data

Continuous Data Protection (CDP)

CDP, also known as continuous backup or synchronous mirroring, involves backing up data by automatically saving a copy of every change made to those data. This creates an electronic record of storage snapshots, with one storage snapshot for every instant that data modification occurs, allowing the administrator to restore data to any point in time.

Parity Protection

Parity protection involves creating a parity disk from all the available disks in the array. If any disk in the array fails, the parity disk can be used to recover the data from the failed disk. Parity protection represents a low-cost and low-maintenance mirroring infrastructure, but if two drives fail simultaneously, then the data will be lost completely. Also, any threat that affects one disk could also affect the parity disk.

Backup Schedules

The following are two backup schedules:

1. *Intraday data protection*: In an intraday data protection system, data are backed up several times during the day. The data can be copied onto the same disk or onto a remote disk. Backup strategies using intraday data protection include:

   - Snapshots
   - Application dumps (where application data are backed up every few hours)
   - Continuous data protection

2. *Weekend and nightly backups*: There are three types of weekend and nightly backups, as previously mentioned:

   - Full backups
   - Differential backups
   - Incremental backups

Removable Backup Media

Some types of removable backup media are:

- CD-ROM
- DVD-ROM
- Tape drive
- USB drive
- External hard drive

One of the main disadvantages of using removable backup media is that it requires the user to perform data backup and take the media off-site, which may increase the risk of data loss. Removable backup media contains limited storage space, and there is a risk of media damage.

Disks Versus Tapes

Tape backups have the following features:

- Cheap method for archiving data
- Slow, cumbersome, labor intensive and expensive
- Takes more time to restore the data after the disaster event
- Used when deep archiving is required, such as maintaining important financial documents for tax or other purposes
- Require the user to intervene only when a tape change is needed
- Little chance of human error because tape is not changed daily
- Minimum number of tapes required for fully restoring

Disks have the following features:

- More reliable than tape backup
- Provide faster backup and faster restores by sending multiple backup streams to a disk target
- Shelf life of disks is far longer than that of tapes

- Less prone to errors and corruption
- Used to access data quickly in the event of a disaster
- Provide higher speed and higher storage capacity than tapes
- Provide greater access to information
- Reduce costs due to increased automation

Potential Risks

There are several risks in the backup and retrieval process. For instance, data backed up at a remote location can be a target for thieves and attackers, so the data should be encrypted. Other risks include the following:

- Storage media may be stolen from the delivery vehicle.
- Storage media on the return trip from the centralized storage site may be delivered to the wrong customer.
- The tape system could be destroyed.

The following steps can help manage these risks:

1. Carefully scrutinize contracts with the off-site backup provider.
2. Use locked containers to transport tapes.
3. Encrypt all data prior to writing to backup tapes, or selectively encrypt only sensitive data.
4. Include backup procedures in the corporate strategy.

Challenges in Backup and Recovery

Some of the challenges include the following:

- Increased complexity and burden
- Limited capabilities of conventional solutions
- Time requirements
- Reliability
- Size of data
- Expensive new technologies
- Lack of a simple disaster recovery process
- Maintenance

Backup and Recovery Checklist

The following is a backup and recovery checklist:

- Keep the backup plan as simple as possible.
- Establish reliability through automation. Minimize the potential for human error.
- Implement immediate, granular recovery options.
- Allow users to securely recover individual files.
- Make disaster recovery plans flexible.

When purchasing a third-party data backup solution, organizations should keep the following considerations in mind:

- Does it meet the organization's recovery objectives, including RTO and RPO?
- How easy and reliable is data restoration?
- Does it store data off-site in case of a disaster?

Item	Yes	No	Applicable	Not Applicable	Comments
Select the purpose of the test. What aspects of the plan are being evaluated?					
Describe the objectives of the test. How will you measure successful achievement of the objectives?					
Meet with management and explain the test and objectives. Gain their agreement and support.					
Have management announce the test and the expected completion time.					
Collect test results at the end of the test period.					
Evaluate results. Was recovery successful? Why or why not?					
Determine the implications of the test results. Does successful recovery in a simple case imply successful recovery for all critical jobs in the tolerable outage period?					
Make recommendations for changes. Call for responses by a given date.					
Notify other areas of results. Include users and auditors.					
Change the disaster recovery plan manual as necessary.					

Figure 8-1 This template can be used to conduct a data recovery test.

- Does it comply with the organization's existing disaster recovery plan?
- Are the data secure and encrypted?
- What is the labor and maintenance requirement?
- When will the data be backed up?
- How much does the solution cost, including labor, maintenance, and support?

Testing Data Recovery

It is important to regularly test the backup and recovery solution, perhaps as often as every month. Organizations can use the template in Figure 8-1 to conduct a data recovery test.

Data Backup and Recovery Tools

Norton Ghost

Norton Ghost is a comprehensive disk imaging solution. It is shown in Figure 8-2 and includes the following features:

- Full system backup (disk image)
- File and folder backup
- FTP backup
- Off-site backup
- Remote management over LAN
- Google Desktop integration
- Advanced compression and encryption

Norton Online Backup

Norton Online Backup delivers automatic file backup over the Internet using a secure Web portal. It stores files on separate storage arrays at the data center for added file safety. It is shown in Figure 8-3, and its features include the following:

- Automatically backs up files to one central, secured location
- Quickly recovers data in case of hard drive crashes, file system damage, or natural disasters
- Allows access and file restoration from any Web-connected PC

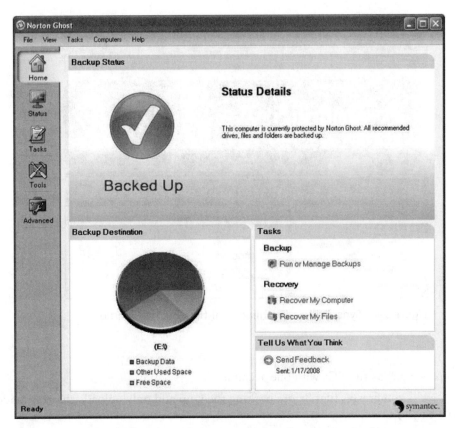

Figure 8-2   Norton Ghost uses Drive Image to make accurate backups.

Figure 8-3   Norton Online Backup allows file access from any
Web browser.

Figure 8-4 Syncplicity is an online, real-time backup solution.

- Backs up as many as five PCs with one account
- Automatically compresses files before backing them up and only uploads changes made since previous backups
- Uses 256-bit government-grade encryption
- Eliminates relying on external backup drives and memory cards

Syncplicity

Syncplicity, shown in Figure 8-4, is an online backup solution with the following features:

- Real-time backup
- Share any folder with anyone
- Access anytime, anywhere
- Uses 128-bit SSL

Handy Backup Server

Handy Backup Server for Windows performs automatic backup, restoration, and synchronization of multiple servers and workstations. All workstation backup tasks are managed by a central server and require no user intervention. It supports image backup for both servers and workstations on CD/DVD, external USB and Firewire drives, FTP, SFTP, LAN, and more.

Handy Backup Server is shown in Figure 8-5, and its features include the following:

- Centralized backup, operated from a single server and invisible for users on remote workstations (running as a Windows service)
- Full and incremental backup of workstations and the central server
- Backs up ODBC databases (MySQL, Microsoft SQL, Oracle, FoxPro, Microsoft Access, etc.)
- Plug-ins that save Microsoft Exchange Server, Oracle, Microsoft SQL, DB2, and Lotus Notes/Domino data during remote workstation backup and local server backup
- Minimal consumption of system resources, allowing workstation backup tasks during working hours
- Image backup of server and workstations (backing up of the entire hard drive including all primary, logical, and extended partitions, as well as system and boot records)
- Backs up Microsoft Word documents, Excel files, PowerPoint files, etc. (using file filtering)

Source: http://www.handybackup.net/backup-screenshots/ftp1.shtml. Accessed 9/2009.

Figure 8-5 Handy Backup Server performs automatic backup on Windows machines.

- Excludes temporal, system, and other files from backup (using file filtering)
- Bidirectional synchronization of network computers
- Allows task scheduling and launching other applications before or after backup tasks
- Verifies images
- E-mail notification after backing up remote workstations
- Remote task management by a central server
- Direct backing up to the central server, requiring no disk space on client computers for backup files

NovaBACKUP

NovaBACKUP is designed for small offices running an SQL and/or Exchange Server. It works with Microsoft's Volume Shadow Copy Service (also known as VSS) in order to back up open files online. It is shown in Figure 8-6, and its features include the following:

- Free and premium off-site backups
- Users can backup and recover data anywhere
- Disk imaging
- Microsoft SQL 2008 and Exchange 2007 support
- Flexible scheduler
- E-mail reporting
- Virus protection and updates

BackupAssist

BackupAssist performs automatic scheduled backups of Windows servers. It is able to back up everything from individual files to complete servers (including Active Directory, Exchange, and SQL). It is shown in Figure 8-7, and its features include the following:

- Simple restoration of individual e-mails, calendars, tasks, notes, contacts, or entire mailboxes
- Automatically backs up Exchange mailboxes

Figure 8-6   NovaBACKUP uses VSS to back up open files.

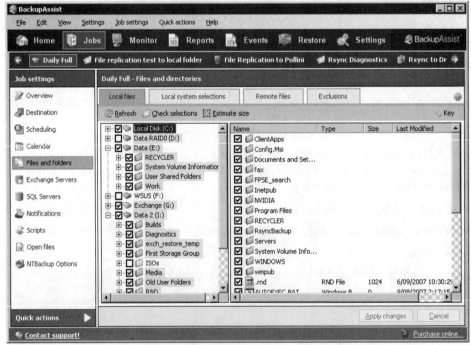

Source: http://www.backupassist.com/images/tour/screenshots/system_files.png. Accessed 9/2009.

Figure 8-7   BackupAssist automatically backs up Windows servers.

- Live, online backups of SQL Server databases
- Backs up open files using an open-file manager
- Straightforward restore wizard for individual databases and complete servers
- Allows user to restore data from different points in time

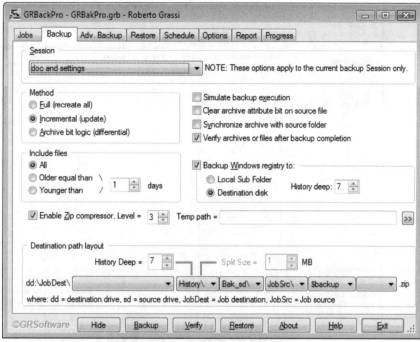

Figure 8-8   GRBackPro creates backups in Zip files.

GRBackPro

GRBackPro can run as a service while the user is logged off and has an integrated scheduler to plan backups. It supports standard Zip compression to save disk space and allow backups with any Zip-compatible software. The program supports network shares, hard drives, CDs, DVDs, and other removable storage.

GRBackPro is shown in Figure 8-8, and its features include the following:

- Supports network UNC names
- Can run as a Windows 2008/Vista/2003/XP/2000/NT service process
- Can span across multiple removable media
- Supports PKZIP 2.0 standard password protection scheme
- Allows user to copy files or compress them into a single archive or one archive per folder
- Re-creates source directory structure
- Synchronizes user backup archives with source files and folders
- Runs in the background and can be run from the system tray

Genie Backup Manager Pro

Genie Backup Manager Pro backs up an entire system to a secure location, and recovers it instantly. It supports 256-bit encryption and can be set up to run automatically at preset time intervals and rotate various backup types. Genie Backup Manager Pro is shown in Figure 8-9.

Veritas NetBackup

Symantec's Veritas NetBackup is a data backup solution for UNIX, Windows, Linux, and NetWare environments. It is shown in Figure 8-10, and its features include the following:

- Advanced disk-based data protection features that include data deduplication, virtual tape library (VTL) controls, support for third-party disk appliances, and snapshot capabilities
- Integrated data protection and recovery for virtual environments, critical applications, databases, and servers
- Single platform to manage, protect, and recover data across storage tiers, locations, and operating systems

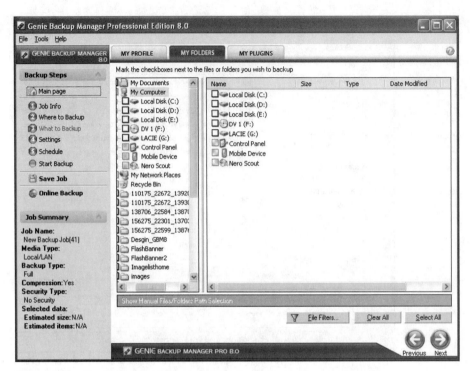

Figure 8-9 Genie Backup Manager Pro supports government-grade 256-bit encryption.

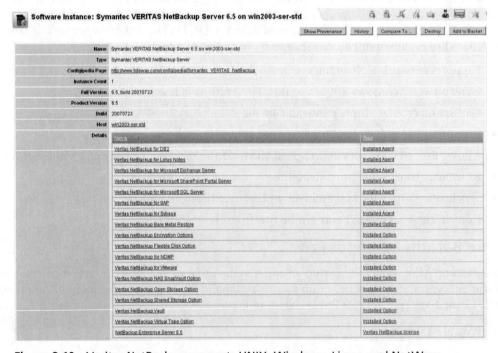

Figure 8-10 Veritas NetBackup supports UNIX, Windows, Linux, and NetWare.

- Automate and manage snapshots for VMware virtual machines from host-based and array-based providers
- Provides desktop, remote office, and data center protection across the entire enterprise
- Advanced protection for VMWare environments, e-mail applications such as Microsoft Exchange Server 2007, and large databases

Off-Site Data Backup

Off-site backup involves storing backup data at a separate, secure location, so that if any disaster occurs at the primary site, the backup data will remain safe. Data can either be physically moved to the secondary site using storage media, such as DVDs or backup tapes, or it can be transmitted using a network such as the Internet.

Figure 8-11 shows how off-site data backup over the Internet works.

Advantages of Off-Site Data Backup

Some advantages of backing up data off-site include:

- Protects data in the event of a disaster
- Automatically performs the backup operation
- Encrypts data
- Eliminates the necessity of tapes
- Protects data from damages such as hardware failure, database corruption, and natural disasters
- Can be cheaper than tape alternatives
- Convenient
- Dependable
- Efficient
- Data can be accessed from other remote systems

FTP Backup

File Transfer Protocol (FTP) is typically used to reliably transfer large files over the Internet. Data can be accessed on an FTP server from a backup program, a special FTP client, or a standard Web browser. Private FTP servers require authentication, which provides a layer of security.

Advantages of using FTP servers for backup include the following:

- Users can view the files stored on the FTP server any time using any FTP client or Web browser.
- Mobile users can back up data from anywhere in the world with an Internet connection.
- FTP backup is less expensive than a specialized remote backup service.

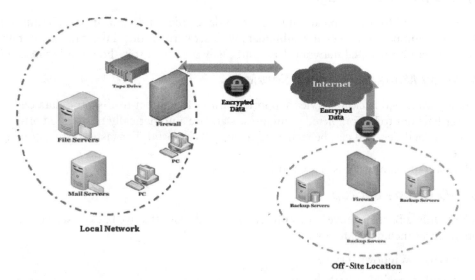

Figure 8-11 Be sure to encrypt data before transmitting it over an open network like the Internet.

Figure 8-12 EMC Remote Office Backup catches duplicate data before it is transferred.

The main disadvantage in this method is data security. FTP is not a secure protocol, and anyone who discovers a legitimate user's username and password can easily access files. Data must be manually encrypted before transferring it to the FTP server, or else it could be intercepted and viewed.

One option is to store data in a standard password-protected Zip archive. The data can then be extracted using any Zip client, many of which use strong encryption algorithms, such as AES or Blowfish.

Off-Site Backup Services

EMC Remote Office Backup

EMC Remote Office Backup uses EMC Avamar software, which catches duplicate data before they are moved across the enterprise network, reducing bandwidth demand. It includes Mozy Enterprise software, which backs up data over the Internet with a monthly subscription. EMC Remote Office Backup is shown in Figure 8-12.

Egnyte Online File Storage

Egnyte is designed for easy upload and storage of large files and data. It provides an online file server, which supports any number of folders and subfolders with set permissions. Files can be securely accessed using either a Web browser or a mapped network drive and easily searched. It is shown in Figure 8-13.

DataReady Managed Backup Service

DataReady Managed Backup Service supports features like direct-to-disk and data deduplication, which allow full server backups to be completed in minutes. Data are automatically transferred off-site every night to secure data storage facilities, and can be recovered using a Web portal. For faster restoration, a client-side program is available.

A diagram of DataReady is shown in Figure 8-14.

DriveHQ Online Backup

DriveHQ Online Backup delivers a secure, reliable, and cost-effective backup service. It is shown in Figure 8-15, and its features include the following:

- Runs as a Windows service
- Scheduled weekly or daily backups
- Real-time backups as change occurs

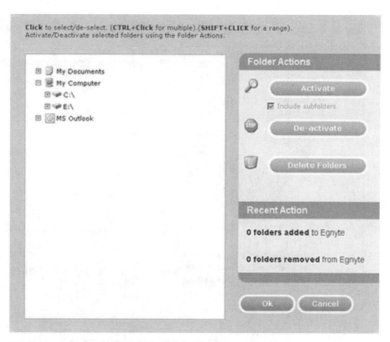

Figure 8-13   Egnyte Online File Storage is designed to handle large files.

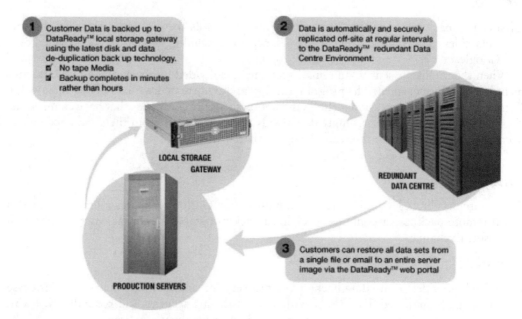

Figure 8-14   DataReady backs up servers in minutes.

- Incremental backups, saving time and storage space
- Easy and reliable restore through Web, DriveHQ Online Backup, or FileManager
- Quick launch from Windows Explorer through right-click menu
- Encryption of backup data
- Secure data transfer through HTTPS/SSL

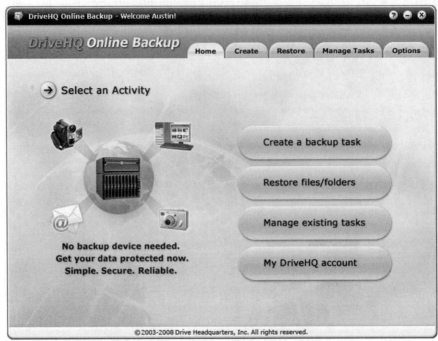

Source: http://www.drivehq.com/Downloads/OnlineBackupScreenshots/main.htm. Accessed 9/2009.

Figure 8-15　DriveHQ Online Backup backs up data to a remote server.

Offsiter

Offsiter is a backup utility that compresses files and sends them as encrypted attachments to off-site e-mail accounts. Files can be stored using any e-mail account, including free accounts provided by Yahoo!, Microsoft, and Google.

When the archive is sent to an e-mail account, it is divided into separate e-mail attachments. Each attachment is strongly encrypted. The program can use archives created with any compression application; however, Offsiter's own Zip compression includes the option to archive only files that have changed since the last backup. To recover an archive, a user simply downloads the attachments from the e-mail account and uses Offsiter to decrypt and merge them to re-create the original archive.

Offsiter is shown in Figure 8-16.

Ahsay

Ahsay supports brick-level Exchange backup (including Outlook e-mails, contacts, and calendars) for Internet-based remote backups. It contains specialized backup databases such as Microsoft SQL Server, Oracle, and Microsoft Exchange.

Rhinoback

Rhinoback provides secure data backup and recovery for small and medium-sized businesses. It stores data in a professionally managed data center with state-of-the-art security and redundancy. It can perform backups automatically every day, and data can be restored immediately at any time.

Rhinoback is shown in Figure 8-17, and its features include the following:

- User-configurable incremental backup mode
- Offline backup mode and logout backup reminder
- Customizable backup schedule
- Compresses and encrypts data automatically
- Incremental backup strategy
- Supports both full and incremental backups
- Runs on Windows, Mac OS X, Linux, NetWare, UNIX, and all other platforms supporting a Java 2 Runtime Environment

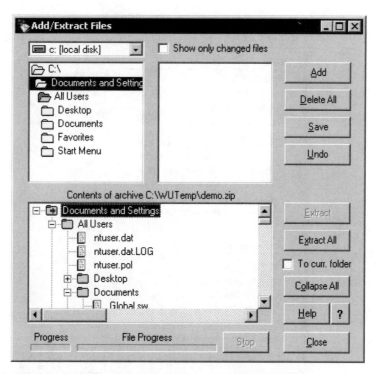

Figure 8-16   Offsiter stores backups in e-mail accounts.

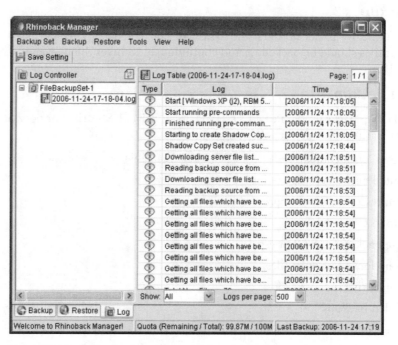

Figure 8-17   Rhinoback is designed for small and medium-sized businesses.

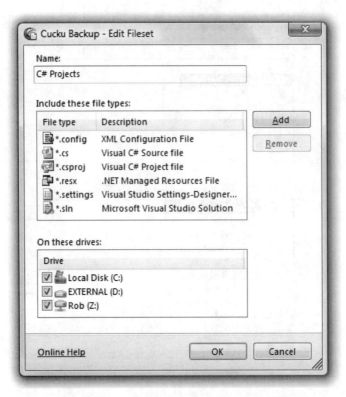

Figure 8-18 Cucku backs up data and sends them to a trusted friend.

Cucku Backup

Cucku automatically backs up data and sends an encrypted copy to a trusted friend or family member. It chooses what files should be backed up and continuously archives them, even if they are in use. Cucku is shown in Figure 8-18.

Safe Data Backup

Safe Data Backup backs up data to a CD, DVD, local drive, USB drive, or network drive. It is shown in Figure 8-19, and its features include the following:

- Windows Vista compatible
- Unlimited backup configurations
- Uncompressed or Zip-compressed backups
- Backup to CD or DVD
- Remote backup via FTP or e-mail
- Backs up locked or open files
- Network drive support
- Scheduled backups
- Saves revisions of modified files
- Saves deleted files

Backup Platinum

Backup Platinum creates backups on any type of storage media: hard drive, CD, DVD, Blu-ray disc, or FTP server. It provides 128-bit encryption with Blowfish and Zip compression on the fly. A built-in CD/DVD engine allows for erasing a rewritable disk before burning and automatically splitting large backups into several parts using disk spanning.

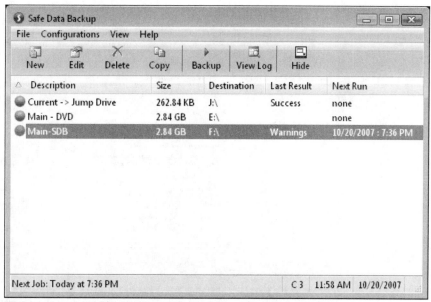

Figure 8-19   Safe Data Backup works with network drives.

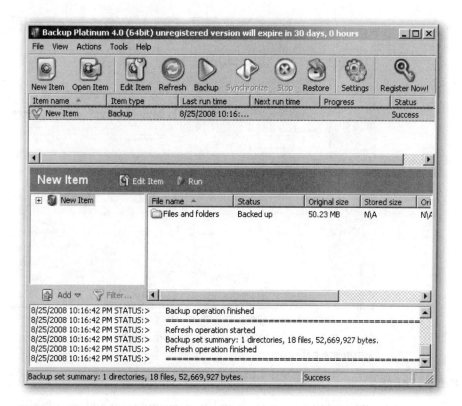

Figure 8-20   Backup Platinum can perform backup tasks in Windows
service mode.

Backup Platinum is designed for Windows. The program comes with a flexible scheduler to provide automatic backups and can run in service mode under Windows NT/2000/XP/2003 to execute scheduled tasks even when no one is logged in.

It creates detailed logs of all operations and can back up open files. Restoring files is as easy as clicking a button. Backup Platinum is shown in Figure 8-20.

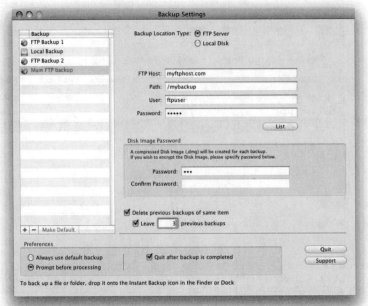

Source: http://zevrix.com/screenshots/ib/ib-web.jpg. Accessed 9/2009.

Figure 8-21 Instant Backup is a simple FTP backup utility.

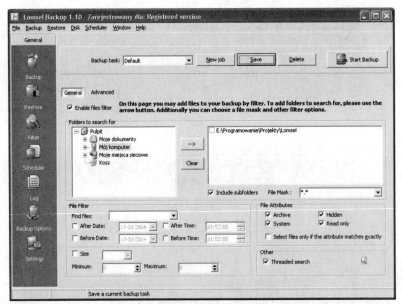

Source: http://www.lomsel.net/index.php?action=shotspl&lng=en&progid=1. Accessed 9/2009.

Figure 8-22 Lomsel Backup uses Windows Scheduler to automate backups.

Instant Backup

Instant Backup is a simple solution to back up and archive important and sensitive files to a password-protected FTP site. It is not a replacement for complete backup systems; its main draws are its ease of use and flexibility. Instant Backup is shown in Figure 8-21.

Lomsel Backup

Lomsel Backup works with Windows Scheduler to automate backup processes. It is shown in Figure 8-22, and its features include the following:

- Simple and intuitive interface
- Fast access to the most important options

- Shell integration
- Backup settings adjustment
- Backs up open files
- Registry backup
- Windows shell backup
- Incremental backup
- Backup password protection
- Export/import backup job settings
- Wizards for backup and restore
- Spanned backup files
- Strong 256-bit encryption

Enterprise Backup Tools

Symantec Backup Exec System Recovery

Backup Exec System Recovery is a complete disk-based system recovery solution for Windows-based servers, desktops, and laptops. It captures a recovery point of the entire live Windows system, including the operating system, applications, databases, all files, device drivers, profiles, settings, and registry, without disrupting the user. A recovery point can be saved to various media or storage devices such as SAN, NAS, DAS, RAID, and Blu-ray disc/DVD/CD.

Backup Exec System Recovery can be managed remotely either by a licensed copy of Backup Exec System Recovery or Backup Exec System Recovery Manager. Backup Exec System Recovery Manager can be used to centrally deploy, modify, and maintain recovery activities, jobs, and policies for local and remote systems. It can be used to constantly monitor and resolve problems. Backup Exec System Recovery works together with Google Desktop and Backup Exec Retrieve to recover end-user files without IT support. The Symantec Backup Exec System Recovery Granular Restore option can be used to restore an individual's Microsoft Exchange e-mails, folders, and mailboxes.

Figure 8-23 shows the steps of running Symantec Backup Exec System Recovery.

Key Features and Benefits

Benefits of Symantec Backup Exec System Recovery include:

- Rapid and reliable recovery, even with dissimilar hardware or virtual environments
- Flexible off-site protection and enhanced recovery capabilities
- Integration with other leading technologies

It also includes the following features:

- Flexible restoration options
- Enhanced virtual support
- Easy remote system recovery
- Enhanced Exchange, SharePoint, and file/folder recovery
- Scalable, centralized management

Symantec Backup Exec for Window Servers

Symantec Backup Exec for Windows Servers delivers disk-to-tape backup and fast, efficient recovery. In Backup Exec, backup, restore, and utility operations are known as *jobs*. These jobs are performed through the administration console. Administrators run the administration console from the media server or a remote computer. Once jobs are created, the Backup Exec server components begin backup, restore, and utility operations on the media server.

Figure 8-24 shows a diagram of Symantec Backup Exec.

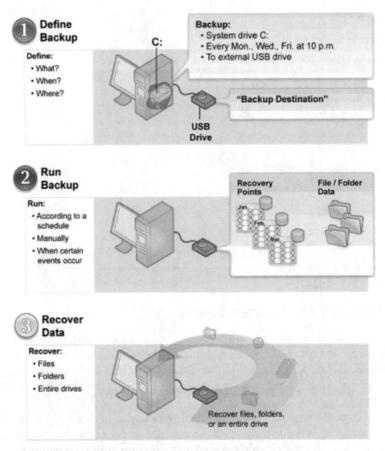

Figure 8-23 Symantec Backup Exec System Recovery captures a live recovery point of the entire Windows system.

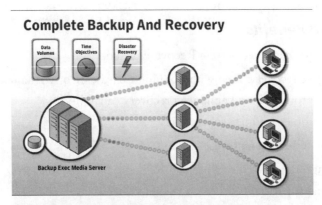

Figure 8-24 Symantec Backup Exec provides fast, efficient recovery.

Key Features and Benefits

Key features of Symantec Backup Exec include:

- Comprehensive data protection for VMware Infrastructures and Microsoft Virtual Servers
- Data protection for Microsoft Windows 2008 Server
- Expanded granular recovery benefits for SharePoint Server

- Backup Exec infrastructure manager
- Enhanced protection for NDMP-enabled NAS devices
- Acts as a remote media server agent for Linux servers
- Complete data and system protection for Windows environments
- Protects data for physical and virtual server environments
- Granular Recovery Technology (GRT) recovers critical Microsoft application data in seconds
- Centralized three-tier setup, reporting, and patch management
- Scalable heterogeneous support through remote agents and options
- Continuous data protection for Exchange, SQL, and file servers
- Multiproduct integration
- Online storage

Benefits include:

- Fast and reliable
- Eliminates backup windows
- Enables faster backups
- Recovers individual files, Exchange messages/mailboxes, and SharePoint documents within seconds
- Provides file retrieval for the end user without any IT intervention
- Provides complete disk- and tape-based data protection
- Increases Windows application availability
- Offers simple, scalable, and centralized management
- Provides certified compatibility across Microsoft Windows 2000 and Windows Server 2003 environments
- Provides complete data and system protection
- Provides granular recovery and continuous protection

AmeriVault-AV

AmeriVault-AV is an online data backup service that delivers automated, one-step online backup and off-site storage. It is shown in Figure 8-25, and its key features include the following:

- Continuous data protection (CDP)
- Total automation
- Point-and-click restores
- Centralized management
- Redundant storage
- End-to-end encryption
- Compliant processing
- Integrity verification
- Supports Windows, UNIX, Linux, Mac, VMware, System i, Novell NetWare, and Sun/HP UX/AIX
- Automatic upgrades

MozyPro

MozyPro is a simple Internet backup system, shown in Figure 8-26, containing the following features:

- 128-bit SSL encryption using AES and Blowfish
- Automatically detects and backs up new and changed files
- Provides automatic or scheduled backups

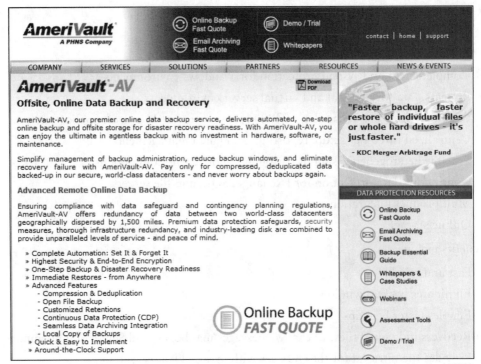

Source: www.amerivault.com. Accessed 9/2009.

Figure 8-25 AmeriVault-AV is a one-step online backup service.

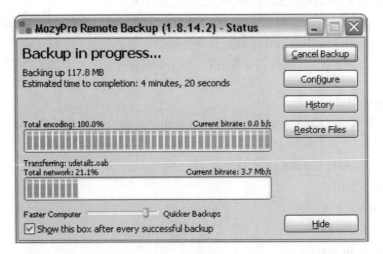

Figure 8-26 MozyPro is a simple Internet backup system.

- Provides block-level incremental backups
- Supports SQL, Exchange, network drives, Windows, and Mac

PC Backup Pro

Migo PC Backup Pro is an image-based backup and recovery tool. It backs up open files and scans the backups for viruses. PC Backup Pro is shown in Figure 8-27.

Auto Backup

Auto Backup can automatically or manually back up critical data to a local disk, network drive, or remote FTP server. It allows full, incremental, and differential backups on Windows systems with 256-bit encryption. Auto Backup is shown in Figure 8-28.

Figure 8-27   PC Backup Pro can scan backups for viruses.

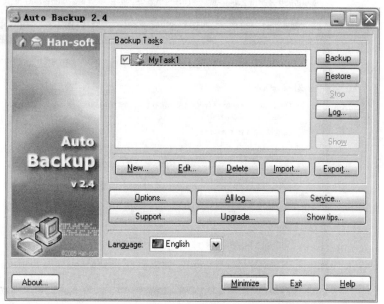

Figure 8-28   Auto Backup allows full, incremental, and differential backups.

SyncBackPro

SyncBackPro can be used for backing up and synchronizing files on local drives, network drives, removable drives, or FTP servers. It supports backups spanning multiple CDs or DVDs, and can synchronize files with an e-mail server. Users can even write their own scripts to control the program. SyncBackPro is shown in Figure 8-29.

Kabooza

Kabooza is an online backup service that automatically backs up files and photos without user interaction. It encrypts files before transfer and stores multiple copies of files in several geographical locations to ensure protection. It also maintains a file's history for 30 days to restore accidentally deleted or damaged files. Kabooza is shown in Figure 8-30.

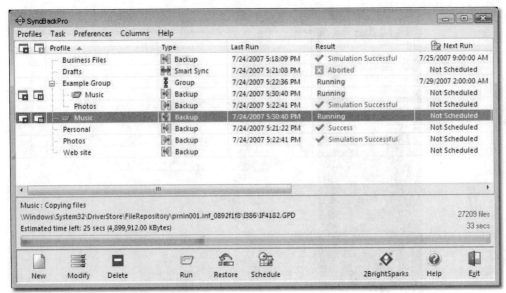

Source: http://www.2brightsparks.com/syncback/sbpro-screenshots.html. Accessed 9/2009.

Figure 8-29   Users can write their own SyncBackPro scripts.

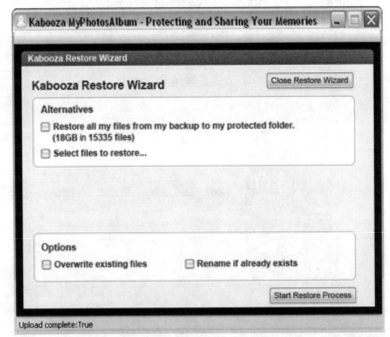

Source: http://www.kabooza.com/images/kabooza_restore_wizard.jpg. Accessed 9/2009.

Figure 8-30   Kabooza keeps a file's history for 30 days.

iStorage

iStorage features unlimited storage space for photos, files, and critical data. It features redundant data storage with 256-bit encryption and stores large files using the included WhaleMail tool. iStorage is shown in Figure 8-31.

SOS Online Backup

SOS Online Backup backs up files to a global network of SOS datacenters. Data are compressed using proprietary delta compression. It is shown in Figure 8-32, and its features include the following:

- Continuous data protection
- Integrated local backup

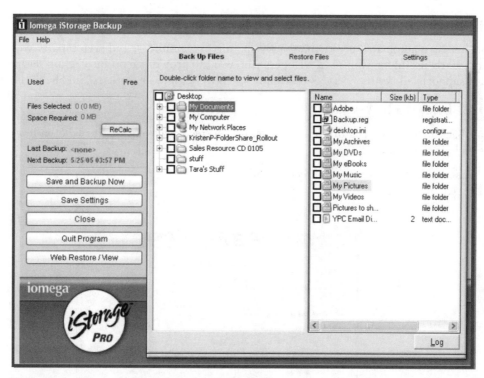

Figure 8-31   iStorage provides unlimited storage space.

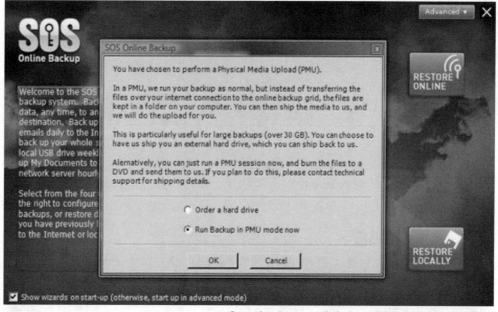

Source: http://www.sosonlinebackup.com/features.htm. Accessed 9/2009.

Figure 8-32   SOS Online Backup stores files on a global network of datacenters.

- Complete privacy protection
- Allows 20 to 30 GB of data
- Supports multiple computers
- Intelligent file filters
- Powerful recovery
- Scheduled backups

SiteShelter

SiteShelter is an automated utility that backs up, mirrors, monitors, and even repairs Web sites and FTP sites. It is particularly useful for Web site developers who want to provide an online backup service for their client's Web sites. It supports all types of servers—Windows, UNIX, Linux, and others. SiteShelter is shown in Figure 8-33.

EVault Backup Software

EVault Backup Software is a disk-to-disk backup and recovery solution. It is shown in Figure 8-34, and its features include the following:

- Ensures data availability and recoverability
- Scalable and efficient

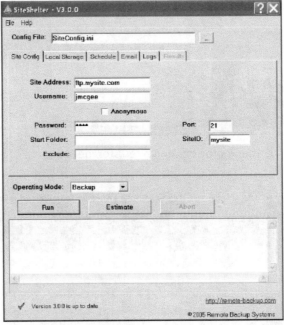

Source: http://www.remote-backup.com/siteshelter/docs/sitesheltorwt.htm.
Accessed 9/2009.

Figure 8-33   SiteShelter is useful for Web site developers.

Source: http://www.evault.com/site. Accessed 9/2009.

Figure 8-34   EVault is a disk-to-disk backup program.

- Encrypts the data before and during over-the-wire transmission
- Web-based centralized management for distributed environments
- Compliance with industry and corporate governance requirements
- Broad platform support

IDrive

IDrive online backup provides automated protection for critical data. It can restore data from either its desktop client or its Web client. Users can drag and drop files to restore from the online drive to the local system. IDrive Pro is shown in Figure 8-35, and its features include the following:

- Allows access to files anywhere, anytime
- Supports multiple systems
- Encrypted backups
- Retains 30 individual versions of the backed-up data
- Drag-and-drop restore using the optional IDrive Explorer interface in addition to IDrive Classic options

Backup2net

Backup2net is an automated backup program, shown in Figure 8-36, that has the following features:

- Local and remote secure server backup
- Easy-to-use interface
- Easy file and folder selection
- Built-in task scheduler
- Intuitive backup and restore
- Secure shell data transfer

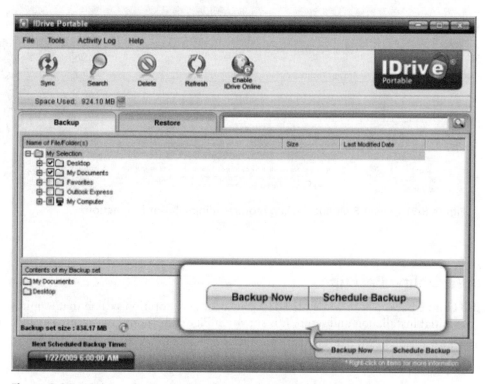

Figure 8-35 IDrive can restore data from either its desktop client or its Web client.

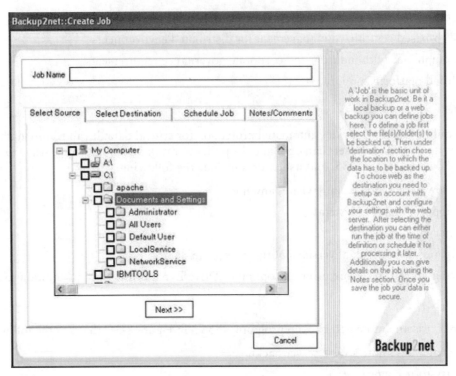

Figure 8-36   Backup2net is a simple online backup and restore program.

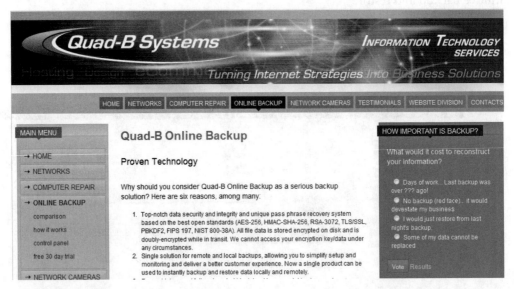

Figure 8-37   Quad-B Online Backup requires minimal user interaction.

Quad-B Online Backup

Quad-B Online Backup is an automated data backup and restoration system that requires no human interaction after the initial installation and setup. It is shown in Figure 8-37, and its features include the following:

- Easily scheduled online backups
- Low bandwidth requirements and adjustable bandwidth settings
- Flexible version control to define which versions to store

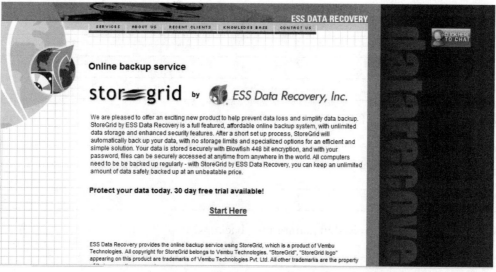

Source: http://www.datarecovery.com/backup_service.asp. Accessed 9/2009.

Figure 8-38 StoreGrid provides unlimited data storage and enhanced security.

- High encryption and security
- Backs up individual files or entire directories
- All data are compressed and encrypted locally before being sent to the server
- All data on the server are stored in a compressed and encrypted format
- Supports the backup of local files, network files, and open databases (VSS compatible)

StoreGrid

StoreGrid is an online backup system with unlimited data storage and enhanced security features. It stores data securely using Blowfish 448-bit encryption, and it allows the user to access files securely anywhere in the world. StoreGrid is shown in Figure 8-38.

Chapter Summary

- It is extremely important to regularly back up data.
- Backups can be done to a local tape drive, but it is safer to use off-site storage.
- Use encryption on backups.
- Disk backup is used to recover data quickly in the event of a disaster.
- Removable media backup refers to the use of CDs, DVDs, tape drives, USB drives, and external hard drives.
- Most online backup solutions are highly reliable.
- Files can be backed up online using File Transfer Protocol (FTP) servers.

Review Questions

1. What is disk mirroring?

_____

_____

_____

_____

2. What are some challenges faced in maintaining backups and recovering data?

_____
_____
_____
_____

3. What are some causes of data loss?

_____
_____
_____
_____

4. What are some risks involved in maintaining backups?

_____
_____
_____
_____

5. Why is it necessary to secure backups with encryption?

_____
_____
_____
_____

6. What is off-site backup?

_____
_____
_____
_____

7. What are the advantages of off-site backup?

_____
_____
_____
_____

8. What is online backup?

_____
_____
_____
_____

9. What is a disadvantage of using FTP for backup?

_____
_____
_____
_____

10. What are some services that provide online backup?

_____

_____

_____

_____

Hands-On Projects

1. Use Norton Ghost to back up files and folders.

   ■ Navigate to Chapter 8 of the Student Resource Center.

   ■ Install and launch the Norton Ghost program.

   ■ Select **Back up selected files or folders** and click the **Next** button.

   ■ Select the files and folders to back up and click the **Next** button.

   ■ Select a destination folder and click the **Next** button.

   ■ Select a schedule option and click the **Next** button.

   ■ Select **Run Backup Now** and click the **Finish** button to run the backup.

2. Use Norton Online Backup to back up files online.

   ■ Navigate to Chapter 8 of the Student Resource Center.

   ■ Install and launch the Norton Online Backup program.

   ■ Enter the name of the computer in the **Display Name** field and click **OK**.

   ■ Add files and folders for backup, and create a schedule to run the backup.

   ■ Click **Back up Now** to back up immediately.

   ■ Click **Restore** to recover the files.

   ■ Check the activity log by clicking **View Log**.

3. Use BackupAssist to manage backups.

   ■ Navigate to Chapter 8 of the Student Resource Center.

   ■ Install and launch the BackupAssist program.

   ■ Select the type of backup and click the **Next** button.

   ■ Select the destination backup directory and click the **Next** button.

   ■ Select the files and folders to back up and click the **Next** button.

   ■ Enter a name for this job and click the **Finish** button.

   ■ Go to the **Jobs** menu, select the job that was just created, and click the **Run** button.

   ■ Click the **Events** tab and view the events that have occurred.

   ■ Click the **Restore** tab and click on **Restore using NTBackup**.

   ■ Click **Recent job reports** to view reports.

4. Use Genie Backup Manager Pro to back up data.

   ■ Navigate to Chapter 8 of the Student Resource Center.

   ■ Install and launch the Genie Backup Manager Pro program.

   ■ Click **Backup** to create a new backup job.

   ■ Select the backup media and location for the backup, and click the **Next** button.

   ■ Select the files to back up and click the **Next** button.

   ■ Select the settings for backup and click the **Next** button.

- View the report.
- Click **Restore** to recover the backup files.
- Select the files to recover and click the **Next** button.
- View the report.

5. Use Handy Backup to schedule data backups.

- Navigate to Chapter 8 of the Student Resource Center.
- Install and launch the Handy Backup program.
- Select the task type and click the **Next** button.
- Choose the files to back up and click the **Next** button.
- Select the backup location and click the **Next** button.
- Enter the backup name and click the **Finish** button.
- Check the settings and click the **OK** button.
- Click the **View** tab and click **Save Log** to save the log.
- Select **Restore task** and click the **Next** button.
- Select the restore location and click the **Next** button.
- Click the **Finish** button to recover the files.

Chapter 9

Certification and Accreditation of Information Systems

Objectives

After completing this chapter, you should be able to:

- Understand certification and accreditation
- Enumerate the guidelines for certification and accreditation
- Understand the role of risk assessment in the certification and accreditation process
- Compare different certification and accreditation processes
- Implement physical security requirements
- Understand how threat and vulnerability analysis applies to the certification and accreditation process

Key Terms

Accreditation   the official approval to operate an information system for a specific period of time

Approval to operate   an official permission granted by a designated approving authority (DAA) to operate automated information systems (AIS) or networks in a particular security mode

Certification   the process of assessing whether the technical and nontechnical safety features of an IS satisfy the minimum security requirements

Introduction to Certification and Accreditation of Information Systems

Certification and accreditation are important aspects of maintaining and strengthening the security of an information system. This chapter introduces you to the concepts of certification and accreditation. It covers what is involved in the process and how other processes contribute to the certification and accreditation process. The chapter also covers how threats and vulnerabilities are related to the certification and accreditation process.

Certification and Accreditation

The risk involved with operating an information system (IS) can never be completely eliminated, but it can be reduced using a risk management approach. Certification and accreditation authorities are appointed to effectively manage the risk associated with operating an information system.

Certification

Certification is the process of assessing whether the technical and nontechnical safety features of an IS satisfy the minimum security requirements. Security certifications for information systems provide an assurance to their various stakeholders that the system is operating under acceptable risk limits and proper controls are implemented to handle and respond to an information security incident.

Certification should:

- Validate that the security measures meet the minimum security requirements of an IS
- Test the security safeguards
- Evaluate the technical security measures in terms of functionality and assurance

The certification process supports the risk management process in the information system's security program. This certification process is divided into two tasks: security control assessment and security certification documentation.

Security control implementation deals with the implementation of the security requirements in an organization. The objectives of the security requirements implementation are to:

- Prepare for the security assessment
- Conduct the security assessment
- Document the results

Preparation for security assessment involves generating and gathering appropriate planning and supporting materials such as system requirements and design documentation, security control implementation evidence, and results from previous security assessments, security reviews, or audits.

System certifiers and accreditors are the individuals responsible for providing security certifications or assessing management.

Accreditation

Accreditation represents the official approval to operate an information system for a specific period of time. It is the official declaration by a responsible senior manager that an automated system is permitted to process information up to a maximum sensitivity level, under specified controls and operating procedures. It signifies senior management's official approval of the residual risk.

Procedures and Controls to Detect or Prevent Unauthorized Access

Table 9-1 describes procedures and controls for detecting or preventing unauthorized access to information systems.

Certification and Accreditation Guidelines

An organization should follow these guidelines to pass the certification and accreditation process and get certified. These guidelines provide an overview of measures to achieve certification and accreditation.

The guidelines are as follows:

- Apply consistent, comparable, and repeatable evaluations of the security controls to information systems.
- Understand and recognize the mission risks resulting from the operation of information systems.
- Create more complete, reliable, and trustworthy information for the authorizing officials.
- Achieve secure information systems.
- Create a documentation policy and document all the procedures and controls implemented in the organization in a clear, concise manner.

Procedures and Controls	Focus On
Information Security Policies	Definition of the appropriate security controls
	Assessment of the current security controls
	Guidelines to report, assess, respond to, and handle organizational security incidents
	Recommendations for the appropriate controls to safeguard sensitive information
Awareness and Training	Development of the required skills in security teams
	Creating awareness among end users regarding roles and responsibilities related to the system and information access
Access Controls	Use of relevant logical and physical security controls such as identification and authentication, and privilege assignments
	Creating user groups and granting differentiated permissions according to their roles and duties in the organization
	Password protection of all access points
	Installation of physical security controls such as biometric scanners and smart-card readers
	Deployment of security personnel, fencing, and surveillance
Disaster Preparedness	Development of procedures to protect information systems from unlawful destruction and accidental loss
	Preparedness to overcome natural disasters and environmental hazards
Information Encryption	Encrypting information in all its states, i.e., during collection, processing, and transmission
	Encrypting all communication channels
Use of Automated Tools	Automated tools to manage access to information systems and resources
Evaluation and Audits	Audit of all the access control measures to ensure their effectiveness
	Evaluation and audits lead to certification and accreditation of information systems

Table 9-1   These are procedures and controls for detecting or preventing unauthorized access to information systems

Certification and Accreditation Documentation

Organizations should maintain documents that contain information about the corrective and security measures applied in the organization to achieve certification and accreditation. The set of documents should also include the result of applying the controls and the extent to which the desired outcome has been achieved.

The documentation should include the following:

- System categorization statement document
- System description document
- Network diagram and data flows
- Software and hardware inventory
- Business risk assessment
- System risk assessment
- Contingency plan
- Self-assessment document
- System security plan

Organizational Certification and Accreditation Process

A typical organizational security certification and accreditation process consists of four phases:

1. *Initiation phase*: This phase ensures that an organization's information security manager is in agreement with the contents of the information system security plan. This phase consists of three tasks:
   - Preparation
   - Notification and resource identification
   - Information system security plan analysis, update, and acceptance

2. *Security certification phase*: This phase ensures that security controls in the information system are implemented correctly and produce the desired outcome. This phase consists of two tasks:
   - Security control assessment
   - Security certification documentation

3. *Security accreditation phase*: The purpose of this phase is to find out if the remaining known vulnerabilities in the information system pose an acceptable level of risk to the organization's operations, the organization's assets, or individuals. This phase consists of two tasks:
   - Security accreditation decision
   - Security accreditation documentation

4. *Continuous monitoring phase*: The purpose of this phase is to provide complete information system security monitoring on an ongoing basis and to inform the organization's information security manager when any changes occur in the information system. This phase consists of:
   - Configuration management and control
   - Security control monitoring
   - Status reporting and documentation

Role of Risk Assessment in the Certification and Accreditation Process

Risk assessment is an important activity in an organization. An information security program supports security accreditation and is needed by the security certification and accreditation authority. Information security policies and procedures based on risk assessment help to reduce security risks. Thus, risk assessment is important to the certification and accreditation process. Risk assessment cost-effectively reduces the information security risks to an acceptable level and ensures that information security is addressed throughout the life cycle of each agency information system. It enables more consistent, comparable, and repeatable assessments of the security controls in an information system.

Comparison of Different Certification and Accreditation Processes

The following are three methodologies used for certification and accreditation initiatives:

1. Defense Information Technology Security Certification and Accreditation Process (DITSCAP)
2. National Information Assurance Certification and Accreditation Process (NIACAP)
3. National Institute of Standards and Technology (NIST)

Defense agencies primarily use DITSCAP, though civilian agencies may also use it. It is based on a process published by the National Security Telecommunications and Information System Security Instruction (NSTISSI). Most civilian agencies instead use the NIST methodology.

NIST and NIACAP establish a framework to provide certification and accreditation to an organization. NIST and NIACAP both stipulate definitions and requirements for a system's characterization, risk assessment, verification and validation of the security controls, and testing.

All certification and accreditation processes consider the entire system, network, and application life cycle from a security standpoint. The certification and accreditation process is a manual audit of policies, procedures, controls, and contingency planning. NIST is designed for unclassified information.

The following are the four phases of the NIST model:

1. Initiation
2. Certification

3. Accreditation

4. Continuous monitoring

The following are the four phases of the NIACAP model:

1. Definition

2. Verification

3. Validation

4. Postaccreditation

DITSCAP also involves the same four phases as NIACAP. Though there is a difference in the nomenclature of phases in the certifications listed and accreditation methodologies, the underlying basic principles are the same. They all evaluate the security controls implemented in an organization.

Monitoring the Certification and Accreditation Process for Vulnerabilities

The certification and accreditation process determines the security of an information system; it suggests the means to protect information from vulnerabilities. The security of information can be protected by implementing countermeasures that are selected according to the possible threats and the importance of the data. Threat analysis is performed during the certification and accreditation process, and the sources of any vulnerabilities are continuously monitored. An effective continuous monitoring program requires the following:

- Configuration management and configuration control processes
- Security impact analysis on changes in the information system
- Assessment of selected security controls in the information system

Vulnerability detection can be carried out at any phase in the system development life cycle. The vulnerability detection process can be performed through various means such as questionnaires, interviews, document reviews, and automated scanning tools.

Vulnerability sources can be located in the following places:

- Previous risk assessment reports
- Audit log reports
- System anomaly reports
- Vulnerability scans and penetration-testing reports
- Security testing and evaluation reports
- Hardware/software security analyses

Relationship Between Vulnerabilities, Risks, and Attacks

Vulnerabilities, risks, and attacks on an information system are interrelated. Risks are compounded by vulnerabilities in the system and in controls implemented to overcome attacks. Attacks often involve the exploitation of system vulnerabilities. The risk of attack increases with the presence of vulnerabilities in a system.

Approval to Operate (ATO)

Approval to operate is an official permission granted by a designated approving authority (DAA) to operate automated information systems (AISs) or networks in a particular security mode. Before granting permission, the DAA verifies an accreditation statement to make sure that the residual risk is within the acceptable limits. The DAA ensures that each AIS fulfills the AIS security requirements, as reported by the information systems security officer (ISSO). Responsibilities of an ISSO include the following:

- Establish and manage security for systems operated by an agency, contractors, and command personnel
- Appoint the person who will directly report to the DAA
- Assign levels of classification required for applications operating in a network environment
- Verify the accreditation plan and sign the accreditation statement for the network and AIS
- Verify the documentation for AIS security requirements, which are defined in the AIS network security program

Security

Security Laws

The following are some of the security laws that regulate and are referred to by certification and accreditation authorities:

- *Federal Information Security Management Act (FISMA)*: It sets guidelines for conducting annual reviews of an agency's information security program and reporting the results.
- *Health Insurance Portability and Accountability Act (HIPAA)*: It sets strict guidelines to ensure the integrity and confidentiality of individually identifiable health information and helps protect information against reasonably anticipated threats and unauthorized disclosure.
- *Sarbanes-Oxley Act (SOX)*: It provides guidelines to improve the accuracy and reliability of corporate disclosures.
- *Gramm-Leach-Bliley Act (GLBA)*: It sets guidelines for the security and confidentiality of a customer's financial information.

Physical Security Requirements

The physical security of systems and data is important in an organization. It includes measures to protect personnel, critical assets, and systems against deliberate attacks and accidents. The intent of physical security is to prevent the unauthorized access of information and other assets of a company. It can be achieved by means of securing data and systems through physical access controls and restricted entry to the server and data storage rooms. The first and foremost security measures to be implemented in an organization are the physical security measures.

The following are some physical security measures organizations typically implement:

- *Lock up the server room*: Management implements policies to keep the server room locked and to allow only authorized personnel to open the lock and enter the server room.
- *Set up surveillance*: There may be the chance of misuse of authority by an authorized person, so a logbook should be maintained to keep track of who goes in and out and when. Surveillance equipment should also be installed in areas containing highly sensitive information.
- *Place valuable devices in a locker*: All network devices and important data disks should be kept in a locker; this protects the devices and helps prevent theft.
- *Use rack-mount servers*: Rack-mount servers are small and easy to secure.
- *Protect portable devices*: The physical security of portable devices is important, as they can be easily stolen by anyone.
- *Pack up backups*: Backup tapes, disks, or discs can be stolen and used by outsiders; backups should be kept off-site in a secured place.
- *Disable drives and ports*: Information can be stolen with the help of removable media. When the organization is not using them for business purposes, it is advisable to disable or remove floppy drives, USB ports, and other means by which external drives can be connected.
- *Protect printers*: Printers store information concerning recently printed documents in memory. It is important to protect printers, as they may lead to important information leakage if not protected properly.

Physical security measures vary according to needs and circumstances and depend on the cost of what is being protected. A prudent mix of physical, technical, and operational measures helps ensure sufficient physical security.

Security Inspections Covered During the Certification and Accreditation Process

The objective of the security inspections conducted during the certification and accreditation process is to determine the risk to organizational operations, organizational assets, or individuals and to determine if the organization-level risk is acceptable. During this process, the planned or completed corrective actions to reduce or eliminate vulnerabilities are checked. The final risk to the organization and the acceptability of that risk is determined during this security inspection process.

The security inspection process can be divided into the following phases:

- Preparing for the security assessment
- Conducting the assessment of the security controls
- Preparing the final security assessment report

Security Policies and Procedures Implemented During the Risk Analysis/Assessment Process

The following are some of the security policies and procedures implemented during the risk analysis/assessment process:

- Identifying threats that harm and affect vital information security operations and assets
- Estimating the likelihood that such threats will occur, based on past information
- Identifying and ranking the value of operations and assets
- Estimating the cost for potential losses, damage, and recovery
- Identifying cost-effective actions to reduce potential risk
- Documenting the results and developing an action plan

Vulnerabilities Associated with Security Processing Modes

The security processing mode of an information system is determined based on the classification of data, clearances, access approval, and need-to-know of the users of the information system. Only authorized persons are allowed to access information and make changes to that information. Management is responsible for deciding who is allowed to access and modify which information.

Depending on management policies, security processing is differentiated into the following modes:

- *Dedicated security mode*: In this mode, all users must have the required security clearance, formal access approval, and a need-to-know for all information processed by the system. All users can access all information on the system, which could lead to information leakage.
- *System high-security mode*: In this mode, all users must have the required security clearance and formal access approval, but they do not need to have a need-to-know for all information processed by the system. Users only have to have a need-to-know for some of the information. This could lead to a user accessing or modifying information he or she should not access.
- *Compartmented security mode*: In this mode, all users must have the required security clearance. However, all users do not need to have formal access approval and a need-to-know for all information processed by the system, just for some of the information.
- *Multilevel security mode*: In this mode, all users do not need to have the required security clearance, formal access approval, and need-to-know for all information processed by the system, just for some of the information. This is the most secured mode.

Threat and Vulnerability Analysis Input to the Certification and Accreditation Process

An organization prepares a system security plan for the certification and accreditation process that contains complete information about the information system, security categories, potential threats, and vulnerabilities.

Threat analysis input to the certification and accreditation process includes:

- List of all potential threats that affect the information system
- Threat information such as capabilities, intentions, and resources of potential adversaries
- Threat detection information that is documented in the risk assessment process

Vulnerability analysis input to the certification and accreditation process includes:

- Flaws or weaknesses in an information system
- Vulnerability identification information that is documented in the risk assessment process
- Vulnerability information associated with the information system and common security controls

How Certification and Accreditation Provide Assurance That Controls Are Functioning Effectively

The certification and accreditation process considers the vulnerabilities, processes, and solutions to deal with the vulnerabilities. The certification and accreditation authorities check the suggested and implemented solutions in an organization to overcome vulnerabilities and counter attacks.

The process of security control assessment consists of three phases:

- *Phase I*:
  - Prepare for the assessment of security controls.
  - In the first phase, proper planning and collection of supporting material takes place, after which methods and procedures are developed for assessing security controls.

- *Phase II*:
  - Assess the security controls.
  - In the second phase, the developed methods are implemented for the assessment of solutions that are suggested and implemented in the organization.

- *Phase III*:
  - Document the final results of the assessment.
  - This is the assessment phase in which the assessment of the results of the control measures takes place; the outcome is compared with the expected result documents and corrections, if any, are suggested for better results.

Protections Offered by Security Features in Specific Configurations

Depending on the organization's policies and the security measures applied to the system, the protection provided to the system is divided into the following four categories:

1. *High*: This system profile is recommended for systems that contain sensitive data and are accessed by many users. All networking services are disabled for this type of system. Only the transfer of information to other systems is allowed, and receiving data is not allowed.

2. *Improved*: This system profile is recommended for systems accessed by groups of users who can share information. User IDs can be reused as desired. Only limited networking services are enabled.

3. *Traditional*: This system profile is recommended for compatibility with other systems. Passwords are necessary to access the system, but they are not configured to expire. All networking services are enabled.

4. *Low*: This system profile is recommended only for systems that are not publicly accessible. It is also implemented in systems having a small number of cooperating users.

Threat/Risk Assessment Methodology Appropriate for Use with System Undergoing Accreditation

The threat/risk assessment methodology used for a system undergoing accreditation focuses on the following:

- *Prioritization of risk*: Risks anticipated by an organization need to be prioritized according to their seriousness. The more serious and potentially damaging risks are attended to first and given higher priority. The countermeasures applied to counter the risks are dependent on the expected damage caused by the risks and the impact of the damage on the organization.

- *Categorization of recommended safeguards*: The countermeasures to be applied are categorized according to their urgency and cost effectiveness.

- *Feasibility of implementation of solutions*: It is the responsibility of the organization to use the most appropriate means to safeguard against damage caused by a threat. Appropriate and useful countermeasures should be selected to effectively control an attack.

- *Other risk mitigation processes*: Often, lessons learned from previous risk management are used to implement countermeasures. Lessons learned from previous mistakes are taken into consideration when designing new countermeasures.

Information Technology Security Evaluation Criteria

The Information Technology Security Evaluation Criteria (ITSEC) is a UK scheme in which security features of IT systems and products are tested independently of suppliers to identify logical vulnerabilities.
ITSEC defines the following security criteria:

- A security target and informal architectural design must be produced.

- An informal detailed design and test documentation must be produced.

- Source code or hardware drawings should be produced.

- A formal model of security and semiformal specification of security-enforcing functions, architecture, and detailed design should be produced.

- Architectural design explains the interrelationship between security-enforcing components.

- A formal description of the architecture and security-enforcing functions should be produced.

Questions Asked by the Certifier During the Certification and Accreditation Process

Authorizing officials must consider the suitable factors and decide to either permit or reject the risk to their respective agencies. The following are some of the questions asked during the certification and accreditation process:

- Are the security controls in the information system effective at maintaining the preferred level of protection?

- What actions have been planned to correct any deficiencies in the security controls for the information system?

- Could any of the modifications to the information system affect the existing, known vulnerabilities in the system?

- Have the resources needed to effectively complete the security certification and accreditation of the information system been recognized and allocated?

- To what extent are information system security controls implemented?

Chapter Summary

- Certifiers are responsible for conducting a comprehensive assessment of an information system.

- Accreditation represents official approval to operate an information system for a specific period of time.

- The certification process supports the risk management process in the information system's security program.

- Risk assessment policies and procedures reduce security risks to an acceptable level.

Review Questions

1. Explain certification and accreditation.

_____

_____

_____

_____

2. List the procedures for detecting and preventing unauthorized access.

_____

_____

_____

_____

3. List the guidelines for certification and accreditation.

_____

_____

_____

_____

4. What are the documents required to prepare certification and accreditation documentation?

_____

_____

_____

_____

5. Describe what happens during the initiation phase.

_____

_____

_____

_____

6. Describe the importance of the security certification phase.

_____

_____

_____

_____

7. What is the role of risk assessment in the certification and accreditation process?

_____

_____

_____

_____

8. Compare the different organizational certification and accreditation processes.

_____

_____

_____

_____

9. List the security policies and procedures implemented during the risk analysis and assessment process.

_____

_____

_____

_____

Hands-On Projects

1. Navigate to Chapter 9 of the Student Resource Center. Open Accreditation+guidelines.pdf. Read the following sections:

   - Becoming Accredited

   - Accreditation standards for all PCIA accredited programs

   - Technical Accreditation Standards

2. Navigate to Chapter 9 of the Student Resource Center. Open taxonomy.pdf. Read the article.

3. Navigate to Chapter 9 of the Student Resource Center. Open CNSSP-6.pdf. Read the following sections:

   - National Policy on Certification and Accreditation of National Security Systems

   - Section II - Definitions

Index